Dependency Syndrome in Marriage

Branny Mthelebofu

Published by Banny Joma Enterprise, 2025.

"Dependency is not devotion—it is the quiet surrender of self.Healing begins when we remember that love cannot growwhere freedom cannot breathe."

Dependency Syndrome in Marriage

"A psychoanalytic journey to decode why love becomes survival instead of connection.

By Branny Mthelebofu

The rise of "marriage syndrome" in modern society. How faith communities, tradition, and modern life can create emotional conflict. The global crisis of loneliness.

1. Acknowledgements

I acknowledge the presence of my colleagues in the film industry, my spouse's motivation and love, which carry me through to write daily, and my family; they are all the pillars of strength.

I acknowledge the International Society of Applied Psychoanalysis (ISAP), the International Psychotherapy Institute, School of Natural Health Sciences, and everyone who is contributing positively in my career.

By Branny Mthelebofu (Branny Smith)

Why rural and urban communities suffer similar emotional wounds?

Why culturally-informed healing is essential in African contexts. Through narrative psychology, cultural insight, and real-life case stories, Branny Mthelebofu reveals how intergenerational trauma, societal expectations, and unspoken memories shape the way people love, choose partners, and cope with suffering. The book also introduces "Emotional Indigestion," a psychological concept developed by Branny Mthelebofu, describing the build-up of suppressed emotions that eventually manifest as illness, depression, or destructive relationships.

2. Preface of this book

Dependency Syndrome in Marriage

Marriage is often imagined as a partnership built on love, trust, and mutual support. Yet, hidden beneath many relationships lies a subtle but powerful force—dependency syndrome—a pattern where one partner becomes emotionally, financially, or psychologically over reliant on the other. This dependency can slowly erode independence, reduce self-worth, and create imbalances that strain even the strongest unions. The intention of this book is to bring this often-ignored reality into clear view.

Over the years, countless couples have struggled in silence, unable to understand why their relationship feels heavy, unbalanced, or emotionally draining. What many fail to recognize is that dependency does not always appear as weakness; sometimes it disguises itself as love, loyalty, sacrifice, or cultural obligation.

In communities where traditional expectations shape gender roles and emotional expression, dependency can even be normalized—making it harder to identify or challenge.

This book emerges from a desire to give voice to those experiences. It is written for partners who feel stuck, for individuals who have lost their independence inside love, and for couples seeking a healthier balance. It is also for professionals—therapists, counsellors, and social workers—who support relationships affected by emotional over-dependence.

Throughout this book, the aim is not to assign blame, but to illuminate the patterns that keep marriages stagnant or unequal.

By understanding the psychological roots of dependency, the cultural forces that reinforce it and the emotional costs it carries, couples can begin to rebuild their partnerships on a foundation of mutual respect and autonomy.

Most importantly, this book is an invitation:

An invitation to reflect, to heal, and to create marriages where both partners can grow—not in each other's shadow, but side by side.

May these pages offer clarity, courage, and hope to all who seek a more balanced and fulfilling love.

— *Branny Mthelebofu*

More information: brannysmithsa@gmail.com
Banny Joma Enterprise Publishers Johannesburg
South Africa
@Branny Smith
@Branny Mthelebofu

3. Dedication

I dedicate this book to all the therapists, lectures, psychoanalysts, psychiatrists, social workers, students and readers in the whole world who are trying to assist clients who are located in the Cities, rural areas, townships, flats, old suburbs, and under privileged areas.

I dedicate these stories to all the people who have grown up from all underprivileged areas and are now faced with the challenges of relieving their own colleagues and everyone who desires to be out of misery of marriage through therapy.

I dedicate this book to all the students who aspire to reach their destiny and are trying so had to be something despite coming out of marriage dependency syndrome.

4. The Author

Branny Mthelebofu is a multifaceted South African creative whose work bridges the realms of storytelling, healing, and music. As a filmmaker, nutrition therapist, holistic counsellor, and musician, he channels his diverse talents into narratives that explore the complexities of the human psyche and the pursuit of inner peace.

Under the pen name Branny Smith, Mthelebofu creates stories that delve into personal challenges, emotional trauma, and the transformative journey toward self-understanding. His literary works, such as The Professor's Descent, Desperation, and Chasing Where There is Love, My Wedding Contract Too, Her Lover is Gone, often feature protagonists grappling with internal conflicts and societal pressures, reflecting his deep interest in mental health and psychoanalysis. Beyond writing, Smith employs his background in holistic therapy to assist clients in achieving emotional well-being through interactive counselling sessions. His approach integrates scriptwriting principles to facilitate character development and personal growth, offering a unique therapeutic experience that resonates with individuals seeking happiness and fulfillment.

As a musician, Branny Smith composes lyrics that address life's challenges, happiness, and the quest for peace of mind, utilizing music as a form of therapy for his audience. His passion for mental health and storytelling converges in his creative endeavors, making his work a compelling exploration of the human condition.

Through his multifaceted career, Branny Smith Mthelebofu continues to inspire and guide others on their journeys toward self-discovery and emotional resilience.

5. Groundbreaking Exploration of How the Body Remembers Pain — and How to Heal

In a world where emotional wounds are often minimized, ignored, or culturally silenced, *Dependency Syndrome in Marriage* arrives as a ground-breaking book that redefines healing for the 21st century. Written by researcher and storyteller Branny Mthelebofu, this deeply human work unpacks how trauma is stored in the body, how relationships repeat our earliest wounds, and why true healing must integrate both emotional and physical well-being.

Set across rural Limpopo villages and global cities like New York, Lagos, and Johannesburg, the book explores the shared emotional struggles shaping modern society — heartbreak, anxiety, silence, self-abandonment, and the desperate need for belonging. This is a book for anyone who has ever carried pain alone.

Through narrative psychology, cultural insight, and real-life case stories, Smith reveals how intergenerational trauma, societal expectations, and unspoken memories shape the way people love, choose partners, and cope with suffering. The book also introduces "Emotional Indigestion," a psychological concept developed by Branny Mthelebofu, describing the build-up of suppressed emotions that eventually manifest as illness, depression, or destructive relationships.

Dependency Syndrome in Marriage is both a mirror and a map: a mirror for readers who see their lives reflected in its pages and a map for those seeking a path toward emotional freedom.

Branny Mthelebofu brings a distinctive African voice to the global landscape of mental health writing, offering a nuanced perspective on how culture, poverty, tradition, and modern identity collide with emotional healing.

This book is poised to become essential reading for students, therapists, community leaders, faith practitioners, corporate professionals, educators, and anyone searching to make sense of their inner world.

6. Purpose of the Book

The purpose of this book is to uncover, explain, and challenge the psychological, cultural, and socio-economic patterns that shape dependency syndrome in marriage—one of the least discussed yet most damaging cycles affecting individuals, families, and communities across Africa and the world. While marriage is often celebrated as a sacred union, a symbol of companionship, and a marker of stability, for many women and men it has become something fundamentally different: a survival strategy, an escape route, or a desperate attempt to fill emotional and identity voids created in childhood.

This book seeks to give language to that reality.

At its core, this book aims to highlight how childhood environments—poverty, overcrowding, violence, substance abuse, the absence of privacy, and exposure to adult sexuality—shape the emotional lives and future relationship choices of young people. Many children raised in cramped RDP houses, townships, informal settlements, or rural villages grow up longing for escape. Marriage becomes the imagined destination of safety and independence, even when the emotional readiness for that union is missing. This book investigates how those early experiences quietly follow individuals into adulthood, gradually forming patterns of dependency, co-dependency, trauma bonding, and identity confusion.

Another purpose of this book is to dismantle cultural myths that pressure women to find worth only through marriage.

In many African, Latin American, Asian, and Western societies, the idea that a woman's dignity or completeness depends on being chosen by a partner is deeply embedded.

This belief keeps many trapped in painful relationships, afraid to leave because returning home means re-entering cycles of poverty, shame, or unresolved trauma. By analysing these social expectations, the book encourages readers to re-evaluate the meaning of love, partnership, and identity.

This book also serves an educational purpose: to explain the psychological mechanisms behind dependency.

Concepts from psychoanalysis, trauma studies, and identity theory are translated into accessible language, helping readers understand why people stay in harmful marriages, why they feel incomplete alone, and how the wounds of childhood reappear in adult relationships. By connecting personal experiences to psychological theory, the book empowers readers to recognise their patterns and begin the work of healing.

Equally important, the book aims to destigmatise therapy and make emotional healing visible and acceptable within communities.

Many individuals avoid therapy due to fear, cultural pressure, or lack of exposure, yet therapy remains the most effective tool for breaking the dependency cycle.

Through real-life scenarios and analysis, this book shows how therapy can help individuals rebuild self-worth, discover their identity, process trauma, and form healthier, non-dependent relationships.

Finally, the purpose of this book is to inspire societal transformation. By understanding the roots of dependency, communities can begin creating healthier homes, reducing childhood trauma, fostering emotional literacy, and empowering young people to build their futures on authenticity rather than fear.

The book calls for a shift from marriages formed as escape routes to marriages formed through healed, whole, emotionally mature individuals.

Ultimately, this book exists to illuminate truth, to promote healing, and to redefine love. It is a call to break cycles, confront painful histories, reshape identities, and build a generation capable of loving freely—not dependently.

7. Introduction- Why This Book Is Important

This book is important because it exposes a silent crisis affecting millions of women and men across Africa and around the world—a crisis often misinterpreted as "relationship problems," when in reality it is rooted in childhood trauma, poverty, cultural expectations, and deeply ingrained emotional wounds. Dependency syndrome in marriage is not merely a personal issue; it is a societal pattern that shapes identity, mental health, family structures, and community wellbeing. Yet, until now, few books have explored this phenomenon with psychological depth, cultural sensitivity, and global relevance.

This book matters because it gives language to experiences that many people have lived through but could never fully articulate. For countless individuals who grew up in overcrowded homes, informal settlements, or unstable environments, the feelings of shame, confusion, and emotional fragmentation have followed them into adulthood. Many never understood why they rushed into premature relationships, why they longed for escape, or why marriage felt like the only viable path to dignity. This book exposes those hidden pathways that trauma creates, allowing readers to finally understand themselves without judgment.

It is important because it breaks the silence around childhood emotional injuries—the subtle, everyday wounds that shape adult identity but are rarely discussed in families, churches, or communities. It helps society recognise that dependency is not weakness; it is the outcome of environments that deprive children of safety, stability, and emotional affirmation. By telling the truth about these origins, the book removes stigma and replaces blame with understanding.

This book is also vital because it challenges cultural and religious misconceptions that pressure women into equating self-worth with marriage. For generations, girls have been taught that marriage is their destiny, their escape, and their validation. This expectation has contributed to cycles of depression, emotional entrapment, and lifelong co-dependence. By confronting these narratives, the book promotes emotional freedom and encourages healthier definitions of womanhood, manhood, and partnership.

Beyond individual relationships, this book is important on a societal level. Dependency syndrome has direct consequences for generational trauma, family instability, parenting styles, and the emotional upbringing of children. When adults enter marriage wounded, they often raise children who inherit the same wounds. Understanding and breaking this cycle is essential for building emotionally healthy communities.

The book also fills a significant knowledge gap by combining psychological theory, African lived experience, socio-economic realities, and global comparisons. Few texts link township life, rural trauma, identity formation, and marriage choices in such a comprehensive and accessible way. This makes it a valuable resource for students, therapists, social workers, community leaders, policymakers, and anyone seeking to understand the deeper emotional architecture of relationships.

Importantly, the book creates a bridge between theory and healing. It not only explains why dependency develops but also offers pathways for recovery—through self-reflection, therapy, trauma processing, and emotional education. It empowers individuals to reclaim their identity, rebuild their self-worth, and make choices grounded in healing rather than survival.

In essence, this book is important because it speaks to the heart of what makes us human: our need for love, belonging, and security. It invites readers to re-examine the foundations of their relationships, confront their pasts with courage, and imagine a future where love is a partnership—not an escape. By shining light on a hidden cycle, the book opens the door for emotional liberation, healthier marriages, and a new generation that loves from a place of wholeness rather than fear.

Chapter 1 : Dependency Syndrome in Marriage

Chapter summary

This chapter introduces the reader to the invisible emotional burdens carried within families and communities, especially in rural contexts. It explores how unspoken histories—loss, migration, abandonment, cultural obligations—shape daily choices and emotional responses. The chapter situates the reader in the world where silence itself becomes a form of inheritance, framing trauma as both personal and collective. It sets the foundation for understanding how individuals internalize pain and how these patterns pass from one generation to the next.

Introduction - The Silent Weight of the Past

The concept of dependency in love has become a defining force in the lives of many women. In many African societies—and increasingly across Western cultures—marriage is viewed not merely as a union, but as a pathway out of poverty, emotional instability, and social limitations.

This pressure has created a psychological pattern known as dependency syndrome in marriage, where marriage becomes the primary route to achieve safety, stability, identity, and social acceptance.

Although cultural and religious traditions encouraged the idea that *"a woman shall leave her home and join her husband,"* this idea, once rooted in protection and continuity of family structures, has evolved into a source of significant social and mental health consequences.

What was meant to be a positive relational bond has now, in many contexts, become a survival strategy.

1. Understanding Dependency Syndrome in Marriage

1.1 Definition

Dependency syndrome in marriage refers to a pattern in which women (and increasingly men) rely on marriage as the sole source of financial support, emotional stability, identity, and social security.

It is not dependency itself that is harmful—healthy relationships naturally involve interdependence. The problem arises when dependency becomes the *only* survival mechanism.

1.2 Why It Develops

Dependency syndrome does not begin in adulthood. It is rooted in:

✓ Childhood trauma
✓ Poor living conditions
✓ Lack of privacy and safety
✓ Emotional neglect
✓ Financial instability
✓ Exposure to abuse
✓ Limited educational opportunities
✓ Cultural pressure to "escape" poverty through marriage

Women internalize the belief that their lives only become complete once they are married. When this does not happen early, many experience anxiety, shame, or a sense of failure.

2. Living Conditions and the Roots of Dependency

2.1 Poverty and Lack of Space

Growing up in overcrowded households—common in townships and informal settlements—leaves children with:

✓ No privacy
✓ Exposure to adult sexual activity
✓ Exposure to parental conflict
✓ Exposure to substance use
✓ High vulnerability to abuse

In communities such as Alexandra Township, Soweto, Gugulethu, Kayelitsha, Zanin, and various Limpopo villages, many children sleep in one-room homes shared with parents and siblings. This environment becomes:

✓ A source of trauma
✓ A trigger for early sexual curiosity
✓ A breeding ground for emotional confusion
✓ A root cause for seeking early marriage as an "escape route"

Women raised in these environments often carry unresolved trauma into adulthood. Marriage becomes a symbol of freedom, privacy, and safety—even when the marriage itself becomes a new form of suffering.

1. Trauma, Sexual Exposure, and Early Sexual

Identity Formation

3.1 Witnessing Sexual Acts
Many women who grew up in single-room homes report that:

✓ They witnessed their parents having intercourse.

✓ They witnessed siblings being intimate.

✓ They developed early sexual curiosity.

✓ They internalised trauma silently because these issues are never discussed.

✓ This silent trauma contributes to:

✓ Depression

✓ Anxiety

✓ Early pregnancies

✓ Early sexual activity

✓ Desire to escape home by "marrying early"

3.2 Sibling Sexual Contact

Lack of space can lead to instances of sibling intimacy, usually unintentional at first but later complicated by trauma and shame. These experiences further push young women towards early relationships—especially with older men—seeking protection, stability, and emotional rescue.

4. Dependency, Love, and Escape

4.1 Marriage as an Exit Strategy

For many girls in poor living conditions, marriage becomes:

✓ A way out of poverty
✓ A way out of parental conflict
✓ A way to gain privacy
✓ A way to feel loved

Not because they love the man— but because they love the exit, he represents.

These results in marriages based on:

✓ Fear of returning home
✓ Need for financial stability
✓ Cultural pressure
✓ Emotional desperation

Such marriages struggle, often within the first year, because they were not built on compatibility.

4.2 The Silent Suffering in Marriage

Women who enter marriages to escape hardship later find:

✓ They are still traumatized
✓ They still feel unloved
✓ They cannot trust their partners
✓ They become emotionally dependent
✓ They cannot divorce because they have nowhere to go
✓ This is the psychological prison of dependency syndrome.

5. Men and Dependency Syndrome

Dependency syndrome affects men too—especially those from:

✓ Poor backgrounds
✓ Violent households
✓ Economically unstable families

Some men marry not out of love, but to escape poverty or to access financial support from women. This creates marriages built on mutual survival, not mutual affection.

6. Global Comparison: Dependency Beyond Africa

Dependency syndrome is not unique to Africa. In:

- New York
- Brazil
- Vietnam
- USA
- Russia
- Australia

Children raised in abusive homes, foster care, poverty, or neglect grow up with a deep desire to seek emotional rescue through marriage or romantic partners. The pattern is global—poverty and trauma create dependency.

7. Identity Crisis and Dependency

7.1 How Childhood Shapes Sexual and Social Identity

Unstable homes create identity confusion in youth.

Lack of:

✓ love
✓ emotional stability
✓ parental guidance
✓ spiritual grounding
✓ safety

✓ ...leaves children unsure of:
✓ who they are
✓ what role they play in society
✓ what love means
✓ what stability looks like
✓ their gender and sexual identity

As psychoanalytic theorists such as Sigmund Freud explain, unresolved childhood conflicts disturb the balance between the id, ego, and superego, resulting in identity confusion.

8. How Therapy Helps

Therapy is essential because it:

✓ Helps individuals understand *why* they married
✓ Helps them identify past trauma
✓ Helps them build healthier, non-dependent relationships
✓ Helps couples communicate honestly
✓ Provides a safe space to rebuild identity

Healing requires:

✓ Individual therapy
✓ Couple therapy
✓ Trauma processing
✓ Workshops on relationships, parenting, identity, and love

Dependency syndrome in marriage is a psychological, cultural, and socio-economic phenomenon rooted deeply in:

✓ Poverty
✓ Childhood trauma
✓ Unstable homes

✓ Cultural expectations
✓ Emotional neglect
✓ To break the cycle, individuals must:
✓ Understand their past
✓ Be honest about their motives for marriage
✓ Seek therapy to resolve trauma
✓ Re-learn love and rebuild emotional independence
✓ True healing begins not in the marriage, but in the self.

Chapter 2: Dependency, Identity, and the Psychological Roots of Marriage Choices

Introduction

Dependency in love has become one of the most complex psychosocial issues affecting women across Africa and globally. In many societies—whether rural villages in Limpopo, dense townships like Alexandra and Khayelitsha, or urban centres in New York and São Paulo—women are socialised to believe that marriage is not simply a partnership, but a primary pathway to security, financial stability, and emotional identity.

This expectation forms what can be described as Dependency Syndrome in Marriage: a psychological pattern where marriage becomes the only perceived escape from poverty, trauma, or social instability. Although marriage should ideally provide support and companionship, it can become a source of mental health strain when used as a survival mechanism.

1. Cultural Origins of Dependency Syndrome

The cultural idea that *"a woman shall leave her home to join her husband"* has been interpreted for generations as an obligation rather than a choice. In many African contexts, a girl's future is imagined through marriage before she even develops a sense of personal identity. This creates:

✓ Pressure to marry early
✓ Anxiety when marriage is delayed
✓ Feelings of failure when not chosen by a man
✓ An emotional link between marriage and survival

As a result, many women—even highly educated and successful ones—tie their self-worth to their ability to secure and maintain a relationship.

2. Living Conditions and the Roots of Psychological Dependency

Townships, Villages, and the Cycle of Escape

In overcrowded households—such as RDP homes, shacks, or one-room structures found in Alexandra, Khayelitsha, and villages like Makholeng or Seshio—children grow up with:

✓ No privacy
✓ Nightly exposure to adult sexual activity
✓ Domestic violence
✓ Parental substance abuse
✓ Emotional neglect
✓ Financial instability

This exposure produces childhood trauma, which later shapes adult behavior and relationship decisions. Many young girls see marriage as the only way to:

✓ Escape poverty
✓ Gain physical space
✓ Find emotional safety
✓ Establish identity
✓ Access financial stability

Thus, marriage becomes an escape route rather than a mutual choice.

3. Trauma, Early Sexual Exposure, and Co-Dependency

In cramped environments, many children unintentionally witness sexual activity among adults or older siblings. This contributes to:

- ✓ Early sexualisation
- ✓ Higher teenage pregnancy rates
- ✓ Vulnerability to older partners
- ✓ Risk of sexually transmitted infections, including HIV

Young people, especially girls, enter relationships prematurely because they associate adulthood and sex with escape, independence, and love.

4. Co-Dependency Beyond Gender

Although women are often the focus, men are equally trapped in co-dependent patterns. Men from impoverished homes may seek marriage for:

- ✓ Housing
- ✓ Emotional support
- ✓ Escape from abusive families
- ✓ Financial relief

Some older women also enter relationships with younger men for emotional escape or companionship. Co-dependency thus becomes multi-directional, affecting both genders and all socioeconomic backgrounds.

5. Marriage as Survival, Not Choice

Many marriages today are formed under pressure, not compatibility. Couples marry to:

✓ Leave unhealthy homes
✓ Gain stability
✓ Escape trauma
✓ Please family expectations
✓ Access better living conditions

This creates marriages that are structurally fragile. During the first years, partners realise they are mismatched, yet remain because:

✓ They cannot afford to leave
✓ They depend financially on each other
✓ Returning home means returning to hardship
✓ Divorce carries shame
✓ Children complicate separation

Thus, people stay in marriages that deepen their trauma, leading to mental health struggles such as depression, anger, anxiety, and emotional exhaustion.

6. Identity Problems and Psychological Confusion

When children grow up with:

✓ constant conflict,

✓ lack of guidance,

✓ lack of love,

✓ overcrowded homes,

✓ parental dysfunction,

✓ they develop identity confusion. They may not know:

✓ what a healthy relationship looks like

✓ whether they want to marry or remain single

✓ what kind of partner to choose

✓ how to understand their gender or sexual identity

✓ Social chaos creates psychological chaos. Exposure to violence, drugs, and neglect leads to:

✓ identity instability

✓ poor self-esteem

✓ attraction to harmful environments

✓ vulnerability to exploitation

Freud's concepts of the id, ego, and superego illustrate how early experiences shape self-identity. Without secure attachment, the child's ego becomes fragile, making adulthood chaotic.

7. Why Therapy Is Essential

People avoid therapy because they fear discovering uncomfortable truths:

✓ Why they actually married

✓ How deeply childhood shaped their choices

✓ Whether their partner fits their true identity

✓ The trauma they bring into relationships

✓ However, therapy provides the only pathway to:

✓ Understanding one's childhood

✓ Healing trauma

✓ Breaking dependency patterns

✓ Re-learning healthy love

✓ Building emotional independence

✓ Both individual and couple's therapy are essential for sustainable marriages.

8. A Global Issue, Not Only African

Dependency syndrome appears worldwide:

✓ Brazil's favelas
✓ New York's foster care systems
✓ Russian orphanage survivors
✓ Vietnamese urban poverty
✓ Australian social care homes

Wherever poverty, trauma, neglect, or instability exist, marriage becomes a psychological refuge. The pattern is global and universal.

Conclusion of the Chapter

Co-dependency in marriage is not simply a relationship issue—it is a psychological, cultural, and economic phenomenon shaped by childhood trauma, living conditions, and social expectations.

To break the cycle:

Women and men must understand the true motives behind their relationships.

Therapy must be accessible and destigmatized.

Individuals must confront their past openly and honestly.

Society must create safe environments for children so they do not grow up using marriage as an escape.

Healing begins with self-understanding. Only through therapy, emotional education, and personal honesty can people build marriages rooted in love—not survival.

Chapter 3: Dependency Syndrome in Marriage – A Cycle of Escape, Trauma, and Identity

Dependency in love has become one of the most powerful forces shaping the emotional, social, and psychological lives of women, particularly in many African communities. While love, partnership, and companionship should ideally be sources of support, the reality for countless young women is that marriage becomes a survival strategy rather than a conscious choice. This chapter explores how *dependency syndrome in marriage*—the core concept of this book—emerges, evolves, and affects women across different social contexts.

From a young age, many girls in rural and township communities are taught, both directly and indirectly, that marriage is their path out of poverty. Whether in Limpopo villages, crowded RDP settlements, or the urban townships of Soweto, Alexandra, and Khayelitsha, young girls grow up absorbing a message: *to be safe, to be secure, to be respected, and to be free, you must marry a man who can provide.* Even in Western settings, similar patterns emerge, where financial security becomes a silent condition for choosing a partner. Although rooted in biblical and cultural traditions that portray a woman "leaving her mother's home to join her husband," this practice has increasingly created unintended psychological consequences.

Introduction

Dependency syndrome in marriage remains one of the most complex psychological and socio-cultural phenomena affecting relationships globally. Although often associated with economic hardship or traditional gender norms, dependency is far more deeply rooted in identity formation, childhood experiences, trauma histories, and cultural expectations. In both Western and African societies, dependency manifests through emotional over-reliance, financial dependence, impaired autonomy, and compromised personal agency.

Drawing on Sigmund Freud's theories of identity formation, projection, and transference, this chapter examines how dependency becomes internalized and reproduced within marital relationships. Furthermore, it explores how this pattern presents differently in **New York (USA), Nigeria, and Mozambique**, revealing both universal mechanisms and culturally specific dynamics.

Chapter 4: The Origins of Dependency

Amara learned early that life's hardships were not optional—they were inevitable. Her mornings began with chores before the sun fully rose, her afternoons filled with the noise and chaos of a crowded home. She had no private space to reflect, no room to explore who she was beyond her roles as daughter, sister, and helper. In her village of Khayelitsha, the message was clear: a girl's value was measured by the stability of the man she could marry. Education mattered, yes—but survival mattered more. Marriage became a blueprint for safety, a ticket out of crowded shacks and daily trauma.

Sipho's upbringing was different but just as confining. Born in a Johannesburg suburb, he had access to education and resources that Amara could only dream of. Yet his father's emotional coldness and high expectations left Sipho navigating adulthood without a clear model of intimacy or emotional safety. From Freud's perspective, Sipho's ego defenses had developed early to manage anxiety: he learned to suppress vulnerability and to perform competence externally, even as internal insecurities shaped his choices in love. In adulthood, he projected unmet childhood needs onto partners, seeking approval and validation where real compatibility was absent.

Meanwhile, Maya in New York City faced a subtler but equally potent set of pressures. In her professional circles, success was celebrated—but personal life was scrutinized. Single women, no matter their achievements, were subtly reminded of societal expectations. Jung's ideas of archetypes illuminate Maya's experience: the "Anima" and "Animus" within her psyche were influenced not only by personal upbringing but by collective societal narratives of what a woman or man "should" be. The pressure to marry, to be chosen, to prove worth through romantic attachment, became an internalized script that dictated her relational patterns.

Across these diverse settings—rural South Africa, urban Johannesburg, and cosmopolitan New York—the roots of dependency syndrome reveal a convergence of trauma, social expectation, and internalized beliefs.

Poverty, overcrowding, and exposure to abuse shape Amara's early dependence. Societal status and parental expectation mold Sipho's emotional hesitancy and conditional relationships. Cultural norms, professional comparison, and media representations intensify Maya's anxiety and attachment struggles.

Eric Fromm's concept of *Freedom of the Self* offers insight into why dependency is so persistent. Fromm argues that genuine love is an active choice, rooted in awareness, respect, and autonomy.

Dependency—whether driven by survival, social pressure, or internalized beliefs—erodes freedom, making love conditional, transactional, and ultimately limiting.

People like Amara, Sipho, and Maya find themselves repeating relational patterns not because they are incapable of love, but because they have not yet reclaimed the freedom to love without fear, expectation, or compulsion.

Understanding these origins is critical for intervention. It is not enough to advise individuals to "leave toxic relationships" or to "be independent." The roots of dependency are deeply psychological, social, and cultural. They require exploration, acknowledgment, and gradual deconstruction.

Therapy, mentorship, cultural dialogue, and narrative reflection provide pathways, but these must be adapted to context: village-based approaches for Amara, urban therapy models for Sipho, and holistic self-awareness practices for Maya.

By tracing these pathways, this book invites readers to reflect: Where do our own choices come from?

How have our childhood experiences, societal norms, and internalized beliefs shaped the way we seek love, safety, and identity? The journey begins with awareness.

Only by understanding the origins of dependency can one begin the process of disentangling survival-driven decisions from authentic desire, reclaiming the freedom to love, and nurturing a self-defined identity.

Chapter 5: Living Conditions, Trauma, and Early Dependence

Amara grew up in a home where the walls were thin, both literally and emotionally. The small two-room house she shared with her mother, grandmother, and three siblings in Khayelitsha was always loud—pots clanging, babies crying, neighbours arguing, radios humming.

Privacy was a luxury no one could afford.

The constant presence of others meant Amara learned early to silence her needs and adapt to the demands around her.

In psychological terms, she developed what clinicians call *hypervigilant caregiving*: a survival strategy where a child becomes overly attentive to others' moods to prevent conflict or violence.

Her grandmother often reminded her, *"Indoda yindlela yokuphila"—"A man is a pathway to survival."*

These words became a quiet script shaping her future relationships. In environments where poverty narrows life choices, dependence is rarely a character flaw—it is a survival architecture.

Researchers in trauma studies describe this as environmental dependency-conditioning, where living conditions, scarcity, and social norms fuse into unconscious behavioural patterns that follow individuals into adulthood.

Sipho, though raised in better physical conditions, was not exempt from trauma. His childhood in Johannesburg involved polished school shoes, after-school programs, and gated security—but inside the home, emotional safety was absent.

His father's unpredictability created a different kind of instability: not loud, but silent; not chaotic, but cold. Sipho learned to read micro-expressions, anticipating whether his father would offer approval or disapproval. The emotional distance taught him that love had to be earned.

In adulthood, Sipho struggled with intimacy. Romantic relationships felt like untested territory because his early experiences had trained him to distrust vulnerability.

According to attachment theory, he developed an avoidant attachment style, marked by self-reliance on the surface and loneliness beneath. His trauma was invisible but persistent—shaping the way he entered and exited relationships without ever feeling fully seen.

On the other side of the world, Maya navigated a different set of cultural forces. Living in New York meant access to therapy, self-help literature, and diverse communities, yet she carried an internal weight she could never quite explain. Her parents, immigrants who had sacrificed everything for stability, often reminded her that success was the ultimate repayment. She excelled academically, built a career, and achieved everything that would make her family proud—yet she felt hollow.

In her romantic life, Maya gravitated toward partners who validated her achievements but never her emotions. Her dependency was not financial—it was psychological. She feared abandonment, over-explained herself, and tolerated emotional inconsistencies because they felt familiar. Jungian psychology frames this as the shadow of the achiever archetype—a part of the self-shaped by societal narratives of perfection, masking deeper insecurities.

Across all three stories, a consistent pattern emerges:

Trauma is not always dramatic. Sometimes it is the accumulation of small, repeated experiences—poverty, silence, shame, or emotional neglect—that shape the architecture of dependency.

Fromm notes that many people cling to relationships not out of love but out of fear: fear of loneliness, fear of meaninglessness, fear of inadequacy. In places like Khayelitsha, partnership becomes a shield against economic uncertainty. In suburban Johannesburg, it becomes a performance of stability. In New York, it becomes a measure of social success.

This chapter highlights a crucial psychological truth:

Dependency does not begin in adulthood. It is born in childhood, shaped by environment, culture, and the emotional climate of the home.

Amara's quiet endurance, Sipho's emotional avoidance, and Maya's chronic self-doubt reflect different faces of the same phenomenon. Each of them learned, in their formative years, that love is conditional: on obedience, on achievement, on resilience.

As their adult stories unfold, so do the lingering effects of these early lessons. Their struggles are not signs of weakness but evidence of how deeply human beings adapt in order to survive. And because dependency is learned, it can also be unlearned—through awareness, compassionate introspection, and the courage to break inherited emotional patterns.

1. The Psychological Foundations: Freud's Ideology of Identity and Projections in Love

Sigmund Freud's psychoanalytic theory provides a foundational lens for understanding dependency in adult relationships. According to Freud, identity is not a fixed construct—it forms through childhood attachments, internalized family dynamics, and unresolved unconscious conflicts. These early experiences shape the "internal working model" of love, safety, and self-worth.

1. Freud's Identity Theory and the Dependent Self

Freud argued that identity develops through:

- introjection of parental qualities,
- negotiation between the id, ego, and superego,
- internal conflicts between desire, morality, and reality.

When a child grows up in an environment where autonomy is discouraged, affection is conditional, or survival is linked to obedience, the ego develops adaptive mechanisms that later create dependency in adulthood.

For many women globally, marriage becomes the arena where this incomplete identity structure is replayed.

1.2 Relationship Projection and Transference in Marriage

Freud described projection as a process where individuals transfer their unconscious needs, fears, or unresolved emotions onto others.

In dependent marriages, partners often project:

- the need for security,
- fears of abandonment,
- unresolved childhood longing for approval,
- internal emptiness that seeks external filling.

This projection leads to romanticised dependency, where the spouse becomes the symbolic replacement of a parent, protector, or emotional anchor.

2. Dependency as a Cycle of Escape and Trauma

Dependency in marriage is not simply a matter of financial need; it is often a psychological escape from:

- poverty,
- loneliness,
- childhood trauma,
- social expectations,
- internal identity conflicts.

Across cultures, marriage becomes a coping mechanism—a refuge promising stability and validation. However, when the foundation of union is survival rather than partnership, dependency evolves into a cycle that weakens personal identity and autonomy.

3. Comparative Contexts: New York, Nigeria, and Mozambique

Although dependency syndrome manifests universally, each society imposes unique cultural pressures, economic conditions, and relational expectations.

Comparing these regions reveals how dependency is shaped by local realities and how Freud's theories remain relevant across cultures.

3.1 New York, USA: Emotional Isolation and Economic Anxiety

New York represents a high-income, cosmopolitan environment where women possess legal autonomy, employment opportunities, and access to financial institutions. Yet dependency still persists—often in a subtle psychological form.

Challenges in New York

Emotional Loneliness in High-Pressure Environments

The intense pace of urban life creates emotional gaps that push individuals to seek security in relationships. Dependency arises not from economic need, but from psychological neediness and unresolved identity insecurities.

Economic Competition and Gender Performance Anxiety

High living costs and economic precarity (housing, healthcare, childcare) increase reliance on a financially stable partner. Marriage becomes a buffer against the uncertainty of single life.

Trauma Rooted in Family Histories

Many individuals carry intergenerational trauma, childhood neglect, or parental absence, unconsciously recreating these patterns through dependent attachments.

Freud's conception of transference is particularly evident here: partners unconsciously use each other to fill emotional voids left by earlier relational ruptures.

3.2 Nigeria: Patriarchy, Economic Inequality, and Cultural Obligation

Nigeria presents a socio-cultural landscape where gender expectations and economic structures strongly influence dependency dynamics.

Challenges in Nigeria

- Deeply Entrenched Patriarchal Norms

Marriage is culturally positioned as a woman's ultimate identity marker. This reinforces early socialization where girls are taught to rely on male provision for legitimacy and survival.

- Limited Economic Opportunities for Women

Although progress is emerging, many regions still provide fewer economic pathways for women. Financial dependence becomes a structural consequence rather than a personal choice.

- Bride Price System and Familial Pressure

Practices such as bride price create a transactional view of marriage, intensifying a woman's perceived obligation to remain dependent, loyal, and emotionally submissive.

- Religious Expectations

Religious teachings emphasising obedience, submission, and endurance further complicate autonomy.

Freudian theory interacts with these norms by explaining how early identity development—within obedience-oriented cultures—produces adults whose sense of self is externally defined.

3.3 Mozambique: Post-Conflict Trauma, Poverty, and Social Vulnerability

Mozambique's history, marked by civil conflict, poverty, and displacement, shapes its marital structures and dependency patterns.

Challenges in Mozambique

Post-War Trauma and Gender Vulnerability

Many women who grew up during or after conflict internalized identities rooted in survival, fear, and scarcity. Marriage becomes a protective mechanism, reinforcing dependency.

High Poverty Rates

Economic hardship results in transactional marriages where survival outweighs emotional compatibility.

Early Marriage Practices

In rural communities, early marriage remains common, with girls entering unions before identity formation is complete. This produces lifelong dependency and limited sense of self.

Limited Access to Education and Health Services

Restricted opportunities for women strengthen psychological and financial dependence on male partners.

Freud's theory aligns here with the idea that trauma-filled childhoods shape adult relational patterns grounded in fear, compliance, and emotional fusion.

4. Global Patterns: What New York, Nigeria, and Mozambique Have in Common

Despite vast differences, several universal mechanisms emerge:

Identity Formation Dictates Attachment Style

Incomplete or trauma-shaped identities increase dependency tendencies across cultures.

Socio-Economic Pressure Reinforces Dependency

Whether through poverty (Nigeria, Mozambique) or economic anxiety (New York), financial instability drives people into dependent marriages.

Projection and Transference Are Universal

Across all three contexts, partners project childhood needs and unmet emotional longings onto their spouses.

Marriage as Escape Rather Than Choice

Whether escaping poverty, loneliness, or internal emptiness, dependency marriages are often rooted in psychological need rather than relational readiness.

5. A Cross-Cultural Psychological Reality

Dependency syndrome in marriage is not a uniquely African or Western phenomenon. Instead, it reflects a universal human struggle rooted in identity formation, early emotional experiences, and socio-economic constraints. Freud's theories illuminate how unresolved childhood needs shape adult relational dependency, while global comparisons reveal the powerful role of cultural conditions.

Understanding these patterns is necessary for developing healthier relationships where love is chosen—not used as an escape, replacement, or psychological crutch.

This chapter therefore lays the foundation for the deeper exploration that follows: how partners can break the cycle, reconstruct identity, and rebuild marriage on principles of equality, autonomy, and emotional maturity.

Living Conditions and the Origins of Dependence

For many girls, the push toward marriage begins with their living conditions. Growing up in overcrowded homes—sometimes a one-room shack, an RDP house, or a small four-room township dwelling—exposes them to trauma at an early age. Reconstruction and Development Programme (RDP) house, which is a socio economic policy, launched in 1994 by the government of South Africa under Nelson Mandela to address a social problems like poverty, lack of housing and inequality. The term RDP became most popular for free house to lower income people and unemployed person in South Africa. Although for anyone to qualify for the RDP house, they should be a South African citizen.

Privacy is almost nonexistent: parents engage in sexual activity in the same space where children sleep, siblings share mattresses, and the boundaries between adulthood and childhood dissolve. These conditions silence many girls, who carry shame, confusion, and unresolved trauma into adulthood.

Some girls witness sexual acts daily; others are exposed to sexual assault within the home. In such environments, the desire to "leave home" becomes urgent. Marriage is not simply a romantic ambition—it is an escape route from poverty, noise, sexual exposure, alcohol misuse, and emotional neglect.

The foundation of dependency syndrome in marriage often begins long before a woman enters her first romantic relationship.

In many communities—rural villages in Limpopo, townships in Gauteng and Western Cape, or informal settlements across Africa—living conditions create a complex web of environmental, psychological, and social pressures that shape young girls' perceptions of love, safety, and identity. These pressures are not merely economic; they are profoundly emotional and developmental, influencing relational patterns that can persist into adulthood.

Overcrowding and the Dissolution of Boundaries

For countless girls, homes are overcrowded spaces where privacy is a scarce commodity. One-room shacks, RDP houses, or small four-room township dwellings often house large families, leaving children without separate spaces to sleep, study, or reflect. In these cramped environments, girls routinely witness adult sexual activity—parents may engage in intimacy in the same room where children sleep, siblings may share mattresses, and even discussions about personal boundaries or bodily autonomy are often absent. The natural boundary between childhood and adulthood becomes blurred, fostering confusion about acceptable social and sexual behaviour.

This lack of privacy has profound psychological consequences.

Girls internalize experiences they do not understand, often feeling shame, guilt, or confusion about natural bodily functions and sexual curiosity. These early exposures contribute to an internalization of unsafe relational norms: intimacy is conflated with survival, secrecy, and compliance, rather than mutual respect or emotional connection.

Freud's framework of identity formation is particularly relevant here: the ego, tasked with mediating between desires (id) and societal expectations (superego), becomes fragile when childhood experiences are saturated with unresolved confusion and trauma.

Early Exposure to Sexual Acts and Abuse

Beyond general overcrowding, some girls witness sexual activity on a daily basis, while others are tragically exposed to sexual assault within the home.

Such exposure is not incidental; it profoundly shapes the development of relational templates. When sexual activity occurs in environments marked by neglect, violence, or alcohol misuse, girls may subconsciously equate love and attention with access to safety or protection.

The consistent presence of these experiences can lead to an early, need-based orientation to intimacy, where sexual or romantic relationships are perceived primarily as survival mechanisms rather than mutual, consensual bonds.

The psychological effects of this early exposure are multifaceted:

Emotional confusion

Girls struggle to differentiate between affection, sexual attention, and coercion.

Shame and secrecy

Fear of judgment from family or community reinforces silence, preventing processing or healing.

Internalized trauma

Without adult guidance or safe disclosure, trauma becomes encoded as part of the self, shaping future relational behavior.

These experiences are central to the emergence of dependency syndrome. Women raised in such environments may enter relationships with heightened urgency, prioritizing security, acceptance, and protection over emotional compatibility or personal autonomy.

Marriage as an Escape Route

The effects of overcrowding, early exposure to sexual acts, and neglect are compounded by the socio-economic realities of poverty, unemployment, and limited education. In these contexts, marriage is no longer merely a romantic choice—it becomes a practical and psychological strategy for escape.

The drive to leave home is intensified by:

Noise and chaos

Overcrowded households generate constant stress and emotional overstimulation.

Sexual exposure

Daily exposure to adult sexual behavior or unsafe sexual environments fosters premature sexualization.

Substance abuse in the household

Alcohol or drug misuse by caregivers increases risk of neglect and violence.

Emotional neglect

Absence of parental guidance or nurturing leaves children emotionally unprepared for independent life.

For young girls, marriage is positioned as a pathway to privacy, respect, and safety. Yet, the very mechanism intended to provide escape often perpetuates dependency. Because the need for security precedes emotional maturity, these women may prioritize partner provision over personal growth, autonomy, or self-identity, establishing a lifelong pattern of relational dependence.

Dependency Syndrome: The Worrying Factor

Dependency syndrome emerges when survival needs are internalized as relational imperatives. Girls raised in high-trauma, low-privacy environments learn early that emotional survival is contingent on pleasing, appeasing, or securing a partner. Over time, this internalization manifests as:

High emotional reliance on partners

Women may struggle to maintain individuality or self-esteem outside the marital relationship.

Compromised decision-making

Dependency may lead to tolerance of abuse or suppression of personal desires.

Perpetuation of trauma cycles

Marriages founded on survival needs rather than mutual choice can replicate childhood trauma dynamics.

The syndrome is particularly worrying because it transforms natural human interdependence into a pathological reliance, limiting agency and reinforcing vulnerability across generations.

Freud's theories help explain this process of early unmet needs, combined with blurred developmental boundaries, produce adults who unconsciously seek parental figures in romantic partners, projecting unresolved childhood conflicts onto marital relationships.

Living conditions play a decisive role in shaping dependency syndrome in marriage.

Overcrowding, lack of privacy, exposure to sexual acts, neglect, and poverty converge to produce early need-based intimacy.

When these formative experiences remain unresolved, marriage becomes not a partnership of choice, but a survival strategy—a psychological, social, and economic escape route.

Understanding these dynamics is critical for developing interventions that prioritize therapy, emotional education, and safe environments, helping women—and men—break the cycle of dependency and build relationships grounded in autonomy, respect, and genuine affection.

Early Need-Based Intimacy: Neuropsychological and Attachment Consequences

The early environments in which children—particularly girls—are raised do more than shape behavioral patterns; they imprint physiological and neuropsychological markers that influence relational choices throughout life.

When exposure to intimacy, sexual acts, neglect, and trauma occurs during critical developmental windows, it fundamentally alters attachment strategies, emotional regulation, and identity formation.

Attachment Theory and Neurodevelopment

Attachment theory, pioneered by John Bowlby and expanded by Mary Ainsworth, demonstrates that secure attachment in childhood is foundational for healthy adult relationships. Children who receive consistent emotional support and safe boundaries develop a secure base from which they explore the world. Conversely, children exposed to trauma, neglect, or overcrowding often develop insecure attachment patterns, including:

Anxious-preoccupied attachment – characterized by heightened dependence on caregivers or partners, fear of abandonment, and intense need for validation.

Avoidant-dismissive attachment – characterized by emotional withdrawal, difficulty trusting, and suppression of intimacy needs.

Disorganized attachment – characterized by conflicting behaviours, such as seeking closeness while fearing it, often linked to early abuse or household chaos.

Neuroimaging studies indicate that chronic early stress elevates cortisol levels, disrupts amygdala and hippocampal development, and impairs prefrontal cortex regulation—all of which compromise emotional regulation, impulse control, and fear processing.

Girls raised in overcrowded, unsafe homes therefore carry a biological predisposition toward heightened anxiety in relationships, and a heightened sensitivity to perceived threats to security or survival.

Projection and Dependency in Adult Relationships

Freud's psychoanalytic framework offers insight into how these early experiences manifest in adult relational dynamics. When unmet needs for safety, validation, and emotional recognition are projected onto adult partners, individuals unconsciously seek caregivers rather than equal partners.

This projection of unresolved childhood needs can lead to:

Seeking partners who replicate parental figures, both positively and negatively.

Prioritizing security over compatibility, affection, or mutual growth.

Reinforcing co-dependent relational patterns, where one partner assumes a "provider-protector" role and the other a "dependent-survivor" role.

In scientific terms, these projections are reinforced by neurochemical reward circuits. Dopamine and oxytocin pathways, which are activated by perceived acceptance, attention, or protection, create conditioned responses that associate safety with relational dependence. The stronger the early deficits in nurturing, the more pronounced these neural patterns become, perpetuating dependency syndrome across relational contexts.

Impact on Emotional Regulation and Identity Formation

Early exposure to trauma and sexualized environments not only shapes attachment but also impacts emotional regulation. Chronic hypervigilance, fear of rejection, and internalized shame can disrupt the development of a coherent sense of self.

Psychologically, this manifests as:

- Difficulty setting boundaries or asserting personal needs.
- Reliance on partner validation to manage emotional states.
- Confusion about identity, gender roles, and self-worth.
- Susceptibility to repeated cycles of abusive or unfulfilling relationships.

Neuropsychological, this correlates with overactive limbic system responses, heightened amygdala sensitivity, and weakened prefrontal cortex inhibition, leading to impulsive relational decisions and low tolerance for emotional discomfort. Over time, these patterns solidify into relational habits that underpin dependency syndrome.

Cultural Amplification of Biological and Psychological Vulnerabilities

While biological and psychological factors predispose individuals to dependency, cultural and socio-economic conditions magnify the effect. In communities where marriage is socially and economically framed as a primary route to safety, identity, and respect, young women learn to normalize dependency as both a survival strategy and a moral expectation. This cultural reinforcement interacts with neurobiological predispositions, making dependency syndrome not just a personal challenge but also a systemic phenomenon.

The intersection of early need-based intimacy, trauma, and socio-economic pressure creates a neuropsychological and relational environment where dependency syndrome thrives. By altering attachment patterns, emotional regulation, and identity formation, these early experiences predispose women—and men—to seek survival over authenticity in marriage.

Understanding these mechanisms is critical: therapeutic interventions must address both the psychological imprint of trauma and the neurobiological pathways of dependence to foster emotionally independent, resilient adults capable of forming healthy partnerships.

Cross-Cultural Perspectives on Dependency Syndrome in Marriage

Dependency syndrome in marriage is not confined to any single region; rather, it emerges wherever socio-economic pressures, childhood trauma, and cultural norms intersect. Examining New York, Nigeria, and Mozambique highlights both universal psychological mechanisms and context-specific manifestations of dependency.

1. New York: Urban Survival, Foster Care, and Relational Projections

In New York City, dependency syndrome is often rooted in urban poverty, single-parent households, and the foster care system.

Many young women grow up in crowded apartments, exposed to domestic violence, substance abuse, or neglect. Unlike rural African settings, the dependency is less about formalized cultural expectation and more about survival within highly unstable social structures.

Psychological Mechanisms

Freud's theory of projection is evident: young women unconsciously seek partners who fulfill unresolved parental needs. For example, girls raised in foster care may seek older partners who replicate nurturing figures, prioritizing stability over compatibility.

Socio-Economic Influence

Economic insecurity, housing instability, and educational gaps increase reliance on partners for financial and emotional support. Dependency syndrome becomes a coping mechanism to avoid homelessness or repeated trauma.

- **Marriage vs. Cohabitation**

Many women enter cohabiting relationships rather than formal marriages; yet the psychological patterns of dependency—emotional reliance, fear of abandonment, and difficulty asserting boundaries—mirror those seen in marriage-dependent contexts globally.

2. Nigeria: Cultural Expectation and Socio-Economic Pressure

In Nigeria, particularly in urban centers like Lagos and rural regions, marriage is deeply intertwined with cultural and familial expectations. Young women are often socialized to view marriage as a marker of social respect, security, and adulthood. Familial pressure, combined with poverty and limited educational opportunities, amplifies dependency.

Cultural Norms and Gender Roles

Societal narratives stress that a woman's value is tied to her marital status.

Freud's identity theory helps explain how young women internalize these expectations, projecting their need for validation and social acceptance onto potential husbands.

Economic Constraints

Limited access to employment or independent income increases reliance on partners, reinforcing dependency patterns. Women may accept marriages with older men for financial stability or social elevation, even if emotional compatibility is lacking.

Psychological Implications

Trauma from childhood neglect, domestic instability, or sexual exposure contributes to anxious attachment.

Unresolved early conflicts often manifest as fear of abandonment, submissive behavior, and difficulty negotiating emotional needs in marriage.

3. Mozambique: Poverty, Polygamy, and Early Marriage

In Mozambique, particularly in rural provinces like Zambézia and Nampula, dependency syndrome is amplified by extreme poverty, early marriage, and polygamous practices. Many young women marry in adolescence as a survival strategy, escaping overcrowded households, domestic labor, and food insecurity.

Structural Challenges

Early marriage and polygamy limit autonomy. Freud's psychoanalytic perspective suggests that girls project unmet childhood needs onto their husbands, expecting emotional security, protection, and recognition from partners who are often absent, older, or polygamous.

Socio-Economic Triggers

Poverty reinforces transactional aspects of marriage: women are expected to exchange companionship, domestic labour, and fidelity for material security. Dependency becomes both emotional and financial, creating a cycle of subordination and vulnerability.

Impact on Identity

Early marriage interrupts identity development. Young women struggle to differentiate their authentic selves from the roles imposed by family and society, often maintaining a fragmented sense of identity that persists into adulthood.

4. Cross-Cultural Analysis: Universal Patterns and Divergences

Despite contextual differences, several universal mechanisms emerge:

Factor	New York	Nigeria	Mozambique
Childhood Trauma	Foster care, urban poverty, domestic instability	Domestic instability, parental neglect	Overcrowding, domestic labor, early sexual exposure
Cultural Pressure	Low formal expectation, high social instability	High familial and societal pressure to marry	High cultural and economic pressure for early marriage
Economic Dependency	Housing, employment instability	Limited employment, gendered economic roles	Extreme poverty, transactional marriage
Attachment Patterns	Anxious, avoidant, disorganized	Anxious, preoccupied	Anxious, dependent, fragmented identity
Identity Confusion	Moderate to high	High	Very high due to early marriage
Marital Motivation	Emotional rescue, survival	Social respect, financial stability	Survival, escape from household, economic security

Freud's Identity Theory

Across contexts, unresolved childhood conflicts influence adult relational projections.

Women unconsciously seek partners who symbolize protection, validation, or escape.

The id's desires for security and pleasure are mediated by the ego's pragmatic negotiation with socio-cultural pressures, while the superego reflects internalized societal norms around marriage and propriety.

Dependency Syndrome as a Global Phenomenon

Although the triggers vary—urban instability in New York, familial expectations in Nigeria, early marriage in Mozambique—the psychological mechanism remains consistent: early trauma + socio-cultural reinforcement = dependency in adult relationships.

5. Implications for Therapy and Policy

Understanding the cross-cultural manifestations of dependency syndrome is essential for effective interventions:

Therapeutic Approaches

Individual and couple therapy should address early trauma, attachment patterns, identity confusion, and relational projections. Psychoanalytic insight can help individuals recognize unconscious motives for dependency.

Policy Interventions

Governments and NGOs must focus on early childhood protection, educational access, safe housing, and community support systems to reduce socio-economic triggers for dependency.

Global Learning

Practices effective in one context—e.g., mentoring programs in urban New York—can be adapted to low-resource settings in Nigeria or Mozambique, considering cultural specificity.

Dependency syndrome in marriage is both a psychological and socio-cultural phenomenon, transcending borders and economic status. By comparing New York, Nigeria, and Mozambique, it becomes evident that while socio-economic conditions and cultural norms shape its expression, the underlying psychological mechanisms—rooted in childhood trauma, attachment patterns, and Freud's identity theory—are universal.

Interventions must therefore combine trauma-informed therapy, socio-economic support, and culturally sensitive education to break the cycle and foster relational autonomy.

Chapter 6: Trauma, Memory, and the Body

Chapter Summary - The Roots of Emotional Dependency

This chapter explores emotional dependency as a survival strategy formed through childhood experiences, family dynamics, and cultural pressure. It examines how lack of emotional validation, poverty, and instability can lead to adulthood patterns such as fear of abandonment, clinginess, self-sacrifice, or difficulty functioning alone. Through examples from diverse contexts—villages in Limpopo, urban Johannesburg, Lagos, and New York—the chapter shows how dependency may look different but originates from similar emotional gaps.

Introduction

The body remembers what the mind tries to forget.

This truth—ancient, biological, and quietly universal—sat at the centre of all three characters' lives, shaping their relationships, decisions, and even their illnesses.

Trauma was not just in their stories; it pulsed beneath their skin, lived in their breathing, and expressed itself through the diseases they carried.

1. The Weight of Memory on the Body

Amara always assumed her exhaustion came from long work hours and stress, but the nurses at the community clinic saw something else. Elevated blood pressure. Uncontrolled glucose levels. Constant dizziness. The doctor explained it gently: *"Your body is fighting battles you haven't named yet."*

At first, she didn't understand.

How could her childhood fight-or-flight instincts still be active decades later?

In trauma psychology, this is known as body memory—the way the nervous system stores emotional pain not as thoughts but as physical reactions. For Amara, the years of hearing midnight fights, waking to uncertainty, and living with scarcity had taught her nervous system that safety was temporary. Her body stayed ready for danger, even when danger no longer existed.

- Her heart raced at harmless sounds.
  Her muscles tightened at the hint of conflict.
  Her digestive system rebelled whenever she tried to rest.

Branny Mthelebofu's concept of Emotional Indigestion Disease became painfully real in her body. The suppressed emotions—the grief she swallowed, the fear she ignored, the disappointments she tried to outrun—sat inside her like unprocessed food. Her heart was tired not from love, but from holding everything in.

2. When the Mind Splits to Survive

For Sipho, trauma never screamed—it whispered.

His memories were not chaotic moments of abuse but prolonged emotional emptiness. Freud would describe this as the formation of ego-defences—psychological strategies the mind develops to cope with unmet emotional needs.

Sipho became a master at dissociation. When conflict arose, he did not argue or shout; he simply disappeared into himself. His girlfriends often complained:

"Talk to me."

"You shut down when I need you."

"You act like everything is fine when you're hurting."

But shutting down *was* Sipho's language of safety.

In neuropsychology, the brain numbs itself in the face of emotional overload by disconnecting consciousness from the body.

He felt sadness only as tightness in his chest, anger as migraines, fear as stomach pain. He was a man who lived outside his own feelings.

His body was speaking a language he had never learned to translate.

3. When Success Fails to Heal

Maya—educated, employed, independent—carried her trauma in more subtle ways. She was the embodiment of modern pressure: a woman who could lead teams and mobilize resources but couldn't calm her own heart at night.

Her therapist once told her:

"You are constantly performing safety—your body doesn't believe you're safe."

This was the modern epidemic: high-functioning trauma.

Her anxiety manifested as:

heart palpitations,

stress eating,

sleeplessness,

and bursts of self-doubt.

She often paused at her reflection, confused:

How can a body that looks whole feel so broken inside?

The answer lay in trauma physiology. When emotional wounds remain unaddressed:

cortisol levels rise,

inflammation increases,

appetite dysregulates,

and the body begins to deteriorate.

This is why diabetes, obesity, and hypertension disproportionately affect those carrying deep emotional burdens. The body becomes a battlefield where memories and survival instincts collide.

4. How Trauma Shapes Love and Intimacy

Despite growing up in different worlds, Amara, Sipho, and Maya shared the same internal war. Their bodies had learned to confuse love with survival. Trauma alters the brain's memory centres—the amygdala, hippocampus, and prefrontal cortex—making unhealthy relationships feel familiar and stable relationships feel threatening.

Amara gravitated toward controlling partners because predictability felt like safety.

Sipho withdrew from partners because intimacy felt dangerous.

Maya over-accommodated partners because abandonment felt unbearable.

Trauma determines:

what feels attractive,
what feels dangerous,
what feels like "home."

It is not the heart that chooses bad partners—
it is the nervous system seeking what it learned to survive.

5. The Village Therapy Method: Healing When People Refuse Therapy

In the rural communities Branny Mthelebofu studied, many people avoided therapy, believing it was:

for "weak people,"
for "Western minds,"
or a sign of "craziness."

This resistance inspired the concept of Village Therapy—a culturally rooted, community-sensitive approach that heals through everyday living rather than formal clinical spaces.

Village Therapy blends:

- **Cultural familiarity**

Healing through storytelling circles, traditional songs, church women's groups, and grandmother-led conversations.

Psychological principles

Stepped exposure, reflective self-awareness, emotional naming, boundary-setting.

Somatic healing

Walking groups, communal gardening, dancing, and body-based stress release.

Social safety

Healing through belonging—because trauma is often born from isolation.

Village Therapy teaches people to process emotional pain in community.

Healing happens not in a therapy room, but in:

the field,
the kitchen,
the church bench,
the neighbour's stoep,
the storytelling fire.
It is therapy disguised as life.

6. The Body's Call for Liberation

Every character reaches a point where the body becomes louder than the mind.
For Amara, it was a sudden collapse at work.
For Sipho, a panic attack that felt like a heart attack.
For Maya, the burnout that left her unable to get out of bed.
These moments were not failures—they were messages.

The body was saying:

"You cannot carry this alone anymore."

Trauma accumulates, compresses, and eventually erupts.

However, this eruption is also the beginning of healing.

7. The Path Forward

In the next chapter, each character will learn to reinterpret their body signals:

Anxiety becomes a sign of a story untold.

Insomnia becomes a protest for silence and rest.

Weight gain becomes a shield the body uses for emotional protection.

Emotional numbness becomes a sign of past survival.

Trauma does not define them.

But understanding trauma allows them to reclaim their lives.

Memory lives in the body—but so does healing.

Three Lives, One Struggle

Amara woke up to the sound of children crying in the crowded one-room shack she shared with her parents and three siblings in Khayelitsha. The sun barely lit the small space, yet the heat and smell of dampness made it feel suffocating.

From an early age, she had learned that escape meant marriage. Watching her mother silently endure her father's drinking and occasional violence, Amara had internalized a silent code: to survive, she must find a man who could provide safety, food, and stability.

Love, she thought, was a luxury; survival was a necessity.

At fourteen, she found herself drawn to older men who offered the security her home never could.

Thousands of kilometers away, in Johannesburg, Sipho sat in his sleek corporate apartment overlooking the city skyline. He had a high-paying job, a degree from a prestigious university, and social respect. Yet, his personal life was a maze of anxiety and half-formed relationships.

Despite his success, he struggled to commit fully. From childhood, he had learned to hide vulnerability—his father had been distant, emotionally cold, and exacting. He sought partners not only for companionship but as a way to satisfy societal expectations.

Divorce or being single was a mark of failure in his social circles. Even with money and education, Sipho realized he was trapped in what Branny Mthelebofu would call *Emotional Indigestion*—a constant mental and emotional strain where achievement could not compensate for unresolved inner conflict.

Across the Atlantic, in New York City, Maya, a mid-level executive in a competitive media firm, scrolled through her social media feeds late at night. Every image of her colleagues with partners, every story of a friend's engagement or wedding, fed a creeping anxiety inside her.

Despite her independence, her accomplishments did not shield her from cultural expectations she had absorbed: being chosen, being partnered, being "complete." She had endured a series of relationships that mirrored her unresolved childhood experiences.

She realized, almost painfully, that she had projected unmet needs onto her partners—seeking affirmation, love, and security in ways that were never truly reciprocal.

Across continents and contexts, a pattern emerged.

Each of these lives reflected the profound impact of *dependency syndrome in marriage*. For Amara, it was survival; for Sipho, societal pressure; for Maya, internalized expectations compounded by modern urban culture. Yet, despite the differences in geography, education, and socioeconomic status, their challenges were strikingly similar: unresolved childhood trauma, societal pressures, and internalized beliefs about love, identity, and worth.

Psychologically, these patterns can be traced through Freud's lens: the id's unmet desires, the ego's fragile defenses, and the superego's moral judgments all interacting to shape adult relationships. Jung's ideas of archetypes and collective cultural narratives illuminate how societal expectations subtly influence the choices people believe are theirs to make.

And as Eric Fromm reminds us, love is an art and a practice, but it requires freedom—freedom from dependency, fear, and projection. Without this freedom, love becomes transactional, conditional, and constraining.

This book will journey with Amara, Sipho, and Maya—not as a distant study of cases but as a mirror for readers to recognize themselves in the patterns of dependency, projection, and survival.

Through narrative, practical exercises, and psychological insight, readers will explore ways to reclaim autonomy, rebuild identity, and cultivate the freedom to love authentically.

Healing is not linear; freedom is not instant. Yet, by understanding the roots of dependency and the forces that shape relational choices, one can begin to untangle the emotional chains and step toward a life where love is chosen, not endured, and where happiness is no longer a source of fear but a lived reality.

Therapeutic Pathways and Psychoanalytic Interventions for Dependency Syndrome in Marriage

Dependency syndrome in marriage, as explored across diverse socio-cultural contexts, is fundamentally rooted in unresolved childhood trauma, socio-economic pressures, and internalized cultural norms. Breaking this cycle requires a multidimensional therapeutic approach—one that combines psychoanalytic insight, trauma-informed care, relational therapy, and practical interventions for emotional and social empowerment.

1. Psychoanalytic Foundations: Freud and Identity Development

Sigmund Freud's psychoanalytic theory provides a foundational lens to understand the psychological mechanisms behind dependency in marriage:

Id, Ego, and Superego

The id represents instinctual drives seeking pleasure, security, and love. Women and men affected by dependency syndrome often unconsciously project these unmet needs onto partners.

The ego mediates these desires within social and environmental constraints, negotiating survival in contexts of poverty, trauma, and cultural pressure.

The superego internalizes societal norms—marriage as a mark of success, gender roles, or moral expectations—which reinforce dependency patterns.

Identity Formation

Childhood trauma—exposure to violence, neglect, or sexualisation—distorts identity development. Individuals may unconsciously select partners who recreate familiar emotional patterns, seeking resolution through external relationships rather than internal healing.

Transference in Relationships

Freud's concept of transference explains how unresolved childhood conflicts are projected onto marital partners. For example, a spouse may unconsciously be perceived as a parental figure, providing security or fulfilling emotional gaps, perpetuating co-dependency.

2. Attachment Theory and Relational Patterns

Building on psychoanalytic theory, attachment theory **explains how early caregiver-child interactions influence adult relational behavior:**

Insecure Attachment

Anxious attachment manifests as fear of abandonment, excessive clinging, and emotional overdependence on a partner.

Avoidant attachment involves emotional withdrawal, reluctance to rely on partners, and fear of intimacy.

Disorganized attachment—common in severely traumatized backgrounds—combines anxious and avoidant tendencies, creating chaos in marital interactions.

Dependency Syndrome as a Coping Mechanism

Individuals with insecure attachment patterns often interpret marriage as a safe haven, compensating for unresolved childhood insecurity. This dynamic reinforces dependency rather than mutual interdependence.

3. Trauma-Informed Therapeutic Interventions

Therapy for dependency syndrome must prioritize trauma-informed approaches, acknowledging that dependency is a survival strategy rather than moral failure.

a. Individual Therapy

Objective

Facilitate self-awareness, emotional regulation, and identity reconstruction.

Methods:

- Psychoanalytic exploration of childhood trauma and relational projections
- Cognitive Behavioural Therapy (CBT) to challenge maladaptive beliefs about self-worth and marriage
- Narrative therapy to reconstruct personal stories and foster agency

Expected Outcomes

- Recognition of unconscious motives for dependency
- Improved self-esteem and emotional autonomy
- Enhanced capacity for healthy choice-making in relationships

b. Couple Therapy

Objective

Address relational dynamics, communication, and co-dependency patterns.

Methods

- Emotionally Focused Therapy (EFT) to identify attachment needs and fears
- Conflict resolution and boundary-setting interventions
- Psychoeducation on the impact of childhood trauma on marital interactions

Expected Outcomes

- Reduction in unhealthy dependency behaviors
- Improved empathy, communication, and mutual understanding
- Shift from survival-based marriage to partnership-based marriage

4. Group and Community Interventions

In addition to one-on-one therapy, group and community-level interventions are crucial, especially in contexts with limited access to mental health services:

Peer Support Groups

Provide safe spaces for women and men to share experiences, normalize struggles, and learn coping strategies.

Educational Workshops

Address healthy relationships, emotional literacy, conflict management, and financial independence, empowering participants to reduce dependency patterns.

Cultural Sensitization Programs

Integrate traditional leaders and community stakeholders to challenge harmful norms, promote emotional education, and facilitate supportive community structures.

5. Global Applicability of Therapeutic Strategies

New York

Trauma-informed therapy addresses the impact of foster care, urban violence, and socio-economic instability. Cognitive-behavioral techniques can complement psychoanalytic interventions.

Nigeria

Couple-focused and community interventions must consider cultural expectations and familial pressures. Psychoeducation and identity reconstruction are vital for enabling autonomy.

Mozambique

Early marriage and polygamy necessitate interventions that combine individual therapy with community advocacy, aiming to delay marriage, reduce dependency, and promote personal identity development.

6. Practical Steps for Healing Dependency Syndrome

Awareness

Individuals must understand the origins of their dependency and recognize unconscious relational patterns.

Self-Exploration

Psychoanalytic and attachment-based therapy can uncover unresolved trauma and distorted identity constructs.

Skill Building

Emotional regulation, boundary-setting, and communication skills reduce co-dependent behaviors.

Empowerment

Economic, educational, and social support increase autonomy and reduce survival-based marital decisions.

Cultural Engagement

Challenging societal norms that tie women's identity solely to marriage is essential for long-term change.

Dependency syndrome in marriage is a complex interplay of psychological, cultural, and socio-economic factors. Psychoanalytic insights, particularly Freud's identity theory and concepts of transference, illuminate how unresolved childhood trauma shapes adult relational choices. Attachment theory further clarifies patterns of co-dependency and insecure relational behaviors.

Effective therapy must integrate individual insight, relational repair, community support, and structural empowerment. By addressing the root causes of dependency—trauma, identity confusion, and social pressure—therapy allows individuals to transition from survival-based marriages to authentic partnerships grounded in emotional maturity, autonomy, and mutual respect. Ultimately, healing begins not in the marriage but within the self.

Preventive Strategies and Social Policy Recommendations for Dependency Syndrome in Marriage

The phenomenon of dependency syndrome in marriage, while deeply rooted in psychological, socio-economic, and cultural factors, can be mitigated through targeted prevention and structural interventions. Preventive strategies must address the individual, family, community, and policy levels to break cycles of trauma, identity confusion, and relational dependence.

1. Early Childhood Interventions

Preventing dependency syndrome begins with the early developmental environment:

Safe and Stable Home Environments

Governments and NGOs must prioritize policies that reduce overcrowding, improve housing quality, and provide family support services. Studies show that children raised in private, stable, and nurturing environments demonstrate higher emotional resilience, autonomy, and self-esteem—protective factors against future dependency.

Parenting Education Programs

Training caregivers in emotional literacy, conflict management, and positive discipline equips children with secure attachment patterns. Early interventions reduce the likelihood of anxious or avoidant attachment styles that contribute to adult co-dependency.

Access to Quality Education

Educational empowerment, particularly for girls, delays early marriage, strengthens identity development, and enhances financial independence. Scholarships, school retention programs, and mentorship can reduce economic pressures that drive dependency-based marital decisions.

2. Adolescent and Youth-Focused Programs

Adolescence is a critical stage for identity formation and relational learning:

Life Skills and Emotional Intelligence Training

Teaching young people emotional regulation, communication skills, and decision-making fosters self-efficacy and resilience. Programs that integrate psychoeducation about healthy relationships, gender equality, and sexual health equip youth to enter adulthood with informed choices.

Mentorship and Role Models

Exposure to mentors who model healthy, interdependent relationships provides aspirational examples. Mentorship programs in New York, Lagos, and Maputo have demonstrated reductions in early marriage and improved relational decision-making.

Sexual and Reproductive Health Education

Comprehensive, culturally sensitive sexual education reduces early pregnancies, prevents exploitative relationships, and fosters healthy sexual identity development, decreasing the urgency to seek marriage as a survival strategy.

3. Community and Cultural Interventions

Dependency syndrome is reinforced by social norms and cultural expectations.

Community-level interventions are essential:

Challenging Harmful Norms

Programs engaging traditional leaders, religious institutions, and community influencers can redefine social perceptions of marriage, shifting the narrative from survival and status to mutual partnership and personal choice.

Safe Spaces for Dialogue

Establishing women's and youth groups where individuals can discuss relational pressures, identity issues, and cultural expectations promotes critical reflection and peer support.

Public Awareness Campaigns

Media and social campaigns highlighting the psychological consequences of dependency in marriage, including depression, anxiety, and relational dissatisfaction, encourage societal accountability and supportive norms.

4. Psychoanalytic and Therapeutic Integration

Therapeutic intervention should move beyond crisis management and integrate preventive strategies:

School-Based Counseling

Embedding trauma-informed counseling in schools helps adolescents process emotional and identity challenges before they influence relational decisions.

Community Mental Health Clinics

Accessible, culturally sensitive mental health services prevent dependency from escalating into harmful marital patterns. Psychoanalytic and attachment-informed therapy enables early intervention.

Training for Counselors and Social Workers

Professionals must be trained to recognize early signs of co-dependency, identity confusion, and trauma-related relational projections, providing early guidance and support.

5. Policy Recommendations

Structural change is critical to prevent dependency syndrome at scale:

Legal Protection and Enforcement

Enforce laws against early and forced marriage. Strengthen protections for children and women in vulnerable households, including access to safe housing and legal advocacy.

Economic Empowerment Programs

Government and NGO programs offering vocational training, microfinance, and entrepreneurship opportunities provide financial independence, reducing the perceived need to marry for economic survival.

Data-Driven Interventions

Governments should monitor the prevalence of dependency-driven marriages, early unions, and related mental health outcomes. Evidence-based policies can target the most vulnerable communities, from Soweto to Maputo to New York's underserved neighbourhoods.

6. Global Comparative Lessons

Examining preventive approaches in different countries provides transferable insights:

New York, USA

Foster care reforms, school counseling, and youth empowerment initiatives reduce the risk of dependency syndrome stemming from early trauma.

Nigeria

Legal enforcement against child marriage, community advocacy, and educational sponsorships delay marital entry and promote autonomy.

Mozambique

Grassroots awareness campaigns, integration of traditional leadership in social change, and women's cooperatives strengthen identity and reduce economic dependence.

7. Integrating Therapy, Education, and Policy

Prevention is most effective when therapeutic, educational, and policy approaches converge:

Therapy addresses internalized trauma and identity issues.

Education empowers informed choice, delays marriage, and builds economic independence.

Policy ensures structural protections, challenges harmful norms, and creates sustainable social systems.

Together, these interventions reduce the psychological, emotional, and social drivers of dependency syndrome, enabling individuals to pursue relationships based on love, compatibility, and mutual respect rather than survival.

Dependency syndrome in marriage is preventable. Addressing it requires holistic, multi-level strategies that empower individuals, transform communities, and reform social structures.

Early interventions, youth education, therapeutic access, and culturally sensitive policy measures collectively reduce the cycle of trauma, identity confusion, and relational dependence.

By fostering emotional independence, promoting informed choice, and redefining the meaning of marriage, society can create environments where relationships thrive not as escapes from hardship, but as partnerships grounded in mutual growth, love, and psychological health.

Chapter 7: Healing Adult Relationships – Therapeutic Models and Rebuilding Emotional

Autonomy

Introduction

Dependency syndrome in marriage often originates in childhood and adolescence, yet its effects persist into adult relationships. Couples and individuals enter marriages carrying unresolved trauma, internalized identity confusion, and patterns of co-dependency. Healing these relationships requires targeted therapeutic interventions, emotional education, and practical strategies to foster autonomy, self-esteem, and relational health. This chapter explores scientifically grounded therapeutic models, psychoanalytic frameworks, and practical approaches to rebuild emotional independence in adults affected by dependency syndrome.

1. Understanding the Adult Impact of Dependency

Adults trapped in dependency-driven marriages often exhibit:

Emotional Over-Reliance

Seeking constant validation and approval from partners.

Identity Fusion

Equating self-worth with marital status or partner approval.

Relationship Projections

Replaying childhood trauma and relational patterns onto partners.

Avoidance of Conflict

Suppressing needs to maintain stability, resulting in resentment.

Difficulty with Boundaries

Struggling to define personal space, autonomy, and limits.

Psychoanalytic theory, particularly Freud's concepts of the id, ego, and superego, helps explain these dynamics. Unresolved childhood conflicts—such as neglect, abuse, or inconsistent attachment—shape adult projections. Individuals unconsciously seek partners who replicate early experiences, repeating cycles of dependence and relational dysfunction.

2. Therapeutic Models for Healing Dependency

2.1 Individual Therapy

Goal: Foster self-awareness, process trauma, and rebuild emotional autonomy.

Psychodynamic Therapy

Explores unconscious patterns, relational projections, and unresolved childhood conflicts. Helps clients recognize how early experiences influence partner choice, dependency behaviors, and relational expectations.

Cognitive Behavioral Therapy (CBT)

Identifies maladaptive thoughts and beliefs that drive dependency, e.g., "I cannot survive without my partner." CBT equips clients with practical tools to challenge these beliefs, set boundaries, and make autonomous decisions.

Trauma-Informed Therapy

Focuses on processing past abuse, neglect, and emotional wounds that drive co-dependent behaviors. Techniques include grounding exercises, mindfulness, and expressive therapies (e.g., journaling, art, or movement therapy).

2.2 Couple Therapy

Goal: Rebuild mutual respect, communication, and healthy interdependence.

Emotionally Focused Therapy (EFT)

Targets attachment patterns within the relationship, helping couples identify negative cycles and foster secure emotional bonds. EFT emphasizes understanding each partner's vulnerabilities and creating safety in expressing needs.

Gottman Method Therapy

Focuses on communication, conflict management, and building shared meaning. Couples learn to navigate disagreements without triggering dependency dynamics.

Behavioral Couple Therapy

Encourages shared goal-setting, cooperative problem-solving, and reinforcement of positive relational behaviors, helping couples transition from survival-based interaction to partnership.

3. Rebuilding Emotional Autonomy

Independence in relationships does not mean isolation; it requires **healthy interdependence**—where both partners maintain selfhood while contributing to the relationship.

Self-Reflection and Emotional Literacy

Clients are guided to identify emotional triggers, personal needs, and patterns of dependence. Self-reflection reduces automatic dependency behaviors.

Boundary Setting

Teaching individuals to establish limits, assert preferences, and resist over-accommodation strengthens autonomy and reduces resentment.

Identity Reinforcement:

Clients explore personal interests, professional goals, and social networks outside the marriage, reclaiming identity beyond the partner.

Decision-Making Skills

Encouraging independent problem-solving enhances self-confidence and reduces reliance on partners for validation or security.

4. Integrating Psychoanalytic Concepts

Freud's theory provides insight into dependency behaviors:

Id: Drives emotional impulses and immediate need fulfillment. In dependency-driven relationships, the id seeks the partner as a source of constant reassurance.

Ego: Mediates between impulses and reality. Therapy strengthens ego function, enabling individuals to balance personal needs with relationship dynamics.

Superego: Represents internalized societal and familial norms. In dependency syndrome, the superego may impose guilt or shame for asserting autonomy. Healing requires recalibrating these internalized rules to prioritize self-care and healthy relational choices.

By integrating psychoanalytic insights, therapy addresses both conscious and unconscious drivers of dependency, enabling lasting change.

5. Cultural and Contextual Considerations

Healing interventions must account for social and cultural contexts:

African Communities

Traditional expectations about marriage and gender roles may reinforce dependency. Culturally sensitive therapy incorporates community norms while challenging harmful scripts.

Western Settings (e.g., New York)

Economic pressures, foster care histories, or high mobility may compound dependency patterns. Interventions must integrate practical life skills, financial independence, and trauma processing.

Global Relevance

Case studies from Nigeria, Mozambique, and Brazil show that while cultural specifics vary, underlying psychological mechanisms—trauma, identity confusion, and relational projections—are universal. Therapy can be adapted to local contexts while maintaining core principles of emotional autonomy.

6. Practical Steps for Individuals

Commit to self-awareness: Journaling, reflection, and therapy to identify dependency triggers.

Practice assertive communication: Express needs and emotions without fear of rejection.

Build support networks outside the marriage: Friends, mentors, and support groups reduce overreliance on a partner.

Engage in continuous self-development: Education, career, and hobbies reinforce identity and resilience.

Seek therapeutic support: Professional guidance accelerates healing and ensures safety when navigating complex relational dynamics.

Healing adult relationships in the context of dependency syndrome **is** both psychological and relational work. By integrating psychoanalytic understanding, evidence-based therapeutic approaches, and culturally sensitive interventions, individuals can rebuild emotional autonomy and foster healthy partnerships.

Emotional independence empowers individuals to enter marriages not out of fear, survival, or societal expectation, but from a place of authentic love, self-confidence, and mutual respect.

Chapter 8: Case Studies and Success Stories – Overcoming Dependency Syndrome Across Cultures

Introduction

Dependency syndrome in marriage is a global phenomenon, shaped by childhood trauma, cultural expectations, socio-economic pressures, and relational projections. While theory and therapeutic models provide frameworks for understanding the syndrome, real-world examples offer insight into how individuals navigate, confront, and ultimately overcome dependency. This chapter presents case studies from diverse contexts—South Africa, Nigeria, Mozambique, and the United States—to illustrate the universality of dependency syndrome and the pathways to emotional autonomy, healthier relationships, and self-reclamation.

1. South Africa: Alexandra Township – Escaping Poverty and Emotional Confinement

Background

Thandiwe, a 28-year-old woman from Alexandra, grew up in a one-room RDP home shared with her parents and three siblings. She witnessed domestic violence, parental substance abuse, and unregulated sexual behavior from an early age. By adolescence, she viewed marriage as the only way to escape emotional neglect and overcrowding.

Dependency Patterns

Emotional reliance on her husband for self-worth.

Fear of leaving marriage despite frequent abuse.

Inability to set personal boundaries or make independent decisions.

Intervention and Outcome

Thandiwe engaged in individual trauma-informed therapy and couple's counseling.

Therapy addressed childhood trauma, normalized her feelings of fear and shame, and taught communication and boundary-setting skills. Over 18 months, she developed self-confidence, began part-time work, and renegotiated her marital roles.

Lesson:

Early trauma and poverty create strong dependency drives, but therapy combined with skill-building and financial independence can restore autonomy without destroying the marital bond.

2. Nigeria: Lagos – Negotiating Cultural and Familial Expectations

Background

Aisha, 32, from Lagos, was raised in a polygamous household where affection was contingent on behavior and compliance. Cultural norms emphasized marriage as a social milestone; single women faced intense scrutiny and social pressure.

Dependency Patterns

- Belief that marriage equates to social acceptance.
- Anxiety and depression when marital problems arose.
- Tendency to suppress personal needs to maintain the relationship.

Intervention and Outcome

Aisha participated in cognitive-behavioral therapy (CBT) and joined a women's empowerment group. Therapy addressed maladaptive beliefs, reinforced self-worth independent of marital status, and introduced conflict-resolution techniques. Within two years, Aisha reported higher emotional resilience, clear boundaries, and an improved marital partnership grounded in mutual respect rather than survival.

Lesson

Cultural pressures exacerbate dependency, but structured support systems and psychoeducation empower women to reclaim agency while honoring cultural identity.

3. Mozambique: Maputo – Overcoming Trauma and Economic Reliance

Background

Lucia, 29, grew up in Maputo's informal settlements, experiencing extreme poverty and parental neglect. At 17, she married an older man who provided financial security but emotionally manipulated her.

Dependency Patterns

- Over-reliance on husband for shelter and finances.
- Internalized shame and guilt for asserting independence.
- Repetition of childhood trauma patterns in marital interactions.

Intervention and Outcome

Lucia accessed trauma-focused therapy and community-based economic training programs. Through therapy, she confronted unresolved childhood trauma and developed strategies to communicate assertively. Economic training allowed her to contribute financially, reducing the power imbalance. She gradually transitioned to a healthier relational dynamic and established a strong sense of personal identity.

Lesson

Dependency often stems from the intersection of trauma and economic vulnerability. Combining psychological therapy with practical life skills promotes autonomy and equitable relationships.

4. United States: New York – Navigating Foster Care and Relational Patterns

Background

Maria, 27, grew up in foster care in New York City, experiencing frequent relocations, inconsistent attachments, and neglect. By early adulthood, she sought romantic relationships as a primary source of emotional security.

Dependency Patterns

- Intense fear of abandonment and rejection.
- Repeatedly choosing partners who mirrored past instability.
- Difficulty establishing boundaries or emotional self-regulation.
- Intervention and Outcome

Maria engaged in psychodynamic therapy focusing on identity reconstruction and relational projections. She explored unconscious patterns linking childhood instability to adult choices. Group therapy provided peer validation and relational modeling. Over time, Maria cultivated self-reliance, learned to identify unhealthy partners, and built emotionally sustainable relationships.

Lesson

Attachment disruptions in childhood lead to profound dependency, but therapy targeting relational projections and identity rebuilding can break intergenerational cycles.

5. Cross-Cultural Patterns and Insights

Across these diverse contexts, several universal themes emerge:

Childhood Trauma as a Root Cause

Overcrowding, neglect, abuse, and unstable homes create dependency drives.

Marriage as Survival: Early relationships often serve as an escape rather than mutual partnership.

Identity Confusion

Dependency is reinforced by unclear personal boundaries, low self-esteem, and internalized societal pressures.

Therapy as a Catalyst for Change

Both individual and couple's therapy—integrating psychodynamic, CBT, and trauma-informed approaches—are critical.

Practical Empowerment

Financial skills, social support, and autonomy-building activities reinforce therapeutic gains.

6. Recommendations for Breaking Dependency Cycles

Early Intervention

Identify dependency patterns in adolescence through psychoeducation and mentorship programs.

Culturally Sensitive Therapy

Tailor interventions to reflect social norms, religious beliefs, and family structures.

Holistic Approach

Combine psychological support with economic and social empowerment.

Public Awareness

Reduce stigma around therapy and challenge cultural scripts linking marriage to survival.

Community Support Systems

Establish safe spaces for women and men to explore identity, relationships, and independence.

Dependency syndrome in marriage transcends geography, culture, and socio-economic status. The cases presented demonstrate that while dependency can create profound emotional and relational challenges, healing is possible through therapy, self-awareness, and practical empowerment. Individuals can reclaim autonomy, rebuild healthy relationships, and redefine marriage as a space of love, choice, and mutual respect rather than survival or escape.

Chapter 9: Preventive Strategies – Educating Young People to Avoid Dependency Syndrome in Future Relationships

Introduction

Dependency syndrome in marriage is not an inevitable outcome. While early trauma, poverty, and cultural pressures create strong predispositions toward relational dependency, preventive interventions can equip young people with the knowledge, skills, and emotional resilience to form healthy, autonomous relationships. This chapter explores evidence-based strategies to prevent dependency, drawing on psychoanalytic theory, developmental psychology, and cross-cultural research. The focus is on education, therapy, mentorship, and community engagement as critical mechanisms for change.

1. Understanding the Risk Factors Early

Before prevention can occur, young people and caregivers must understand the roots of dependency syndrome.

These include:

- Childhood trauma
- Exposure to violence, abuse, neglect, or unstable households.

Economic vulnerability

Lack of financial independence creates reliance on others for survival.

Cultural expectations

Social norms linking marriage to identity, respect, or escape from hardship.

Identity confusion

Uncertainty about self-worth, gender roles, and relational expectations.

Sigmund Freud's identity theory and his concepts of the id, ego, and superego provide a useful framework.

Children growing up in unstable environments develop ego defences to manage anxiety, often projecting unresolved inner conflicts onto future partners. By addressing these dynamics early, preventive strategies can mitigate maladaptive patterns.

Understanding the Risk Factors Early – How

Dependency Grows in the Shadows

Before we can prevent dependency syndrome, we must understand where it begins. It does not suddenly appear on the day a woman or man enters a relationship. It has roots—deep, tangled, and often invisible—stretching back to childhood memories, cultural teachings, trauma, and the quiet formation of identity.

To bring these patterns to life, imagine a young woman named Amahle.

1. Childhood Trauma – The First Script Written on the Mind

Amahle grew up in a house where chaos was the daily rhythm. Her father drank to silence his own childhood wounds, and her mother stayed because she had nowhere else to go. At night, arguments exploded like storms, and Amahle learned early that silence could be a shield. She often lay awake beneath the thin blanket, listening to her parents fight, feeling her heartbeat echo every scream, every crash.

This is where dependency begins—not in adulthood, but in childhood.

A child raised in instability learns to interpret love through fear.

Freud's theory of the id, ego, and superego explains this perfectly.

In such homes:

The id absorbs fear, chaos, and unmet needs.

The ego learns to survive by tiptoeing, pleasing, hiding emotions.

The superego becomes punishing, whispering, *"You must be perfect to be loved."*

Later in life, these early lessons create adults who mistake anxiety for passion and control for care.

Amahle did not understand this. She only knew that love felt like walking on broken glass—careful, fragile, dangerous.

2. Economic Vulnerability – How Poverty Becomes a Chain

By the time she turned sixteen, Amahle already felt trapped. Her mother had no job. The electricity was cut off almost monthly. Amahle's school shoes had holes, and her stomach often growled through class.

When Mandla, a 28-year-old taxi driver, started giving her attention, she felt seen for the first time. He brought food, helped buy her stationery, and sometimes gave her money for lunch. He even told her she was beautiful—a word she had never heard at home.

But Mandla had one hidden advantage:

He could offer what she lacked—security.

When someone grows up without financial stability, economic vulnerability becomes a doorway through which dependency enters. Poverty whispers:

"Do not leave him, he is your only chance."

"You cannot survive on your own."

"Respectability comes through marriage."

This is how abusive relationships tighten their grip—not through love, but through financial leverage.

Abusers know this.

And they use it.

When Mandla started showing controlling behavior—checking her messages, isolating her from friends, demanding obedience—Amahle tolerated it. Leaving him meant returning to hunger and uncertainty.

Poverty had prepared her to accept abuse—because survival always came first.

3. How Abuse Deepens Economic Dependency – The Invisible Trap

Abusive partners slowly create environments where the victim becomes financially and psychologically dependent. Mandla insisted that Amahle stop looking for jobs because "a good man provides." He paid her transport, bought clothes, and made sure she depended on him for every need.

But each gift had a price.

Each act of generosity came with new rules.

Soon, Amahle's world shrank to Mandla's room, Mandla's moods, Mandla's expectations.

Economic support became economic imprisonment.

When he withheld money during arguments, she felt punished.

When he threatened to kick her out, she felt terrified.

When he reminded her she had "nowhere else to go," she believed him.

This is the psychological economy of abusive relationships:

The abuser becomes the only provider.

The victim becomes financially crippled.

Dependence becomes a lifestyle.

Freedom becomes unimaginable.

Erich Fromm calls this the Escape From Freedom—

the idea that people sometimes cling to bondage because independence feels overwhelming.

Amahle was not staying because she loved Mandla.

She was staying because she feared a life without him.

4. Cultural Expectations – The Social Programming of Dependency

Growing up, Amahle heard elders say:

"A woman without a man is nothing."

"Your husband will take you out of poverty."

"Every woman needs a man to build her future."
These cultural narratives are powerful.
They shape identity.
They define what success looks like.
They make marriage seem like the ultimate prize.

So even when Mandla's abuse worsened—when he slapped her for questioning him, or when he prevented her from visiting her family—Amahle stayed.

Culture had taught her that endurance is the duty of a "good woman."

Leaving meant being judged, shamed, and seen as "failed."

5. Identity Confusion – The Lost Self (Carl Jung)

Carl Jung believed that all humans possess a shadow—the hidden part of ourselves filled with wounds, fears, and suppressed memories.

Amahle's shadow was overflowing:

- fear from childhood,
- shame from poverty,
- confusion about love,
- longing for validation,
- terror of being alone.

When a person has not formed a strong identity, they are more likely to merge into another person—losing themselves in the process. Jung describes this as identity diffusion, where the boundaries between self and partner blur.

For Amahle:

Mandla was not just a boyfriend.

He was:

- a provider,
- a father figure,

- a protector,
- an escape route,
- and a mirror reflecting her insecurities.

Her own identity had never fully formed.
So she borrowed his—
even when it hurt her.

6. The Cycle Repeats Unless Interrupted

Amahle's story reflects many young women and men around the world:

- trauma teaches them fear,
- poverty teaches them dependence,
- culture teaches them obedience,
- abusive partners teach them submission,
- and society teaches them silence.

This combination becomes a dangerous formula that breeds dependency syndrome.

- Unless someone intervenes—
  a teacher,
  a counselor,
  a supportive relative,
  a community leader—
  the cycle continues into the next generation.

Dependency is not a choice.
It is a survival response to layered disadvantages.

Conclusion – Awareness Saves Futures

Understanding these risk factors gives us the power to prevent dependency syndrome:

- by healing childhood trauma,
- by creating economic opportunities,
- by challenging cultural expectations,
- by teaching identity formation,
- and by creating safe spaces for young people to speak.

Dependency is learned.

But so is freedom.

And with knowledge, empathy, and early intervention, we can help young people choose freedom over fear.

The Psychology of Leaving – Why It Is So Hard to Walk Away From a Toxic Relationship

People often ask why someone stays in a relationship that is clearly breaking them. Outsiders imagine that the decision to leave should be simple—"If it hurts, walk away." But human psychology is not built on logic alone. It is shaped by memory, fear, longing, and the unconscious bonds that form long before adulthood.

Leaving a toxic relationship is not just an act of walking out the door; it is an internal war. It is a battle between the wounded child inside and the adult trying to survive outside.

The Invisible Chains: Emotional and Psychological Bonding

Toxic relationships rarely start toxic. They usually begin with love-bombing, affection, and promises. The abuser may create moments of intense connection—moments that act like emotional magnets. These moments become the anchor that keeps the victim hoping, *"Maybe things will go back to how they were."*

Carl Jung would say that this kind of bond activates a powerful archetype—the *wounded healer*, the part of a person that believes they can fix someone else as a way of healing themselves. The inner child tries to repair what was broken in childhood by repairing a partner who is emotionally unavailable, unpredictable, or hurtful.

Thus, leaving feels like abandoning not just a partner, but a mission, a hope, a dream.

Fear Disguised as Loyalty

Erich Fromm wrote that humans fear freedom because true freedom forces us to make choices—and choices bring uncertainty. Walking away from a toxic relationship means stepping into the unknown: new responsibilities, new identity, new survival strategies.

Many people stay because the relationship, even with abuse, feels *familiar*. Abuse that resembles childhood dynamics can feel like "home," not because it is safe, but because it is known. The unpredictability of an abusive partner mirrors the unpredictability of an inconsistent parent. The psyche recognizes the pattern and confuses familiarity with security.

Fromm calls this the escape from freedom: the mind chooses the cage it knows rather than the open sky it fears.

Internal Conflicts: Freud's Id, Ego, and Superego

Freud helps explain why leaving feels like tearing the self in three directions:

- **The Id** wants comfort, affection, and the emotional highs that occasionally return in the cycle of abuse.
- **The Superego** is filled with cultural expectations: "A good woman stays." "A man must not fail." "You don't give up on marriage."
- **The Ego** tries to survive between these forces, constantly negotiating fear, guilt, shame, and desire.

This inner tug-of-war exhausts the person to the point where leaving feels more overwhelming than staying.

Economic Dependence as a Psychological Trap

For many women—and increasingly for men—economic vulnerability becomes another lock on the cage. Abuse often comes with financial control: limiting access to money, preventing employment, or creating debts. Economic dependence makes leaving dangerous and returning appear safer.

But this economic trap is also psychological.

A partner who controls the money slowly becomes the "provider"—not just financially, but emotionally. The victim starts to believe they cannot survive without that person. It is a learned helplessness born from years of being told, shown, or manipulated into believing:

"You need me."

And over time, the mind accepts it as truth.

Trauma Bonds and the Fantasy of Change

A trauma bond forms when pain and affection are delivered in unpredictable cycles. Neuroscience shows that this combination creates addiction-like attachment. The brain starts craving the moments of relief after the abuse ends.

This is why people say things like:

"He's not always like this."

"She only acts this way because she loves me."

"Maybe if I change, the relationship will improve."

They are not irrational—they are neurologically trapped.

The Cultural Weight of Staying

In many communities, leaving a marriage carries more shame than staying in violence. Families advise endurance. Religion encourages forgiveness. Society celebrates the appearance of stability more than the reality of emotional safety.

Thus, the act of leaving becomes a rebellion—not just against a partner, but against an entire belief system.

The Moment of Awakening

Most people do not leave because they stop loving their partner. They leave because something finally breaks the illusion: a child's cry, a hospital visit, an unbearable humiliation, or the quiet realization that they are disappearing into someone else's darkness.

Leaving requires a psychological shift—an inner liberation.

Erich Fromm would call it *the reclaiming of freedom.*

Carl Jung would call it *the integration of the shadow.*

Freud would call it *strengthening the ego.*

Whatever the language, the meaning is the same:

The person finally chooses themselves.

The Stages of Leaving – How People Finally Break

Free From Toxic Relationships

Leaving a toxic relationship is never a single moment. It is a slow, painful unfolding—a psychological journey made up of emotional turning points, inner conflicts, and moments of clarity that gradually gather enough power to push someone toward freedom.

These stages are not linear. People move forward, fall back, get stuck, and rise again. Yet, almost everyone who eventually leaves passes through some version of these stages.

1. The First Cracks – When the Illusion Begins to Break

The relationship does not collapse all at once. It begins with tiny cracks:

A moment during an argument when the person asks themselves, *"Is this normal?"*

A humiliation that lingers longer than usual.

A realization that the loving moments have become rare.

The feeling of walking on eggshells every day.

Carl Jung would say that the unconscious begins sending signals—dreams, discomfort, subtle anxieties—that something is deeply wrong. The psyche starts resisting the false story it once accepted.

This is the beginning of awakening, though the person often still clings to hope.

1. Bargaining With Reality – The Stage of Self-Blame

During this period, the person tries to save the relationship by sacrificing themselves:

"Maybe if I stop arguing, things will change."

"Maybe I'm asking for too much."

"Maybe I provoked him/her."

This is not weakness; it is the ego trying to maintain emotional stability inside chaos. Freud's concept of defense mechanisms is alive here. The person tries denial, rationalization, and even fantasy to cope.

They blame themselves so they can keep the illusion of control:

"If it's my fault, I can fix it."

But this stage drains self-esteem and deepens the psychological trap.

1. The Breaking Point – When Pain Becomes Unavoidable

Every survivor has a moment—sometimes dramatic, sometimes quiet—when the reality becomes undeniable:

- A physical incident that goes too far.
- A public humiliation too heavy to excuse.
- A child asking, "Why are you crying again?"
- A growing fear that staying is more dangerous than leaving.

The breaking point is not just an event; it is an emotional threshold. The person realizes:

"This is not love. This is destroying me."

In Jungian terms, this is the psyche refusing to carry the shadow any longer. The pain becomes consciousness.

4. Planning the Escape – Secret Steps Toward Freedom

Leaving requires strategy—especially when economic vulnerability is present.

This stage may involve:

Hiding money.

Reconnecting with family or friends.

Seeking a job or income source.

Quiet research on shelters, legal options, or safe spaces.

Mentally rehearsing what leaving will look like.

People often leave symbolically before they leave physically. Emotionally, they start detaching, distancing, imagining life outside the relationship.

Erich Fromm would say this is when a person begins reclaiming the "freedom of the mind"—the inner liberation that must occur before any external action.

1. The Act of Leaving – The Most Dangerous Moment

Statistically, leaving is the most dangerous phase, because the abuser senses the loss of control.

Many leave during moments when the abuser is:

- at work,
- distracted,
- asleep,
- or after receiving help.

It is rarely clean, never simple, and always terrifying. The person does not leave because they are strong—they leave because they finally choose survival.

6. Grief, Guilt, and Withdrawal – The Emotional Aftershock

Even after leaving, the victim does not feel free right away.

They feel:

- guilt,
- shame,
- loneliness,
- doubt,
- longing,
- confusion,

- and even love.

This is the emotional withdrawal stage, similar to addiction recovery. The brain craves the familiar patterns, even the painful ones. Trauma bonds break slowly.

People often return temporarily. Not because they are weak, but because the psychological bonds are deep.

Healing begins when they forgive themselves for this struggle.

7. Rebuilding Identity – The Slow Return to Self

Once safety is established, the true journey begins: rediscovering the self that was silenced in the relationship.

This stage involves:

- rebuilding financial independence,
- learning emotional boundaries,
- therapy or spiritual support,
- reconnecting with community,
- and exploring personal dreams again.

Freud would see this as strengthening the ego.

Jung would see it as the beginning of individuation.

Fromm would call it the embrace of inner freedom.

The person begins to feel:

"I am becoming myself again."

8. Integration – Turning Pain Into Wisdom

With time, the survivor gains perspective. The toxic relationship becomes a chapter, not a cage.

They learn to:

- recognize red flags,
- value emotional safety,
- trust themselves,
- form healthier relationships.

The pain turns into insight. The trauma becomes a story of triumph—not over the abuser, but over the psychological traps that once held them.

The Hidden Cost of Love – How Abuse, Poverty, and Identity Collapse Shape Dependency Syndrome

In every society—whether in the outskirts of Maputo, the crowded suburbs of Lagos, the busy immigrant communities of New York, or the rural villages of Limpopo—there are women whose lives quietly revolve around one emotional truth:

they remain in toxic relationships not because they do not see the danger, but because the idea of leaving feels even more terrifying than staying.

This fear is not irrational.

Childhood wounds, cultural expectations, and a lifetime of economic vulnerability craft it.

And so dependency syndrome becomes the invisible thread woven through their relationships, decisions, and sense of self.

A Story at the Heart of Many Women

Consider *Nomsa*, a 29-year-old teacher in Limpopo.

Her story is fictional, but the emotional and psychological reality reflects thousands of real lives.

Nomsa grew up in a crowded RDP house where privacy did not exist. At night she pretended to sleep while her parents argued, reconciled, fought again, or made up in the same one-room space. When she was 12, she witnessed her older sister being beaten by a boyfriend who promised marriage. Her mother simply said:

"Endure, my child. Every woman must suffer before she is chosen."

By the time Nomsa reached university, she was academically brilliant—yet emotionally starving. She sought a partner, not for love, but for identity. According to Carl Jung, the unmet elements of the psyche search for completion in the "Other." Nomsa was not looking for a boyfriend; she was looking for a piece of herself.

When she met *Thabo*, a charming man with no job but endless confidence, she felt seen. For a while, attention was enough. But slowly, the relationship shifted. Thabo began controlling her money, dictating her clothing, isolating her from friends.

Nomsa tried to leave three times.

Three times she returned.

Not because she loved him—

but because she feared being no one without him.

Economic Vulnerability – The Silent Glue That Holds Toxic Love Together

Across Nigeria, Mozambique, New York, and South Africa, abusive partners often understand one thing:

If you control a woman's finances, you control her life.

Economic vulnerability is the strongest predictor of dependency syndrome.

It explains why:

- women with degrees stay with unemployed partners who drain them,
- women in abusive marriages fear divorce,
- young girls become pregnant for security,
- and why leaving feels like a fall into bottomless uncertainty.

In Lagos, some women endure violence because their husbands pay rent.

In Maputo, others remain because family members believe "divorce is shameful."

In New York, immigrant women fear losing visas, housing, or stability.

Erich Fromm, in *The Fear of Freedom*, describes how people often cling to systems that oppress them simply because the alternative—freedom—feels too overwhelming.

Freedom demands self-definition.

Dependency provides identity, even a painful one.

To the abused woman, leaving feels like stepping into a void.

The Psychological Trap – How the Mind Becomes Its Own Prison

Freud's structure of the psyche explains why dependency takes root so deeply.

The Id

seeks safety, connection, and basic survival.

When childhood lacked safety, the id becomes desperate for external protection.

The Ego

tries to maintain stability. It tells the woman:

"At least here, I know what to expect. Outside, I might fall."

The Superego

echoes society:

"A good woman stays. Marriage is success. Leaving is shame."

These forces collide inside her daily, creating chaos and paralysis.

Meanwhile, Jung's theory of shadow projection shows how women often attract partners who reflect their unhealed inner world. A woman raised in chaos unconsciously gravitates toward chaos—because it feels familiar, even when it hurts. She confuses pain with love, struggle with commitment.

Abuse and the Economy of Power

Abusive relationships operate like economic systems:

- One partner becomes the "resource provider."
- The other becomes the "resource dependent."
- The abuser uses fear, shame, and occasional affection to maintain control.
- This is why women with salaries still feel poor.
- The poverty is emotional.

The wealth belongs to the abuser:

A wealth of dominance, attention, unpredictability, and psychological manipulation.

When a woman tries to leave, she is not walking away from a man—

she is walking away from the entire structure that keeps her identity intact.

Why Leaving Feels Impossible – The Science Behind the Struggle

Leaving a toxic relationship is not simply a decision.

It is a neurological, emotional, cultural, and economic battle.

Women stay because:

Trauma bonds mimic addiction—the brain becomes chemically attached to the cycle of pain and relief.

Fear of loneliness outweighs fear of abuse.

Financial instability makes independence feel unrealistic.

Cultural pressure punishes divorced or single women.

Identity confusion makes the relationship feel like the only stable part of their life.

Fromm describes this as *escape from freedom.*

Jung describes it as *an unhealed shadow seeking recognition.*

Freud describes it as *repetition compulsion*—the unconscious drive to recreate childhood wounds in adulthood.

Together, they explain why intelligent, educated, powerful women remain trapped.

The Way Forward – Healing Through Awareness

To prevent dependency syndrome, society must focus on early intervention:

- teaching emotional literacy,
- creating economic opportunities,
- breaking cultural silence,
- and addressing childhood trauma long before marriage enters the picture.

Dependency does not begin in adulthood.

It begins in the living room of a crowded house, in unspoken pain, in stolen childhoods, and in the moment a young girl realizes:

"My future depends on someone choosing me."

Healing begins when she learns a different truth:

"My future depends on me choosing myself."

Chapter 10: The Psychology of Leaving – Why It Is So Hard to Walk Away From a Toxic Relationship

Introduction

Walking away from a toxic relationship is not simply a matter of willpower; it is a complex interplay of psychological, emotional, cultural, and economic factors. Many individuals remain trapped in harmful partnerships long after the initial love has faded, not because they want to, but because leaving threatens their sense of identity, survival, and social belonging.

This chapter explores why separation is so difficult, drawing on psychoanalytic theory, Jungian concepts of the shadow and projection, and Eric Fromm's *Freedom of Love*, to provide a multidimensional understanding of dependency syndrome.

1. The Invisible Chains of Trauma

Consider Thandi, a young woman from an RDP settlement in Soweto. From an early age, Thandi learned that love was conditional, wrapped in sacrifice and endurance. Her father, distant and emotionally unavailable, and her mother, overburdened and anxious, modeled relationships where conflict went unresolved and silence prevailed.

As Thandi grew older, she gravitated toward a partner who seemed protective but exhibited controlling and manipulative behaviors. Leaving him was not simply a choice—it felt like abandoning the only model of love she had ever internalized. Freud's concept of the *id, ego, and superego* explains part of this: Thandi's ego defenses had developed to survive chaotic environments, and now her id's unmet needs for safety and affection were projected onto a partner who mirrored her unresolved childhood patterns.

2. Economic Dependence and Fear of Survival

Economic vulnerability is one of the most concrete barriers to leaving. Many women, like Thandi, remain in marriages not because of love, but because independence seems impossible. Rent, food, school fees for children, and societal pressure combine to make departure a daunting task.

Similarly, men like Sipho, previously discussed, may stay in relationships to maintain appearances, financial stability, or social acceptance, even when the marriage causes emotional suffering. For both genders, the *freedom to leave* is curtailed by economic realities, reinforcing the cycle of dependency.

3. Identity, Shame, and Cultural Expectation

In many African and global contexts, marriage is still viewed as a marker of success, maturity, and social respect. Leaving a marriage is thus not only a personal choice but a societal judgment. Individuals fear stigma, gossip, and the perception of failure.

From a Jungian perspective, leaving a toxic partner forces confrontation with the *shadow self*—the parts of identity that have been denied, projected, or suppressed. For example, women may realize their own agency has been stifled, while men may confront insecurities they have hidden behind control or avoidance. Recognizing these truths is terrifying, making staying in the relationship feel like the safer option.

4. Emotional and Psychological Bonding: Why Attachment Persists

Toxic relationships often involve intermittent reinforcement—periods of affection, attention, or calm are interspersed with conflict, manipulation, or neglect. Psychologically, this creates a bond stronger than consistent positivity. Freud's psychoanalytic lens shows that unresolved childhood trauma can make individuals emotionally addicted to partners who mirror early caregivers, even if the experience is harmful.

Eric Fromm's concept of *Freedom of Love* highlights why this is so damaging: when love is not free, it becomes a tool of control. People confuse possession, obligation, or survival with affection. Only when love is recognized as a mutual, liberating force can individuals differentiate between attachment rooted in need and love rooted in freedom.

1. **The Role of Hope, Guilt, and Responsibility**

Hope is another invisible tether. Many individuals stay because they imagine change—believing their partner can improve, or that their efforts will eventually be recognized. Guilt and responsibility further complicate matters: parents, children, and family members are often cited as reasons to remain.

In Thandi's case, leaving would mean navigating societal judgment, economic instability, and the internalized belief that she has failed if she cannot "make the marriage work." These factors illustrate that the psychology of leaving is not a failure of courage, but a reflection of complex internal and external pressures.

6. Breaking the Psychological Chains

Escaping a toxic relationship requires more than a decision; it requires deep psychological work:

Self-awareness

Understanding personal trauma and how it influences relationship choices.

Emotional literacy

Recognizing patterns of attachment, projection, and dependency.

Practical planning

Establishing economic, social, and logistical independence.

Therapeutic support

While therapy is not a universal solution, safe spaces to explore identity, boundaries, and emotional patterns are critical.

Embracing Freedom of Love

Fromm's philosophy teaches that liberation is not about abandoning relationships, but forming connections rooted in autonomy, respect, and authenticity.

1. The Modern Context: Technology, Social Pressure, and Isolation

In contemporary society, social media, cultural narratives, and peer comparison intensify dependency. Couples remain in visible relationships to maintain status, avoid shame, or project a facade of success. Alcohol, escapism, and substance use increasingly serve as coping mechanisms, masking dissatisfaction while deepening psychological entanglement.

Leaving a toxic relationship is not a single act of bravery—it is a layered process requiring emotional, psychological, and social readiness. Dependency syndrome, rooted in trauma, economic vulnerability, and cultural expectation, complicates this journey for both women and men. Freud, Jung, and Fromm collectively offer frameworks to understand why individuals remain, why attachment persists, and how liberation is possible.

True freedom comes not merely from walking away, but from cultivating inner strength, understanding one's own psyche, and learning to engage in relationships as acts of love rather than survival. Only then can individuals reclaim autonomy, dignity, and the authentic joy of connection.

Chapter 11: Why Women Fear Happiness – The Psychology of Self-Sabotage

Happiness is supposed to feel like home.

But for many women who grew up in instability, chaos, or trauma, happiness feels like a stranger—beautiful, inviting, yet deeply suspicious. Instead of embracing it, they stand at the doorway, hesitant, overwhelmed, or ready to run.

Across New York, Lagos, Maputo, Johannesburg, and the villages of Limpopo, you will find women who say:

"I don't know why, but when things go well, I panic."

"When a man treats me well, I lose interest."

"Peace makes me uncomfortable. It feels too quiet."

The world assumes that people fear sadness, but the truth is more complex:

many women fear happiness because happiness is unfamiliar, unpredictable, and vulnerable.

This chapter explores the psychology behind this phenomenon—rooted in trauma, emotional conditioning, identity confusion, and subconscious survival instincts.

1. When Chaos Is Home – How Trauma Teaches Women to Fear Peace

A woman raised in chaos learns that emotional intensity = love.

She grows up in environments where:

- arguments explode without warning,
- parents break up and reconcile repeatedly,
- affection is conditional,
- alcohol controls the home,
- survival requires constant alertness,
- love feels unstable.

Her nervous system becomes wired for unpredictability.

So when life becomes peaceful—when someone loves her gently, speaks calmly, and offers consistency—her body sends signals of danger rather than safety.

Calmness feels foreign.
Peace feels suspicious.
Happiness feels like a temporary illusion.

Carl Jung explains this through the *shadow*: people fear what they have never integrated into their inner world. If peace did not exist in childhood, the psyche cannot recognize it as home.

1. **Emotional Conditioning – When Happiness Becomes Associated With Loss**

In many women's lives, happiness was always followed by pain:

- A joyful day ending in violence.
- A peaceful moment ending in betrayal.
- A loving parent relapsing into chaos.
- A stable period collapsing into trauma.
- Over time, the brain forms a pattern:
  good things do not last.

This leads to a subconscious belief:
"If I get too happy, something bad will happen."

So the woman begins sabotaging good relationships or destroying peaceful situations to protect herself from deeper heartbreak. In psychological terms, this is *anticipatory defense*—hurting yourself before life can hurt you.

3. Freud and the Fear of Pleasure – The Unconscious War Inside

Freud believed that humans have a *pleasure principle* (seeking happiness) and a *reality principle* (avoiding danger).

Trauma disrupts this balance.

A traumatised woman develops what Freud called a "repetition compulsion"—an unconscious drive to repeat familiar pain because it feels safer than unknown joy.

This is why women may choose partners who:

- argue like their parents did,
- withdraw emotionally the way an absent father did,
- love inconsistently like the childhood environment.

They are not weak; they are *psychologically conditioned.*

The woman is not seeking love—
she is seeking familiarity, even when familiarity is destructive.

1. The Identity Crisis – When Happiness Threatens Self-Image

Many women carry an internal script shaped by:

- childhood roles,
- cultural expectations,
- religious guilt,
- family beliefs,
- community narratives.

If her identity was built around suffering, sacrifice, and survival, happiness threatens to erase the version of herself she knows.

Carl Jung said, *"The most terrifying thing is to accept oneself completely."*

To accept happiness, a woman must accept:

- she deserves more,
- she is worthy of peace,

- she can have a soft life.

For women raised to equate worth with endurance and suffering, this is frightening. Joy challenges the identity they learned to wear like armor.

5. Erich Fromm: Freedom, Love, and the Burden of Choice

Fromm believed that humans fear freedom because freedom demands responsibility.

A woman trapped in a cycle of self-sabotage often unconsciously fears:

- the responsibility of maintaining happiness,
- the responsibility of making her own decisions,
- the responsibility of choosing a peaceful partner,
- the responsibility of defining her identity outside pain.

Dependency syndrome becomes attractive because it removes responsibility.
Painful relationships feel easier to understand than peaceful ones.
Happiness demands growth.
Toxicity demands nothing.

1. The Fear of Being Seen – Why Happiness Makes

Women Feel Exposed
Healthy love exposes vulnerable parts:

- your inner child,
- your needs,
- your flaws,
- your fears,
- your real emotions.

For a woman who used strength as a survival mask, being loved gently feels overwhelming.

Peace demands honesty—something trauma survivors struggle with.

- So she may:
- pick fights with a good partner,
- push people away,
- avoid emotional intimacy,
- shut down when feeling loved,
- choose unavailable men instead.

Not because she wants pain—
but because happiness requires emotional nakedness.

1. **The Cycle of Self-Sabotage in Relationships**

When a woman fears happiness, she often:
1. Meets a healthy partner.
2. Feels uncomfortable with peace.
3. Distrusts the calmness.

4. Creates drama to feel "normal."
5. Ruins the relationship.
6. Feels guilt and shame.
7. Falls back into toxic patterns.

This is not a flaw.

It is a trauma response.

8. The Way Forward – Learning How to Feel Safe in Happiness

Healing begins not by forcing happiness, but by teaching the body to feel safe with it.

Women can start by:

• Learning emotional regulation

Rewiring the nervous system to tolerate peace.

• Identifying trauma triggers

Recognizing that discomfort is not danger.

• Challenging internalized beliefs

Replacing "I do not deserve happiness" with "Happiness is my birthright."

• Practicing small doses of peace

Taking micro-steps toward accepting calmness.

• Entering therapy or support groups

To reframe childhood narratives.

• Choosing partners who offer safety, not intensity

Love should not feel like survival.

A New Internal Script

Instead of telling herself:

"Good things never last,"
she begins saying,
"I am allowed to rest."
"I don't deserve happiness,"
becomes
"I am worthy of a soft life."

"Peace is scary,"
becomes
"Peace is healing."

This is the moment women stop running from happiness— and start walking toward themselves.

How Men Fear Vulnerability – The Hidden Side of Dependency Syndrome

This topic explores how men, across rural and urban contexts, silently struggle with emotional dependency and insecurity. Although society often portrays men as emotionally self-reliant, the reality shows a hidden layer of fear, unresolved trauma, and unspoken vulnerability. Many men develop dependency patterns that are masked by anger, withdrawal, or controlling behaviour—mechanisms that hide deep fears of abandonment or inadequacy.

The analysis will examine how social expectations, cultural norms, and pressure to appear strong prevent men from seeking emotional support or expressing tenderness. It also illustrates how economic stress, relationship instability, migration, and childhood socialisation contribute to men's dependency syndrome. The chapter reveals that men, just like women, can become trapped in unhealthy attachments, unable to voice their pain, leading to cycles of emotional violence, silence, or self-isolation.

. Ultimately, this topic challenges stereotypes by showing that men's emotional struggles are real, complex, and often invisible—yet acknowledging them is a critical part of healing, communication, and healthier relationships.

How Men Fear Vulnerability – The Hidden Side of Dependency Syndrome

Introduction

Dependency syndrome is often discussed with a focus on women, particularly in the context of marriage, societal pressures, and economic survival. However, men are not immune to these patterns. Across rural villages, urban townships, and even affluent urban centres, men grapple silently with emotional dependency, insecurity, and identity struggles. Societal norms teach men to suppress vulnerability, equating emotional openness with weakness. Ironically, this suppression becomes the very source of dependency, as men rely on external validation, control, or avoidance strategies to cope with inner fears.

The Roots of Male Dependency

Several factors contribute to male dependency syndrome:

Childhood Trauma and Socialisation

Many men grow up in households where emotional expression is discouraged. Fathers may model emotional detachment, while boys are punished for showing fear or sadness. According to Freud's identity theory, these experiences shape the ego and superego, creating defense mechanisms that mask vulnerability. Boys learn to internalise pain, projecting unresolved conflicts onto romantic partners in adulthood.

Cultural and Social Expectations

In many African and Western communities, masculinity is defined by strength, resilience, and the ability to provide. Men who do not meet these standards often experience shame, self-doubt, or social exclusion. Marriage, then, becomes not only a source of companionship but also a socially sanctioned space to validate one's masculinity, often at the cost of emotional authenticity.

Economic Pressure and Identity Conflict

Financial insecurity magnifies dependency. Men who struggle to achieve societal benchmarks of success—steady employment, homeownership, or status—may cling to relationships as sources of perceived stability. This creates a cycle where dependence is masked as control, protection, or overcompensation.

Fear of Intimacy and Rejection

Vulnerability exposes inner fears: the possibility of being abandoned, judged, or seen as inadequate. Men often avoid intimacy to protect their identity, but this avoidance paradoxically reinforces dependency. They remain in relationships that do not fulfill them emotionally, unable to articulate their needs or step away.

The Psychological Mechanisms

Men's emotional dependency often manifests as:

Control and Dominance – Attempting to dictate a partner's behaviour to compensate for inner insecurity.

Emotional Withdrawal – Retreating from conflict or intimacy to avoid confrontation with their own unresolved trauma.

External Validation – Seeking affirmation from partners, peers, or society to maintain self-worth.

Carl Jung's concept of individuation is useful here. Men often delay self-actualisation by externalising identity validation through relationships rather than integrating their inner and outer selves. The "shadow self" – the repressed fears, insecurities, and vulnerabilities – remains unacknowledged, subtly shaping behaviour and relational dynamics.

Consequences in Relationships

When men fear vulnerability, relationships suffer in subtle but profound ways:

Partners may feel emotionally neglected or burdened with the task of managing the man's insecurity.

Communication becomes transactional, with conflict unresolved and intimacy shallow.

Dependency transforms into co-dependency, where both partners unconsciously fulfill unmet emotional needs, perpetuating cycles of dissatisfaction and resentment.

Breaking the Cycle

Acknowledging male dependency is the first step toward healthier relationships.

Therapeutic frameworks, including trauma-informed therapy, Jungian self-reflection, and psychoanalytic approaches, can help men:

Recognise and integrate their fears and vulnerabilities.

Build emotional resilience independent of external validation.

Communicate authentically with partners.

Establish healthier relational boundaries.

Freedom of the mind, as conceptualized by Eric Fromm, is critical. Men must achieve the internal capacity to love without fear, to engage in relationships without dependency, and to embrace intimacy without losing autonomy.

Conclusion

Men's fear of vulnerability is not a moral failing—it is a complex psychological, social, and cultural phenomenon. Understanding this hidden side of dependency syndrome is essential for breaking cycles of emotional dysfunction, fostering equitable partnerships, and promoting mental well-being. Recognising that men too carry unprocessed trauma, social pressures, and fear allows for a more holistic approach to addressing dependency in marriage and intimate relationships.

How Men Fear Vulnerability – The Hidden Side of Dependency Syndrome

A Storytelling Perspective

In a small village in Limpopo, Sipho had always been seen as strong and capable. From a young age, he watched his father work long hours while suppressing anger and sorrow, never showing vulnerability. His mother, too, had little time for emotional connection; survival came first. By the time Sipho reached adulthood, he had learned a simple rule: emotions are dangerous, weakness is punished, and independence is measured by control.

Across the township in Alexandra, Lerato, a young woman with a university degree, found herself trapped in a similar but opposite bind. She had been taught that success for a woman is measured by securing a man who can provide stability and respect. Despite her education and employment, she feared being alone, believing marriage was the only route to social approval and personal identity.

Both Sipho and Lerato are living examples of dependency syndrome in modern contexts—men and women navigating relationships not out of choice or love, but as a strategy to escape internal and external pressures.

The Roots of Male and Female Dependency

Dependency in relationships is rarely a matter of laziness or immorality. It is a response to trauma, cultural expectation, and identity confusion:

Childhood Trauma and Socialisation – Sipho's fear of vulnerability mirrors Freud's ideas of the id, ego, and superego. His ego developed defense mechanisms to manage anxiety, repressing feelings of fear, loss, and longing. Lerato, on the other hand, learned that emotional survival meant aligning her identity with marriage, internalizing the belief that independence was risky and unfulfilling.

Cultural Pressures – In both rural Limpopo and urban Johannesburg, societal norms dictate that men must be providers and women must be wives. Men are taught to hide weakness; women are taught that being unmarried equals failure. This creates a paradox where even educated men and women often marry to satisfy society, not themselves.

Economic Vulnerability – Whether uneducated or highly qualified, the fear of financial insecurity drives dependency. Sipho feels trapped in a marriage to maintain status and security, while Lerato stays because divorce would mean losing access to safety, property, or social respect.

Abusive Relationships and Dependency

Dependency is amplified when relationships become abusive. Sipho may lash out in frustration, while Lerato bears the emotional and sometimes physical consequences. Both partners, however, remain entangled due to fear, economic necessity, or societal judgment. Carl Jung's concept of the shadow is evident: unresolved fears and unacknowledged traumas are projected onto the partner, creating cycles of blame, guilt, and co-dependency.

Freedom of Love: Eric Fromm's Perspective

Eric Fromm's philosophy of *Freedom of Love* provides a critical lens for understanding this syndrome. Fromm argued that true love requires freedom—freedom from societal expectation, fear, and dependency. In the rural and township context:

For Women – Freedom of love means recognizing that marriage is not a measure of worth. Lerato, despite her education, must confront internalized beliefs that her identity depends on a man. Only by embracing self-awareness and autonomy can she form relationships rooted in choice, not survival.

For Men – Freedom of love requires embracing vulnerability. Sipho must learn that strength is not the absence of emotion, but the ability to love without control or fear. Fromm suggests that love is an act of courage, not a transaction, allowing men to engage authentically without relying on dominance or avoidance.

For Both Educated and Non-Educated – Education alone cannot solve dependency; identity work, self-reflection, and emotional honesty are necessary. Freedom of love is a mental and emotional liberation that allows couples to form bonds of mutual respect, not co-dependence.

A Modern Reality

In contemporary Africa, alcohol, social media, and transactional relationships have become coping mechanisms. Young women like Lerato, even with degrees, feel compelled to display relationship status as proof of success. Men like Sipho, even with employment, fear that revealing emotional neediness will result in judgment. Both are trapped in cycles of fear and social conformity, where dependency masquerades as security.

Breaking the Cycle

- To escape dependency, both men and women must:
- Recognize the difference between survival-driven attachment and authentic love.
- Address childhood trauma and unresolved emotional wounds.
- Challenge societal definitions of success, masculinity, and femininity.
- Embrace Fromm's *Freedom of Love*: relationships are not meant to complete us—they are meant to complement us.

Cultivate emotional literacy and self-awareness, enabling vulnerability without fear.

Dependency syndrome is not limited to uneducated or rural populations; it permeates all social strata, affecting educated and uneducated men and women alike.

The fear of vulnerability, the pressure to conform, and economic constraints trap individuals in marriages and relationships that may not serve them. Freedom of love, as Fromm articulated, offers a way out: a journey toward emotional autonomy, authentic connection, and self-determined partnership. Only when men and women claim this freedom can they transform marriage from a survival strategy into a place of mutual growth, respect, and joy.

Chapter 12: Why Women Fear Happiness – The Psychology of Self-Sabotage

Introduction

Happiness, for many women, is paradoxically terrifying. The very moments when life feels safe, abundant, or peaceful can trigger unconscious anxiety, self-doubt, and a compulsion to sabotage the good they have earned. This phenomenon, deeply rooted in childhood trauma, cultural conditioning, and internalized expectations, is an essential facet of dependency syndrome in marriage. By exploring Freudian and Jungian insights alongside modern social realities, this chapter uncovers why some women unconsciously resist their own joy and how these patterns perpetuate cycles of emotional dependency.

1. The Roots of Fear in Early Experience

Consider Lerato, a young woman from a Limpopo village who, despite being financially independent and well-educated, finds herself sabotaging successful relationships. Lerato grew up in a home marked by conflict, emotional neglect, and exposure to violence.

From a Freudian perspective, her id—responsible for instinctual drives—craved safety and love, but her superego internalized messages of guilt, shame, and unworthiness.

This created a psychological paradox: whenever Lerato experiences moments of joy, her ego—the mediator between instinct and morality—detects a potential threat. Happiness becomes dangerous because it conflicts with her early experiences of instability, teaching her mind that safety is temporary and love is conditional.

2. Cultural and Social Pressures

In many African and global contexts, women are socialized to prioritize others' needs above their own, internalizing messages such as:

"Your happiness is secondary to your family's survival."
"A successful woman without a man is incomplete."
"Sacrifice is proof of love."

These cultural imperatives shape self-perception and emotional patterns. Lerato, for instance, feels guilty enjoying life alone or pursuing personal ambitions, believing that independence threatens social cohesion or risks isolation. This internal conflict reinforces dependency behaviors, as women often remain in relationships that stifle growth because abandoning them would feel morally or socially wrong.

3. Self-Sabotage and Relationship Patterns

Freud's theory of projection offers insight into why women unconsciously undermine their own happiness. Women like Lerato may project unresolved childhood conflicts onto partners, interpreting ordinary interactions as threats, and preemptively sabotaging relationships to maintain psychological equilibrium.

Jungian concepts deepen this understanding: the *shadow self*—parts of the psyche that are denied or suppressed—manifests through self-sabotage. Lerato may unconsciously reject love, intimacy, or success because they trigger recognition of her own unacknowledged fears, insecurities, or anger.

Patterns of self-sabotage may include:

Initiating unnecessary conflicts.

Withdrawing emotionally at moments of intimacy.

Distrusting partners without clear cause.

Engaging in relationships with unsuitable or abusive partners.

These behaviors reinforce dependency, keeping women tethered to relationships that mirror early-life instability.

4. The Paradox of Freedom and Fear

Eric Fromm's concept of *Freedom of Love* is particularly relevant. Fromm argues that authentic love requires freedom—both to receive and to give. For women conditioned to link happiness with obligation, social expectation, or survival, freedom is frightening.

Moments of autonomy or emotional fulfillment feel threatening, as they contrast with learned dependence.

In rural marriage contexts, both educated and uneducated women often marry not solely for affection but as a survival mechanism. Even those with economic and educational freedom may unconsciously reproduce dependency patterns learned in childhood, sabotaging opportunities for genuine connection and happiness.

5. Modern Pressures and the Amplification of Fear

Today, social media, peer comparisons, and societal narratives amplify these dynamics. Successful women are scrutinized for their choices—being single, independent, or ambitious may invite judgment, gossip, or isolation. Many feel pressure to appear fulfilled only through relational attachment.

This external pressure reinforces internalized fear: happiness without a partner becomes socially risky, while self-sabotage becomes a psychological defense mechanism to prevent perceived failure or rejection.

6. Pathways to Healing and Self-Acceptance

Breaking free from the fear of happiness is challenging but possible. Interventions must address both internal and external factors:

Self-awareness

Recognizing the patterns of self-sabotage and tracing them to childhood experiences.

Shadow work

Confronting suppressed fears, anger, and insecurities, following Jungian methods.

Reframing social expectations

Challenging cultural norms that equate happiness with relational dependency.

Freedom of Love

Practicing relationships that honor autonomy, mutual respect, and emotional authenticity, as Fromm suggests.

Support systems

Trusted mentors, peers, or professional support to reinforce emotional growth.

The fear of happiness is not a moral failing—it is a deeply human, psychologically understandable response to trauma, socialization, and cultural expectation. Women trapped in this pattern often reproduce dependency, unintentionally perpetuating cycles of emotional and relational vulnerability.

True liberation arises when women recognize that joy, autonomy, and love are not threats but essential components of a whole, integrated self. By embracing their inner freedom, confronting shadows, and redefining love on their terms, women can break cycles of self-sabotage and claim authentic happiness without fear.

Chapter 13: How Men Fear Vulnerability – The Hidden Side of Dependency Syndrome

Introduction

While discussions around dependency syndrome often focus on women, men are equally susceptible to the psychological and cultural pressures that shape relational dependency. In many communities—rural villages in Limpopo, urban townships like Soweto and Khayelitsha, or global cities such as New York and Lagos—men face expectations to be providers, protectors, and emotionally unshakable pillars. These pressures create a paradox: the very men who are expected to display strength and control often feel insecure, trapped, and emotionally dependent.

This chapter explores how men's fear of vulnerability contributes to unhealthy marriages, co-dependency, and emotional suppression. Using insights from Sigmund Freud, Carl Jung, and Eric Fromm, we examine the psychological patterns that limit men's capacity for authentic love and how societal expectations intensify these dynamics.

1. The Roots of Male Vulnerability

Consider Thabo, an educated young man from Alexandra Township. Thabo holds a university degree and a promising job, yet he feels compelled to marry young and maintain appearances. Deeply, he fears judgment from family, peers, and society if he delays marriage. Freud's concept of the superego explains this pressure: Thabo internalizes societal and familial norms as moral imperatives, equating relational success with personal worth.

Jungian ideas further illuminate male vulnerability. Thabo's *shadow self*—the suppressed aspects of his emotions, including fear, sadness, and uncertainty—remains unacknowledged. To maintain social approval and self-image, he projects strength and independence outward while internally grappling with identity confusion.

2. Economic and Social Pressures

Men are often socialized to link their identity with financial and social success. In rural Mozambique, Nigeria, and parts of South Africa, a man's capacity to provide materially is frequently equated with masculinity. Those who are educated but unemployed or underemployed experience heightened anxiety: their self-worth is undermined, and marriage becomes both a societal expectation and a perceived escape from scrutiny.

Ironically, these same pressures may drive educated men to marry not for emotional fulfillment but to satisfy social norms. Marriage becomes a defensive mechanism to stabilize their social image, conceal insecurities, and adhere to cultural expectations of masculinity.

3. Emotional Dependency and the Fear of Vulnerability

Emotional dependency in men manifests differently than in women but is equally debilitating. Thabo, like many men, struggles to express fear, sadness, or doubt, fearing these emotions will diminish his perceived value.

In relationships, this fear may present as:

- Controlling behavior or rigidity
- Avoidance of intimacy or deep emotional connection
- Anger or irritability as defensive responses
- Reliance on partners for validation rather than shared mutuality

These patterns mirror dependency syndrome in women, creating marriages based on survival, societal approval, or mutual avoidance rather than authentic connection.

4. The Role of Trauma and Early Socialization

Childhood experiences heavily influence adult dependency patterns. Men who grow up witnessing family conflict, substance abuse, or emotional neglect often internalize instability as normative.

Freud's theory of the id, ego, and superego explains that unresolved internal conflicts manifest in adult relationships: the id's desires for security clash with the superego's internalized societal expectations, leaving the ego to navigate fear, obligation, and unprocessed trauma.

Jungian analysis highlights that men often repress the *anima*—the inner feminine, representing emotional openness and vulnerability. Suppression of this aspect leads to difficulties in forming genuine emotional bonds, perpetuating cycles of co-dependency.

5. Freedom of Love and Male Liberation

Eric Fromm's concept of *Freedom of Love* provides a roadmap for breaking dependency. True love, Fromm argues, requires courage to be vulnerable, autonomy to choose freely, and authenticity in emotional expression. For men like Thabo, embracing freedom means acknowledging fears, expressing emotional needs, and rejecting social pressures as the sole determinants of relational decisions.

In rural and urban contexts, whether educated or not, men who marry solely to satisfy cultural or familial expectations often trap themselves and their partners in cycles of mutual dependency. Fromm's principles suggest that liberation arises not from conforming but from cultivating emotional awareness, self-love, and responsible, conscious relational choices.

6. Modern Amplifiers: Technology, Peer Pressure, and Social Media

Contemporary pressures exacerbate men's fear of vulnerability. Social media reinforces ideals of success, masculinity, and relational status. Peer groups and family networks amplify the need to "appear settled" or "successful" through marriage, sometimes encouraging premature or strategic unions rather than emotionally honest ones.

The consequence: many men feel trapped, unfulfilled, and psychologically burdened. They may seek temporary escapes through alcohol, workaholism, or emotional withdrawal—further contributing to marital co-dependency.

7. Pathways to Emotional Freedom

Addressing male dependency syndrome requires interventions at both personal and societal levels:

Self-awareness: Recognizing internalized societal pressures and childhood trauma.

Shadow integration: Following Jungian methods to acknowledge repressed emotions and fears.

Freedom of Love: Embracing Fromm's model of autonomous, responsible, and authentic relational engagement.

Therapeutic support: Counseling, mentorship, and safe spaces to explore emotions and relational needs.

Cultural reshaping: Encouraging societies to value emotional authenticity over rigid social expectations.

Men, like women, are ensnared by dependency syndrome through a combination of trauma, societal expectation, and internalized fears. The fear of vulnerability—whether stemming from early life experiences, cultural norms, or personal insecurities—prevents authentic relational engagement and perpetuates cycles of co-dependency.

True emotional liberation, echoing Fromm's philosophy, requires courage, self-reflection, and a commitment to authentic love. Men who learn to embrace vulnerability, acknowledge internal conflicts, and make conscious relational choices can break these cycles, transforming marriages from survival mechanisms into partnerships grounded in mutual respect, autonomy, and authentic emotional connection.

Chapter 14: Breaking Trauma Bonds – A Practical Guide to Emotional Freedom

Introduction

Across the globe, dependency syndrome in marriage manifests in both visible and subtle ways, shaping lives in urban metropolises like New York City, bustling South African cities like Johannesburg, and the rural townships of Khayelitsha in the Western Cape. While the environments differ, the emotional and psychological consequences are strikingly similar: trapped individuals, struggling to cope with trauma, social expectation, and identity confusion.

This chapter combines narrative storytelling with psychological theory, drawing on Sigmund Freud's identity framework, Carl Jung's concepts of the shadow and individuation, and Eric Fromm's philosophy on *The Art of Loving* and *The Fear of Freedom*. Through these stories, we explore how individuals can emotionally, spiritually, and psychologically disengage from toxic relational patterns, reclaim autonomy, and cultivate authentic emotional freedom.

1. New York City: The Illusion of Glamour

Story of Maya

Maya, 32, lives in a Manhattan high-rise, works as a marketing executive, and appears to have it all. From the outside, her life exudes success: designer clothes, fine dining, weekend getaways, and an elegant penthouse. Yet, behind closed doors, Maya is trapped in a marriage defined not by love but by mutual dependency.

Her husband, David, is emotionally unavailable, frequently critical, and controlling under the guise of protection. Maya's dependence is subtle—she fears leaving because of the social ramifications and financial uncertainty, even though she is fully capable of independence. Every argument, every silent evening, compounds her internalized trauma from childhood neglect and early exposure to domestic instability.

Freud's framework illuminates Maya's dilemma: her superego, shaped by societal expectations of marriage and success, clashes with her id, which seeks genuine emotional fulfillment. Her ego struggles to mediate between the two, resulting in anxiety, depression, and self-doubt.

Jung would argue Maya is living a life misaligned with her *self*—her shadow, containing suppressed desires for freedom and authenticity, remains unacknowledged. Fromm's *Freedom of Love* offers her a path forward: to recognize that true love—including love for oneself—cannot coexist with fear and dependence. By consciously disentangling her self-worth from her marriage and external validation, she begins therapy, journaling, and mindfulness practices that restore emotional agency.

2. Johannesburg: Pressure and Prestige

Story of Sipho

Sipho, 40, is a successful entrepreneur in Sandton, Johannesburg. He grew up in a township where men were expected to provide, protect, and maintain control. His wife, Thandi, is a high-achieving lawyer, and together they present the image of a perfect, affluent couple. Yet beneath the surface, Sipho feels trapped by expectations—both his own and society's.

Sipho's dependency manifests in secrecy, alcohol, and avoidance of emotional confrontation. Jungian analysis suggests Sipho has repressed his anima, the inner feminine representing empathy, emotional awareness, and vulnerability. He cannot engage in genuine intimacy without fear of losing authority, so he maintains a façade while emotional pain accumulates.

Economic status does not insulate Sipho or Thandi from dependency syndrome; it only amplifies it. Fromm's principle that "love is an art" becomes revolutionary: they must learn to express love not as duty, obligation, or prestige, but as conscious, reciprocal care. Counseling, peer support groups, and self-reflection exercises allow them to begin seeing each other as partners, not lifelines, untangling the trauma bonds rooted in fear, societal expectation, and unprocessed childhood experiences.

3. Khayelitsha, Western Cape: Survival and Emotional Entrapment

Story of Lindiwe

In the township of Khayelitsha, Lindiwe, 27, married at 19 to escape overcrowded living conditions and an abusive home. Poverty, lack of educational opportunities, and social norms that equate a woman's worth with marriage pushed her into a partnership with Bongani, a man who promised protection and financial security.

Years into marriage, Lindiwe feels trapped: Bongani is emotionally distant, controlling, and occasionally violent. Every attempt to express needs is met with hostility, reinforcing her dependency. Here, trauma bonds are stark: leaving means confronting poverty, homelessness, and social stigma.

Freud's lens shows Lindiwe's ego constantly mediating between her suppressed fears (id) and the cultural and moral imperatives of her superego. Jungian theory suggests she must integrate her shadow—the suppressed strength, anger, and self-worth—to reclaim autonomy. Fromm's teachings become a practical blueprint: love is not ownership or survival; it is freedom and active engagement with the self.

Through community therapy, mentorship programs, and engagement with women's support networks, Lindiwe begins reclaiming her life, learning to prioritize personal agency over cultural expectation, and cultivating resilience that empowers her beyond the marriage.

4. Common Threads Across Contexts

Despite geographic and socioeconomic differences, these narratives reveal common patterns:

Trauma Bonds

Early experiences of neglect, abuse, or instability anchor individuals to toxic relationships.

Dependency and Identity Confusion

Fear, societal pressure, and internalized expectations compromise the ability to leave or renegotiate relationships.

Illusions of Stability

Marriage or high-status partnerships are often perceived as safety nets rather than mutually fulfilling relationships.

Mental Health Struggles

Anxiety, depression, substance use, and emotional burnout are common outcomes, irrespective of wealth or education.

5. Pathways to Emotional Freedom

Drawing from Freud, Jung, and Fromm, practical strategies emerge:

Self-Awareness

Recognize how trauma and socialization influence relational decisions.

Shadow Integration

Acknowledge suppressed desires, fears, and anger as signals for growth.

Conscious Love

Apply Fromm's *Art of Loving*: love is active, responsible, and autonomous, not a survival mechanism.

Therapeutic Engagement

Individual, couple, or group therapy to process trauma and develop coping skills.

Community Support

Engage with safe networks that provide guidance, affirmation, and practical assistance.

By following these steps, individuals in any context—urban or rural, wealthy or poor—can break trauma bonds, disengage from unhealthy dependency, and cultivate genuine emotional and spiritual freedom.

Breaking free from marriage dependency syndrome is not a simple act of leaving; it is a comprehensive journey of self-discovery, trauma resolution, and conscious relational choices. Across New York City, Johannesburg, and Khayelitsha, individuals who embrace vulnerability, integrate their shadow selves, and cultivate the *freedom of love* discover that liberation lies not in escape alone but in reclaiming identity, agency, and authentic emotional engagement.

Practical Exercises for Breaking Trauma Bonds

These exercises are designed to help individuals, whether in urban or rural settings, begin disentangling themselves from unhealthy dependency patterns in relationships.

They draw from the teachings of Freud (understanding internal conflicts), Jung (integrating the shadow self), and Fromm (developing the *freedom of love*).

1. Mapping Your Dependency

Goal: Identify the roots and patterns of emotional dependency.

Steps:

- **Take a journal and divide a page into three columns:**
- ***Childhood Experiences, Current Relationship Behaviors, Emotional Triggers.***
- **List events from your childhood that caused fear, neglect, or trauma.**
- **Connect these experiences to your current patterns:**
- **Are you seeking approval?**
- **Avoiding confrontation?**
- **Staying because of fear or financial insecurity?**
- **Highlight recurring patterns.**
- **Awareness is the first step toward change.**

Freud emphasized that unresolved childhood experiences influence adult choices. Naming these connections reduces unconscious repetition.

2. Shadow Work – Facing Suppressed Emotions
Goal: Integrate the suppressed or hidden parts of your identity.
Steps:

1. **Find a quiet, safe space. Begin by writing down emotions you feel uncomfortable acknowledging: anger, fear, desire for independence.**

1. **Ask yourself:** ***Which of these emotions have I ignored to "keep the peace" in my relationship?***

1. **Identify behaviors linked to these suppressed emotions—e.g., people-pleasing, avoiding conflict, or overdependence.**

1. **Commit to expressing these emotions in small, safe ways, such as saying "no" or requesting space.**

◈ *Jung argued that neglecting the shadow leads to repeated trauma cycles.*

◈ *Embracing your suppressed emotions empowers self-determination.*

3. The Freedom of Love Practice

Goal: Shift from survival-driven attachment to conscious love.

Steps

Write down the motivations behind staying in your current relationship: love, fear, financial security, social expectation.

For each motivation, ask:

- *Does this promote my growth and authenticity, or is it rooted in fear or societal pressure?*

Begin practicing self-love activities:

Set personal boundaries.

Pursue hobbies or goals independent of your partner.

Affirm your worth daily: "I am complete and capable on my own."

Fromm emphasized that love must be an act of will and freedom. When love is chosen rather than forced, dependency dissolves.

4. Emotional Disconnection Exercises

Goal: Reduce psychological entanglement with toxic partners.

Steps:

- **Mentally visualize the relationship as a cord connecting you to your partner.**
- **Imagine this cord loosening and separating.**
- **Repeat daily for 5–10 minutes.**
- **Replace the emotional energy previously invested in the partner with self-care activities or creative projects.**
- **Gradually limit interactions that reinforce dependency, while maintaining necessary communications.**

Visualization allows the mind to rehearse freedom before physically taking steps, easing the emotional shock of separation.

1. **Community and Support Engagement**

Goal: Build resilience through external validation and guidance.

Steps:

- Join support groups—online or in-person—where others share similar experiences.
- Seek mentorship from individuals who have successfully left dependency-driven relationships.
- Engage in counseling or therapy when possible, understanding it as a tool for empowerment, not restriction.

Both urban and rural survivors often isolate themselves.

Connecting with empathetic communities strengthens identity and reinforces freedom of choice.

6. Creating an Exit Plan (If Needed)

Goal: Safely transition from toxic relationships.

Steps:

- Identify financial, social, and emotional resources.
- Plan a safe location and support network if leaving a physically unsafe environment.
- Set achievable, time-bound goals to regain independence (e.g., open a bank account, secure employment, enroll in education).

Preparing for independence reduces anxiety and empowers individuals to make decisions based on self-determination, not fear.

Conclusion of Exercises

Breaking trauma bonds is a journey, not a one-time act.

By combining self-reflection, shadow work, conscious love, emotional distancing, community support, and practical planning, individuals reclaim autonomy and mental well-being.

These practices apply to anyone—urban professionals in New York or Johannesburg, women and men navigating rural township expectations, and educated individuals bound by societal pressure.

The key principle: *freedom begins within the mind, then extends to the heart and life choices.*

The Science of Trauma Bonds

Why Women Choose the Same Men (Even When They Know Better)

Lerato, a 29-year-old woman living in Johannesburg, often wondered why she kept attracting men who were emotionally unavailable. She had grown up in a cramped, chaotic household where love was conditional, inconsistent, or outright absent. By the time she reached her twenties, her choices in men seemed pre-programmed: partners who mirrored the instability she had known as a child. Even when her friends warned her, or when she herself recognized red flags, she found herself repeating the same patterns—jealousy, neglect, and emotional withdrawal.

This phenomenon is what psychologists call trauma bonding—a paradoxical attachment formed when intermittent abuse or neglect is paired with affection or reward.

Sigmund Freud's concepts of the id, ego, and superego shed light on why these patterns persist: Lerato's unconscious mind seeks the familiar, even when it is harmful. Her id, craving safety and connection, is drawn to the type of attention she received in childhood; her ego rationalizes it as "love," and her superego struggles to reconcile societal expectations that she must be in a relationship to be complete.

Television shows, films, and social media often reinforce these patterns. From romantic dramas to reality shows, women are presented with narratives where emotional pain, infidelity, and neglect are romanticized. The media glamorizes the struggle, making it appear that love must be hard, that passion is inseparable from conflict, and that survival in a relationship is a badge of resilience. For someone like Lerato, these portrayals act as a psychological trigger, normalizing her repeated choices.

According to Eric Fromm, genuine love is an act of freedom, not compulsion. It requires self-awareness, responsibility, and the capacity to distinguish between affection and dependency. Trauma bonds, however, prevent individuals from experiencing this freedom.

The attachment is not rooted in conscious choice or mutual growth; it is a survival mechanism that provides short-term relief from emotional pain but long-term damage to self-esteem, autonomy, and relational health.

Even educated women and men are not immune. Those with high social status or financial independence may still unconsciously seek partners who replicate familiar trauma dynamics.

Likewise, men who fear vulnerability or emotional authenticity may unconsciously cling to women who tolerate their emotional absence, perpetuating the cycle. In both cases, societal pressures—family expectations, peer influence, and cultural norms—further complicate the ability to break free.

Practical Exercise: Mapping and Releasing Trauma Bonds

Objective: To help individuals identify recurring patterns in romantic choices, understand the underlying trauma, and begin practicing emotional freedom.

Step 1: Story Mapping

Write a timeline of your past romantic relationships.

Include:

- Age and context
- Partner behaviors (both positive and negative)
- Your emotional reactions at the time
- Any unresolved feelings or patterns that repeated from previous relationships
- Highlight recurring behaviors in partners or your own reactions.

Step 2: Recognize the Trauma Connection

Next to each relationship, write: *"Which childhood experiences does this mirror?"*

For example, neglect, inconsistency, abandonment, or overprotection.

This step is critical: Fromm calls it recognizing *where freedom is blocked*. You cannot choose genuine love without seeing the chains of the past.

Step 3: Conscious Choice Practice

Imagine a current or future romantic situation.

Ask yourself:

Am I drawn to this partner out of fear, familiarity, or survival?

Am I seeking them because they fulfill my authentic self, or because they replicate my old trauma?

Write a "freedom statement": "I choose partners who nurture my growth, not my wounds."

Step 4: Emotional Rehearsal

- For 10 minutes daily, visualize interacting with a partner who reflects healthy, balanced love.
- Feel the difference between dependency-driven reactions and conscious love.
- Notice any internal resistance; journal your observations.

Step 5: Media Awareness

- Monitor media consumption and identify messages that reinforce trauma-based attachment.
- Replace at least one hour per day with content that models healthy relationships, emotional intelligence, and self-respect.

Narrative Reflection

Lerato began practicing these steps over six weeks. She realized that her attraction to emotionally unavailable men was not a flaw, but a learned survival response. Through mapping her trauma, journaling her choices, and consciously envisioning healthier relationships, she began to feel a sense of emotional freedom she had never known. She started saying no to relationships that replicated pain, and yes to friendships and self-care activities that strengthened her sense of self. Over time, she experienced a profound shift: love was no longer about survival—it was about growth, choice, and mutual respect.

By integrating Freud's insights on projection, Jung's shadow work, and Fromm's philosophy of freedom in love, individuals like Lerato can begin breaking the cycle of trauma bonds, reclaiming autonomy, and creating relationships rooted in genuine connection rather than survival.

Chapter 15: Breaking Trauma Bonds – Stories of Emotional Freedom

Chapter Summary -Trauma, Memory, and the Body

This chapter forms the heart of the book. It highlights how the body becomes the first witness to suffering and the last to forget. Using case-inspired narratives and psychological insights, it shows how physical symptoms—chronic pain, anxiety, fatigue, panic, and disconnection—often originate from emotional wounds.

The chapter discusses how trauma disrupts the nervous system, alters stress responses, and shapes one's sense of safety. It also reflects on cultural beliefs about bodily illness, such as witchcraft, spiritual imbalance, and traditional healing, showing how these frameworks shape a person's understanding of their suffering. Ultimately, the chapter argues that healing must involve both mind and body working in unity.

Introduction

Dependency syndrome in marriage is not confined to rural Africa, nor is it limited to uneducated populations. Its psychological roots transcend geography and class, manifesting wherever childhood trauma, social pressure, and economic vulnerability intersect. While women have historically been highlighted as victims, men too suffer in silence—trapped by societal expectations, identity confusion, and emotional fear.

In this chapter, we examine how individuals in New York City, Johannesburg, and the rural villages of Khayelitsha navigate trauma bonds, and explore practical pathways toward emotional liberation, drawing on Sigmund Freud's identity theories, Carl Jung's shadow work, and Eric Fromm's concept of the Freedom of Love.

Case Study 1: New York City – The Illusion of Affluence

Maria, 32, is a marketing executive living in Manhattan. On the outside, she embodies success: a high-paying job, a luxurious apartment, and a busy social life. Yet, her romantic life mirrors chaos. Maria repeatedly falls for partners who are emotionally distant or controlling. Despite her financial independence, she clings to these relationships as if they provide something her upbringing could not: emotional safety.

Freud would describe Maria's attachment as a projection of unresolved childhood needs: her superego pushes her toward societal "success markers"—marriage, a committed relationship—while her id craves intimacy, and her ego rationalizes harmful behaviors as love. Jung would add that her shadow—the unacknowledged aspects of fear, inadequacy, and trauma—drives her repeated choices.

Eric Fromm's concept of the Freedom of Love illuminates her struggle: Maria mistakes attachment for love. She believes dependence validates her worth, yet it shackles her inner freedom. Therapy offers tools, but Maria finds the process difficult because it forces confrontation with long-buried emotions—her freedom feels threatening. Alcohol and social distractions often become her coping mechanisms, further deepening her dependence.

Practical Insight:

- Recognizing patterns of attraction based on trauma is the first step.
- Maria begins journaling every emotional reaction to her partner's behavior, asking: "Is this love or survival?"

Case Study 2: Johannesburg – The Weight of Cultural Expectation

Lerato, 29, lives in Alexandra Township. She has a university degree and a growing career in communications, yet she feels incomplete unless she is married. Like Maria, her choices in men are influenced less by compatibility and more by the desire to fulfill cultural and familial expectations. In her community, success is measured by partnership; independence without a man is perceived as failure.

Her first marriage was with a man who offered financial stability but little emotional connection. She stayed, even as resentment and emotional exhaustion built, because returning home meant vulnerability, poverty, and social shame.

Lerato's dependency syndrome is compounded by identity confusion: Jungian psychology suggests that when an individual is unclear about their authentic self, they unconsciously seek others to complete it.

Freud's id-ego-superego model further explains her internal conflict: *her id seeks security, her superego enforces societal rules, and her ego negotiates between survival and personal fulfillment.*

Practical Insight

Lerato engages in shadow work, identifying traits in herself she unconsciously projects onto her partner: fear, control, and neediness.

She begins to practice Fromm's Freedom of Love, redefining love as a mutual growth process rather than a survival strategy.

Case Study 3: Rural Khayelitsha – Early Dependency and Trauma Bonds

Nomvula, 21, lives in a rural village in the Western Cape. Her family home is a small two-room dwelling shared with her parents and siblings. Privacy is scarce, and she witnessed domestic conflict from a young age. By 15, she began dating an older man who promised financial security and a way to escape home. By 17, she was pregnant.

Nomvula's story illustrates how trauma bonds form at the intersection of economic vulnerability and early exposure to unstable relationships. Freud would argue that her unconscious mind seeks familiar emotional environments, even if harmful. Jung might interpret her early entanglement as an enactment of her shadow: unresolved fear, shame, and longing manifesting in romantic attachments.

Here, Fromm's principles of Freedom of Love are transformative. Nomvula learns that emotional freedom requires understanding the difference between love and survival, and that autonomy in thought and emotion is necessary before forming healthy partnerships.

Practical Insight:

Nomvula participates in group workshops on emotional literacy and self-awareness.

She practices conscious detachment: recognizing the compulsion to stay in harmful relationships and actively choosing autonomy first.

The Science Behind Trauma Bonds

Across all three contexts, trauma bonds share common characteristics:

Intermittent Reinforcement

Occasional affection or attention keeps the bond alive despite abuse.

Cognitive Dissonance

The mind rationalizes harmful behavior to maintain attachment.

Projection

Unresolved childhood experiences are projected onto partners.

Societal and Cultural Reinforcement

Social norms, media, and peer pressure normalize harmful relational patterns.

The Role of Therapy and Shadow Work:

Freud: Identifies unconscious patterns and projections.

Jung: Encourages integration of the shadow to reveal hidden motives and fears.

Fromm: Offers a framework for understanding love as an act of freedom, not compulsion.

Key Principle

Freedom in love requires
Self-awareness
Autonomy
And courage.

Only by confronting inner wounds and dismantling societal expectations can individuals escape dependency and trauma bonds.

Practical Exercise: Emotional Freedom Mapping

Step 1: Identify the Bond

Write the names of current or past partners with whom you feel stuck.

Describe the emotional highs and lows, noting moments of fear, desire, and dependency.

Step 2: Analyze Trauma Patterns

Next to each partner, note unresolved childhood experiences mirrored in the relationship.

Example: Neglect → Tolerance of emotional withdrawal; Poverty → Dependence on financial security.

Step 3: Freedom Statement

Write: "I am free to love without fear, without dependence, and without repeating trauma."

Read this statement aloud daily, internalizing autonomy.

Step 4: Shadow Work

Journal thoughts, fears, and impulses that arise during conflict.

Identify which are projections of past trauma versus genuine needs.

Step 5: Practice Healthy Detachment

Visualize releasing attachment to unhealthy partners.

Reinforce self-care, hobbies, friendships, and activities that strengthen autonomy.

Across Geography, Class, and Gender

Whether in the bustling skyscrapers of New York, the township streets of Johannesburg, or the rural homes of Khayelitsha, the human struggle with trauma bonds is universal.

Men and women alike suffer from dependency syndrome, often under the guise of societal expectation, love, or survival. By integrating psychoanalytic insight with Fromm's Freedom of Love, individuals can reclaim autonomy, heal old wounds, and approach relationships with conscious choice rather than compulsion.

The journey to emotional freedom begins not with leaving a partner, but with reclaiming the self.

The Role of Culture, Religion, and Society in Normalizing Toxic Love

Introduction

Dependency syndrome in marriage does not develop in a vacuum. It is reinforced and sustained by layers of culture, religion, and societal expectation. Across generations, communities have created a framework in which marriage is more than a union—it is a marker of identity, respectability, and survival. For women and men, this often translates into an unconscious pressure to conform, stay, or settle, even when the relationship is emotionally damaging.

This section explores how these social forces operate, with examples from South Africa, Western countries, and modern Christian churches, showing how cultural and religious norms can inadvertently perpetuate toxic love and contribute to mental health challenges.

Case Study 1: Modern Christian Churches – The Marriage Mandate

Thandi, a 28-year-old woman in Johannesburg, grew up in a charismatic church where teachings emphasized that a woman's ultimate purpose is to find a husband and submit to him. Sermons repeatedly framed marriage as the pinnacle of spiritual and social success, while singleness was subtly equated with failure or divine disfavor.

Thandi fell in love with a man who displayed controlling behavior, often questioning her autonomy and choices. Yet she stayed because church leaders and peers celebrated their union, and she feared judgment if she left. The community's spiritual narrative conflated suffering with devotion: enduring hardship in marriage was presented as proof of faith and resilience.

Practical Issue:

Church teachings often discourage questioning a partner's behavior or leaving a harmful marriage.

Followers internalize guilt for considering separation, linking their faith with emotional dependency.

Mental health challenges, such as anxiety, depression, and low self-worth, emerge silently as congregants navigate the tension between spiritual obedience and personal well-being.

Case Study 2: Cultural Norms in South Africa – The Weight of Tradition

In rural villages of Khayelitsha and Limpopo, marriage has historically been framed as a survival strategy.

Families view women's unions as critical for social mobility, economic security, and the continuity of family lineage. Nomvula, 22, from a small village, was encouraged by her family to marry an older man who could provide for her, despite knowing little about emotional compatibility.

Traditional ceremonies, lobola (bride price), and community celebration reinforced the idea that securing a husband validated a woman's worth.

Leaving a harmful marriage would not only bring shame but also risk social ostracization. Nomvula found herself trapped: cultural expectation required marriage, and divorce threatened economic survival and community standing.

Practical Issue:

Cultural rituals inadvertently reinforce dependency, making women and men feel compelled to stay in unhealthy relationships.

Social reward structures—praise, respect, family approval—are tied to marital status rather than emotional well-being.

Case Study 3: Western Societies – The Social Validation of Romantic Success

In Western countries like New York and London, societal pressures are subtler but equally potent. Marriage is often portrayed in media, television, and social media as a marker of adult success and personal fulfillment.

Maria, a 30-year-old professional in Manhattan, felt compelled to maintain a relationship with a partner who was emotionally distant, fearing the stigma of singlehood among peers and online communities.

Unlike in the South African or church-based context, the pressure is secular, yet it still creates dependency. Success is measured by partnership, Instagram-worthy coupledom, or cohabitation in high-status neighborhoods. Women and men internalize these expectations, equating relational survival with social approval.

Practical Issue

Social media amplifies comparison, jealousy, and self-doubt.

Individuals remain in toxic relationships to avoid perceived failure or social invisibility.

Emotional dependence is reinforced by external validation rather than internal fulfillment.

Cultural, Religious, and Social Mechanisms That Sustain Dependency

Social Reward Systems:

Communities celebrate marriage as an achievement and singlehood as a deficit.

Positive reinforcement for compliance encourages individuals to remain in harmful unions.

Shaming and Judgment

Leaving a marriage, especially as a woman, often triggers family or community shame.

Religious leaders may interpret divorce as sin, reinforcing guilt and entrapment.

Media and Modern Narratives

Television, movies, and social media normalize toxic behaviors as romantic or aspirational.

Cultural and media messages converge, presenting survival through partnership as the standard path to happiness.

Economic Dependence

Financial reliance magnifies the impact of cultural and religious pressures.

Women and men without economic autonomy often cannot challenge harmful relationships without severe consequences.

Mental Health Consequences

Across all three settings—church, rural tradition, and urban Western society—dependency syndrome becomes a cornerstone of mental health crises.

Individuals trapped in marriages for survival, social validation, or spiritual approval often experience:

- Chronic anxiety and depression

- Identity confusion
- Low self-esteem and self-worth
- Addiction or maladaptive coping strategies (alcohol, substance use)

Eric Fromm's concept of Freedom of Love becomes particularly relevant here: the capacity to love freely is obstructed when social, cultural, or religious forces dictate relational choices. The challenge is helping individuals recognize that societal approval or cultural tradition cannot replace authentic emotional autonomy.

Practical Narrative Exercise: Evaluating Social Influence on Relationships

Step 1: Map Your Influences

Draw three circles: Culture, Religion, Society.

Write the pressures, expectations, or narratives each sphere has imposed on your relationship choices.

Step 2: Identify Conflicts

Highlight where your desires, autonomy, or emotional needs conflict with these influences.

Step 3: Evaluate Your Freedom

Using Fromm's Freedom of Love, ask: "Am I staying because of love, or because of expectation, fear, or survival?"

Step 4: Take Incremental Steps Toward Autonomy

Journal daily about small acts of emotional independence.

Seek safe spaces (therapy, support groups, or trusted friends) to discuss conflicts between personal desires and social pressures.

Cultural norms, religious teachings, and societal expectations create invisible chains that normalize toxic love.

Across continents—from South African villages to modern Western cities—people internalize these pressures, often at the cost of their mental health and emotional freedom. By recognizing and mapping these influences, integrating psychoanalytic insight, and embracing Fromm's philosophy of freedom, individuals can reclaim autonomy, break dependency cycles, and approach relationships with conscious choice rather than compulsion.

Breaking Dependency Bonds: Story-Driven Exercises for Emotional Freedom

Introduction: The Invisible Chains of Dependency

Breaking free from dependency syndrome requires more than intellectual understanding; it requires practical, experiential exercises that challenge internalized beliefs, cultural pressures, and emotional attachments. These exercises combine psychoanalytic insight from Sigmund Freud and Carl Jung with Eric Fromm's concept of Freedom of Love. The goal is to help individuals reclaim autonomy, rebuild identity, and approach love as a conscious, free choice.

Case study

Lindiwe sits on the edge of her narrow bed in Khayelitsha, staring at the faded paint peeling off the wall. She married at nineteen, leaving the one-room home she shared with her parents and three siblings. On the surface, she "escaped" the noise, the overcrowding, and the constant exposure to adult conflict. Yet, three years later, she still feels trapped—this time inside a marriage that was meant to save her. Lindiwe's story is not unique. Across the globe—from the high-rise apartments of New York to the bustling streets of Johannesburg—women and men enter relationships seeking freedom and stability, only to discover that dependency binds them in invisible chains.

This chapter explores how trauma, cultural pressures, and social expectations fuel **Dependency Syndrome in Marriage** and offers practical exercises to reclaim emotional, psychological, and spiritual freedom. Drawing on the insights of Sigmund Freud, Carl Jung, and

Eric Fromm, this chapter blends storytelling with psychoanalytic theory and actionable guidance.

The Science of Trauma Bonds

Why Women (and Men) Repeat Patterns

Sara, a thirty-year-old marketing executive in Johannesburg, watches her friends post romantic milestones on social media. She longs for connection but repeatedly chooses partners who are emotionally unavailable or controlling. "I know better," she tells herself, yet the cycle continues.

The phenomenon she experiences is known as trauma bonding—a deep attachment to someone who simultaneously causes emotional pain and provides brief moments of relief or pleasure. Freud's concept of projection helps explain this: unresolved inner conflicts, often stemming from childhood trauma, are projected onto partners. Jung would add that these individuals are unconsciously seeking to complete unresolved aspects of the shadow self in others.

Eric Fromm's ideas of **Freedom of Love** highlight the danger of confusing attachment with love. When love becomes a survival strategy or a means of self-validation, true freedom of choice is lost. In Lindiwe, Sara, and countless others, the inability to disconnect from these bonds perpetuates cycles of emotional suffering and dependency.

Global Perspectives: How Dependency Plays Out

New York City

Michael, 32, grew up in a foster care system, craving stability. He married young, primarily to meet societal expectations and family approval. Despite a lucrative career, he finds himself emotionally hollow, trapped by fear of being alone, and dependent on the relationship to define his worth. Therapy, although available, feels threatening—it asks him to confront inner chaos he has spent decades suppressing. Alcohol often becomes the escape mechanism.

Johannesburg, South Africa

Nomvula, 28, comes from a middle-class township. Cultural norms praise marriage as a rite of passage for women. Financial dependency and social expectations push her into a relationship with an older man. Even with a university degree, she fears being judged for remaining single. Here, dependency is reinforced not by poverty alone but by social validation of marital status.

Khayelitsha, Western Cape

Lindiwe's story reflects rural realities, where marriage is both an emotional and survival necessity.

Overcrowded living spaces, early exposure to adult conflicts, and lack of privacy make marriage a perceived sanctuary. The underlying trauma from childhood, however, travels with her, turning what should be safety into another site of emotional suffering.

Across these contexts, whether urban or rural, educated or less formally educated, the pattern is striking: dependency is not a matter of morality but a response to psychosocial pressure, trauma, and identity confusion.

The Role of Culture, Religion, and Society

Cultural norms, religious institutions, and societal expectations often glorify dependence in marriage. Churches in Johannesburg preach commitment and sanctity of marriage but rarely address emotional autonomy or the dangers of remaining in abusive or unfulfilling unions. In Western countries, media and entertainment portray romantic love as validation of identity, encouraging individuals to conflate self-worth with relationship status.

In South African rural communities, a woman's respect and social standing often hinge on marriage. For men, masculinity may be defined by the ability to provide, further reinforcing dependency structures. The marriage dependency syndrome, therefore, becomes a cornerstone of mental health challenges, driving depression, anxiety, substance abuse, and identity crises.

Practical Exercises for Breaking Dependency Bonds

Exercise 1: The Mirror of Influence

- Identify all cultural, religious, and societal pressures shaping your relationship decisions.

- Reflect: Which pressures are external impositions?
- Which align with your authentic desires?
- Journal a "story of freedom," imagining choices made without external pressures.

Exercise 2: Shadow Work

- Identify recurring relational patterns.
- Journal early memories connected to each pattern.
- Write a compassionate letter to your "shadow self" acknowledging unresolved pain.

Exercise 3: Roleplay Freedom of Love

Dialogue between **Yourself as Free** and **Yourself as Dependent**.

Speak aloud as your Free Self asserting autonomy and emotional boundaries.

Visualize relationships chosen out of compatibility, not fear or survival.

Exercise 4: Map Emotional Anchors

1. *List factors keeping you in your relationship (financial, social, emotional).*

1. *Rank their influence and identify strategies to reduce reliance safely.*

1. *Visualize slowly removing anchors while maintaining safety and dignity.*

Exercise 5: The Freedom Map

Draw a map of your life including relationship status, emotional state, and personal goals.

Identify areas influenced by dependency syndrome.

Create a step-by-step roadmap to regain independence and build emotional resilience.

Conclusion

Breaking dependency bonds is not merely a theoretical exercise; it is an ongoing journey of self-discovery, courage, and practical action.

By combining Freud's insights on projection and the ego, Jung's work on the shadow, and Fromm's principles of **Freedom of Love**, individuals can reclaim autonomy and choose love consciously.

Whether in the crowded apartments of New York, the vibrant streets of Johannesburg, or the rural homesteads of Khayelitsha, the path to freedom is the same: understand your trauma, recognize external pressures, rebuild your identity, and make love a conscious choice, not a survival strategy.

Exercise 1: The Mirror of Influence – Recognizing Hidden Pressures

Narrative Story:

Lindiwe, 26, lives in Khayelitsha and has been in a marriage for three years. She stays because her family praises her husband for providing financially, yet she feels emotionally drained and unheard. Each evening, she scrolls through social media, comparing herself to peers in relationships that appear perfect.

Exercise Steps:

1. **Sit in a quiet space with a journal.**

1. **Draw a three-column table: Cultural Expectations, Religious Pressures, Societal Messages.**

1. **Write all the ways each influence has shaped your decisions in relationships.**

Reflect

- **Are these pressures aligned with your authentic desires, or are you conforming out of fear, shame, or obligation?**

Narrate your feelings as a story in the journal, describing what you would do if these pressures did not exist.

Outcome

Recognizing the hidden forces allows the mind to separate personal desire from external obligation—a first step toward freedom.

Exercise 2: Shadow Work – Facing the Self

Narrative Story:

Michael, 32, an engineer in New York, married young to please family expectations. He constantly doubts himself, masking insecurity with control over his wife's activities. In therapy, he learns that his dependency is a projection of unresolved childhood anxiety and fear of abandonment.

Exercise Steps

1. ***Identify recurring patterns in your relationships—anger, jealousy, over-compliance, or people-pleasing.***

1. *Journal about the earliest memory connected to each pattern. Freud's theory of id, ego, and superego helps here: which impulses are suppressed (id), which rationalizations justify staying (ego), and which moral judgments (superego) enforce conformity?*

1. *Engage in dialogue with your "shadow self," the part of you carrying unprocessed pain. Write a letter to this part, offering compassion and understanding.*

Visualize detaching from your partner's behavior—acknowledge that their actions are separate from your self-worth.

Outcome

By confronting and integrating the shadow, individuals regain self-awareness and reduce projections onto partners, breaking cycles of toxic dependency.

Exercise 3: The Freedom of Love Roleplay

Narrative Story:

Sara, 29, from Johannesburg, has repeatedly chosen partners who abandon her emotionally. She fears being alone because her sense of identity is tied to romantic attachment. Guided by Fromm's ideas, she learns that love cannot flourish where fear dominates.

Exercise Steps

- Create two characters: Yourself as Free and Yourself as Dependent.
- In a journal, write a dialogue between them:
- Free Self asks: "What do you want for yourself?"
- Dependent Self responds with fears, obligations, or excuses.
- Roleplay this dialogue aloud if possible. Speak as the Free Self, asserting autonomy and emotional boundaries.

Imagine scenarios where you choose partners based on emotional compatibility, not survival or societal approval.

Outcome

This exercise strengthens the ability to choose love consciously, rather than out of compulsion or unresolved trauma.

Exercise 4: Mapping Emotional Anchors

Narrative Story:

Nomvula, 25, in Khayelitsha, notices she clings to her husband despite ongoing abuse. She realizes that her financial dependence, family expectations, and fear of loneliness act as "anchors" holding her in place.

Exercise Steps:

- List all factors keeping you in your current relationship

(financial, social, emotional, cultural).

- Rank each anchor by influence: 1 = minor, 5 = dominant.
- For each anchor, identify a practical strategy to reduce reliance:
- Financial: Develop a side income or access social support.
- Social: Build a network of supportive friends outside the relationship.
- Emotional: Practice mindfulness, meditation, or journaling to self-soothe.
- Cultural: Seek dialogue with trusted community members who support autonomy.

Visualize yourself slowly cutting the strongest anchors while maintaining safety and self-respect.

Outcome

Mapping anchors clarifies what keeps individuals trapped and provides actionable steps toward emotional freedom.

Exercise 5: Creating a Freedom Map – Visioning a Life Beyond Dependency

Narrative Story:

John, 30, in New York, realizes that his marriage is a façade: high social status masks emotional dissatisfaction. He dreams of a life where love is voluntary and mutual.

Exercise Steps:

Draw a map of your life including: Current Relationship, Desired Emotional State, Support Systems, Personal Goals.

Identify which areas are influenced by dependency syndrome.

Set clear, measurable steps for reclaiming autonomy:

Attend therapy or support groups.

Build financial independence.

Redefine self-identity outside of relationship status.

Explore personal passions and goals.

Visualize yourself in six months, one year, and five years, living free from compulsion and fear.

Outcome

The Freedom Map creates a mental and emotional roadmap for moving from dependency to autonomy while ensuring safety and self-respect.

Breaking dependency bonds is an ongoing process requiring courage, awareness, and structured practice. Through shadow work, roleplay, anchor mapping, and visioning exercises, individuals can dismantle the psychological chains of culture, religion, and social expectation. By integrating insights from Freud, Jung, and Fromm, these exercises help men and women reclaim emotional freedom, consciously choose partners, and experience love as a creative and liberating force rather than a survival strategy.

Case Studies: Breaking Dependency Bonds Across Contexts

Michael – New York City: Escaping the Illusion of Success

Michael, 32, grew up in the foster care system in Brooklyn. Early abandonment left him craving approval and stability. Despite achieving a successful career in finance, he consistently chose partners who mirrored his childhood instability: emotionally unavailable, critical, or controlling. On the surface, he had everything society celebrated—money, status, and a long-term relationship—but internally, he felt hollow, trapped in a pattern of fear, shame, and dependency.

Step 1: Identifying Trauma Bonds

Michael began therapy reluctantly, initially seeing it as a threat to his autonomy. Using Freud's concept of projection, he recognized that he had been seeking in women the nurturing absent in his own childhood. Jung's shadow work helped him identify parts of himself he had unconsciously projected onto partners, including insecurity, fear of failure, and the need to control outcomes.

Step 2: Practical Exercises

Mirror of Influence: Michael wrote down the societal pressures that shaped his relationships—success defined by partner approval and social image. He realized that much of his attachment stemmed from proving his worth, not genuine connection.

Shadow Work: He journaled the recurring patterns of abandonment and mistrust, writing letters to his "younger self" and his shadow, forgiving the part of him that sought love in toxic ways.

Freedom Roleplay: Michael rehearsed asserting his needs and boundaries aloud, imagining conversations with partners where he prioritized emotional autonomy.

Outcome

Over months, Michael slowly disentangled from his trauma bonds, choosing relationships based on compatibility rather than fear or social expectation. Alcohol, previously a coping mechanism, became unnecessary as he developed internal strategies for emotional regulation.

1. Nomvula – Johannesburg: Navigating Cultural and Economic Pressures

Nomvula, 28, grew up in Soweto, in a family that celebrated marriage as the ultimate symbol of success for women. She earned a university degree but was constantly reminded by relatives that "no husband meant no respect." Feeling pressure to secure both social approval and financial security, she married at 25. Within two years, she discovered her husband was controlling, emotionally distant, and unwilling to share responsibilities.

Step 1: Recognizing Dependency Patterns

Nomvula realized she had married to escape the fear of being alone and to satisfy social norms. Her identity had been tightly bound to the image of a married woman, rather than her personal growth. She reflected on Freud's id, ego, and superego: her ego had been overpowered by cultural superego expectations, leading to decisions rooted in fear, not desire.

Step 2: Applying Practical Exercises

Mirror of Influence: She wrote down the familial, religious, and cultural expectations influencing her marriage.

Emotional Anchors Map

Nomvula listed factors keeping her in the marriage: fear of shame, lack of financial independence, children, and social judgment. She ranked them, identifying which could be safely mitigated.

Freedom Map: She developed a step-by-step roadmap for independence—securing employment, attending therapy, and establishing supportive social networks outside her family and marriage.

Outcome

Through these exercises, Nomvula regained emotional autonomy. She learned to communicate assertively with her husband and negotiate shared responsibilities. While the marriage didn't end immediately, she developed the skills to make conscious decisions rather than remain trapped by fear and cultural expectation.

1. **Lindiwe – Khayelitsha: Breaking Free from Rural Constraints**

Lindiwe, 24, married at nineteen to escape the overcrowded home she shared with her parents and siblings. Her early exposure to domestic conflict, parental substance abuse, and lack of privacy shaped her perception of love and security. Marriage promised safety, but it soon became a space of emotional neglect and control.

Step 1: Understanding Early Trauma

Lindiwe explored her history through journaling, noting how her early experiences of overcrowding and exposure to conflict had formed unconscious beliefs: that love required sacrifice and that independence was dangerous. Jung's idea of individuation guided her, showing how reclaiming her authentic self meant separating from internalized societal and family pressures.

Step 2: Exercises in Freedom of Love

Shadow Work:

Lindiwe identified traits she projected onto her husband: protection, stability, and validation she had never received. She forgave herself for these projections and began reclaiming self-love.

Roleplay Freedom

Practicing boundaries with a friend, she simulated conversations where she could refuse manipulation or control.

Freedom Map:

Lindiwe created a visual plan for gradual financial and emotional independence, including vocational training, therapy sessions, and community support groups.

Outcome

Lindiwe's journey was gradual but transformative. By understanding the trauma bonds that kept her tethered to her husband, she began making choices aligned with her desires, not survival instincts. Over time, she cultivated a sense of internal freedom, allowing her to experience love without dependency.

Key Insights Across Contexts

Trauma transcends geography and class. Whether in Khayelitsha, Johannesburg, or New York, dependency stems from early experiences of neglect, abuse, or societal pressure.

Dependency is a survival strategy. People marry or enter relationships not solely for love but to escape fear, instability, or shame.

Freedom requires practical and psychological tools. Fromm's concept of Freedom of Love emphasizes that autonomy, self-awareness, and emotional resilience are prerequisites for healthy partnerships.

Cultural, social, and religious pressures amplify dependency. Recognizing and navigating these pressures is critical for personal liberation.

Practical Takeaways

✓ Reflect on early experiences and identify trauma patterns influencing relationship choices.

✓ Map emotional anchors keeping you tied to dependency.

Practice boundary setting and assertive communication through roleplay.

Create a freedom roadmap for emotional, financial, and spiritual independence.

Seek therapy or community support to process trauma safely.

Through these narratives, readers can see that breaking dependency bonds is not about leaving marriage blindly, but about cultivating the inner strength, awareness, and freedom necessary to make conscious choices—whether staying, renegotiating, or leaving.

Chapter 16: Rebuilding Love – From Dependency to Emotional Autonomy

Cultural and Global Considerations

This chapter expands the discussion beyond individual experiences, exploring how culture shapes emotional expression and identity formation. It compares rural African expectations of marriage, gender roles, and community approval with Western urban pressures rooted in independence, success, and personal branding. Drawing on experiences from South Africa, Mozambique, Nigeria, and global cities like New York, it shows how the struggle for identity is universal, even when expressed differently. It argues that healing requires balancing cultural expectations with personal autonomy and emotional health.

Love, in its healthiest form, is not about escape, survival, or meeting societal expectations—it is about freedom, choice, and mutual growth. For individuals trapped in dependency syndrome, the journey to reclaiming love begins with reclaiming the self. In this chapter, we follow Michael in New York City, Nomvula in Johannesburg, and Lindiwe in Khayelitsha, demonstrating how emotional autonomy transforms relationships and life outcomes.

1. Michael's Journey: From Social Success to Emotional Freedom

Michael's life in New York was defined by outward success—high-paying job, luxury apartment, and a carefully curated social circle. Yet, beneath the polished exterior, he felt powerless in love. Freud's theory of projection became clear during his therapy sessions: Michael repeatedly chose partners who replicated his early emotional deprivation.

Turning Point

Through Eric Fromm's *Freedom of Love*, Michael realized that love could not coexist with fear or dependency. He began practicing self-love exercises:

Practical Exercise: The Emotional Ledger

Michael created two columns: "Expectations from Partner" and "Expectations from Self."

He listed everything he had been demanding from partners that he could meet internally.

Daily, he practiced fulfilling one item from the "Self" column, reinforcing autonomy and reducing relational dependency.

Outcome

By internalizing Fromm's principles, Michael shifted from seeking rescue to seeking connection. Love became a choice, not a necessity for survival.

1. Nomvula's Journey: Negotiating Cultural Pressure and Autonomy

Nomvula's marriage in Johannesburg was framed by family expectations and cultural norms. She married to avoid social shame, not because of emotional readiness. Jung's theory of individuation helped her distinguish her authentic self from the roles imposed by society.

Turning Point

Nomvula started integrating mindfulness and reflection into daily routines, identifying moments where cultural expectations had dictated her behavior.

Practical Exercise: Cultural Reflection Journal

She wrote down every decision influenced by family, church, or peers.

For each entry, she asked: "Does this serve my growth or my fear?"

She highlighted one change she could implement weekly that aligned with her authentic desires, such as pursuing a career opportunity without needing her husband's approval.

Outcome

Gradually, Nomvula reclaimed agency. Marriage was no longer a prison; it became a partnership built on negotiation, respect, and mutual growth. Her emotional dependency decreased as she strengthened her financial and social independence.

1. Lindiwe's Journey: Escaping Rural Dependency Traps

Lindiwe's rural life in Khayelitsha had conditioned her to view marriage as safety. Early exposure to trauma, poverty, and overcrowding shaped her perception of love. Carl Jung's insights into the shadow self provided the tools to confront and integrate unresolved fears and desires.

Turning Point

Through shadow work, Lindiwe acknowledged her suppressed anger, fear of abandonment, and desire for autonomy. She learned that dependence was a survival response, not a moral flaw.

Practical Exercise: Shadow Dialogue

Each morning, Lindiwe sat in front of a mirror, speaking to the parts of herself that had been silenced.

She asked: "Why do I stay? What do I fear? How can I meet my needs without losing myself?"

She wrote responses and reviewed them weekly, noticing patterns and progress.

Outcome

Lindiwe slowly shifted her marital interactions, setting boundaries, negotiating shared responsibilities, and pursuing personal development. Emotional freedom reduced anxiety, dependence on her husband, and internalized shame.

4. Principles for Rebuilding Love

Across contexts—urban, rural, African, Western—the following principles emerge as critical:

Internal Autonomy is Key

Love cannot heal what is unhealed within. Individuals must first cultivate self-sufficiency in emotion, thought, and decision-making.

Confront Trauma, Don't Escape It

Freud's projection theory and Jung's shadow work both emphasize identifying unconscious patterns and integrating them consciously.

Societal Pressures Must Be Negotiated

Fromm's *Freedom of Love* reminds us that cultural or family expectations should guide values, not trap behavior.

Practical Tools Matter

Journaling, roleplay, shadow dialogue, and emotional ledgers are simple, actionable tools that reinforce autonomy.

Healing is a Process, Not an Event

Recovery from dependency syndrome takes time, patience, and continuous self-reflection. Success is measured by incremental choices aligned with authentic selfhood.

5. Exercises to Rebuild Love and Emotional Autonomy

Exercise 1: Emotional Independence Checklist

Identify areas where you rely on a partner for validation, safety, or identity.

Write alternative ways to meet those needs internally or through supportive social networks.

Exercise 2: Relationship Projection Journal

✓ List recurring conflicts and frustrations in current or past relationships.

✓ Reflect on whether these issues mirror unresolved childhood or trauma-based patterns.

Exercise 3: Freedom of Choice Map

✓ Draw a map of all decisions in your relationship influenced by fear, social pressure, or dependency.

✓ For each, rewrite the choice from a place of conscious desire rather than survival instinct.

Exercise 4: Shadow Dialogue Practice

✓ Speak to your "shadow" daily, acknowledging suppressed fears, desires, and projections.

✓ Record insights and track progress over time.

Rebuilding love is not simply about finding the right partner—it is about creating the right relationship with oneself. Whether in New York, Johannesburg, or Khayelitsha, emotional freedom transforms dependency into connection, fear into choice, and survival into thriving.

Marriage, when rebuilt on autonomy, respect, and self-awareness, becomes a source of joy rather than a cycle of trauma. Through narrative, reflection, and practical exercises, this chapter provides the roadmap for breaking dependency syndrome and reclaiming the art of loving freely.

Chapter 17: Rewriting Identity – Healing the Self Before Healing the Relationship

Identity lies at the core of every human connection. Without a clear sense of self, relationships become mirrors for unresolved pain, dependency, and fear. In communities across the globe—whether in urban New York, the bustling streets of Johannesburg, or rural villages in Khayelitsha—dependency syndrome in marriage often stems from fractured identities formed in childhood, exacerbated by cultural, economic, and relational pressures.

1. The Foundation of Identity and Its Role in Dependency

From early life, identity is shaped by environment, culture, and family structures. Children raised in unstable or traumatic households develop survival strategies that influence adult relational choices. Freud's theory of the id, ego, and superego explains how unresolved conflicts in childhood—fear, longing, shame—are projected onto partners. Jung adds that the shadow self, comprising suppressed desires and fears, drives behavior subconsciously.

For women and men in rural African communities, identity is often entwined with marriage: "Your worth is proven by the man you marry or the household you build." Similarly, in Western societies, social media, television, and cultural messaging create pressure to align with ideals of romantic and material success. The result? Adults enter marriages not as independent selves but as fragmented projections seeking external validation.

Case Study: Lindiwe, Khayelitsha

Lindiwe grew up in a home where conflict and neglect were daily realities. She married at 19 to escape poverty and instability. In her twenties, therapy revealed that her marriage choices were dictated by fear and survival instincts, not personal desire. Healing required Lindiwe to reconstruct her sense of self, separate from her partner, family, and societal expectations.

2. The Cost of Identity Fragmentation

Identity confusion manifests in multiple ways:

- Emotional Dependence
- Feeling incomplete without a partner.
- Compulsive Approval-Seeking
- Constantly trying to meet societal or partner expectations.
- Relationship Projection
- Replaying childhood dynamics in adult partnerships.
- Fear of Abandonment or Success
- Avoiding autonomy to prevent loneliness or judgment.

In both men and women, these patterns lead to marriage dependency syndrome, where marital relationships become survival mechanisms rather than sources of mutual growth. Eric Fromm's concept of the

Freedom of Love emphasizes that love rooted in fear or dependency is not love—it is attachment to survival, not connection.

Case Study: Michael, New York City

Michael, a successful banker, consistently sought partners who mirrored his mother's disapproval and emotional distance. He believed romantic success would validate him. Through shadow work and exercises in self-love, he realized his compulsive relationship patterns were not about love—they were a replay of childhood emotional deprivation.

1. Steps to Rewriting Identity

Healing identity begins with awareness and intentional self-construction.

The following strategies combine Freudian, Jungian, and Frommian principles:

Shadow Work and Self-Awareness

Identify suppressed fears, desires, and unresolved trauma.

Dialogue with your shadow to integrate disowned aspects of yourself.

Separation of Self from Partner

Establish clear emotional boundaries.

Practice making decisions independent of relational approval or survival motives.

Reconnecting With Core Values

List personal values outside societal or familial pressures.

Prioritize these values in daily decisions and relationship interactions.

Therapeutic Self-Intervention

Individual therapy or coaching to process trauma.

Cognitive behavioral exercises to challenge dependency-driven thoughts.

Freedom Through Love and Choice

Adopt Fromm's model: love freely by choosing connection over need, growth over comfort, and authenticity over approval.

1. Practical Exercises for Rewriting Identity

Exercise 1: Identity Timeline

✓ Map significant life events that influenced self-perception.
✓ Highlight moments where survival instincts overrode personal choice.

Reflect on recurring patterns that may impact current relationships.
Exercise 2: Self-Validation Journal

✓ Daily, write three actions you took that were independent of your partner's approval.

✓ Include reflections on feelings of freedom, satisfaction, or anxiety.

Exercise 3: Shadow Dialogue

✓ Identify a recurring behavior or fear in relationships.
✓ Speak to your shadow self: "Why do I act this way?
✓ What am I protecting?
✓ What do I truly need?"
✓ Record insights and consciously practice alternative responses.

Exercise 4: Values Alignment Map

List your top five personal values.

Compare current decisions—career, relationships, social behavior—to these values.

Note misalignments and plan steps to realign.

1. Narrative Integration

Nomvula, Johannesburg

Nomvula realized that every disagreement with her husband reflected unprocessed anger toward her father. By identifying this pattern, she separated past trauma from present reality. She implemented shadow dialogues, values alignment, and self-validation practices. Slowly, Nomvula transitioned from a dependent partner to an autonomous, loving spouse.

Outcome

Her marriage shifted from survival-based co-dependence to a partnership grounded in mutual respect and conscious love. Nomvula experienced the freedom of self, the key to Fromm's vision of mature, liberated love.

6. Healing the Self as the Foundation of Love

Rewriting identity is the first step to breaking the cycle of dependency syndrome. Only by understanding, integrating, and reclaiming the self can men and women approach love freely and authentically.

Across New York, Johannesburg, and Khayelitsha, the journey is the same: confront trauma, reclaim autonomy, and cultivate emotional freedom. Marriage and relationships then become a choice—a partnership of two whole individuals—rather than a survival mechanism born from fear, societal pressure, or past trauma.

Healing the self is not optional; it is the cornerstone of emotional liberation, sustainable relationships, and the genuine experience of love.

Chapter 18: From Survival to Thriving – Practical Steps to Ending Marriage Dependency Syndrome

Marriage dependency syndrome does not develop overnight. It is a complex interplay of childhood trauma, cultural expectations, economic pressures, and identity confusion. For both women and men, the journey from survival-driven relationships to thriving partnerships requires conscious intervention, emotional work, and practical strategies.

This chapter provides a structured, narrative-driven approach for individuals seeking to reclaim autonomy, heal trauma bonds, and foster sustainable, fulfilling relationships.

1. Understanding Survival vs. Thriving in Relationships

Many adults enter marriage or cohabitation not out of love, but as a survival strategy. Survival-driven relationships are marked by:

- Fear of abandonment or poverty
- Emotional dependence and codependency
- Compulsive approval-seeking
- Repetition of childhood trauma patterns
- Thriving relationships, by contrast, are characterized by:
- Emotional independence and self-respect
- Conscious choice of partner based on compatibility
- Healthy boundaries
- Mutual growth and shared values

Narrative Case Study: Thabo, Johannesburg

Thabo married at 24, believing that a stable household would shield him from the instability of his childhood. For years, he stayed in an emotionally distant relationship because leaving meant confronting financial insecurity and familial judgment. Through therapy and self-reflection exercises, Thabo rebuilt his sense of self, established boundaries, and learned to prioritize compatibility over survival. Today, his relationship is voluntary, respectful, and emotionally rich—he has moved from survival to thriving.

2. Step One: Recognizing and Mapping Dependency Patterns

Before change can occur, one must identify and understand personal dependency patterns. This involves reflection, journaling, and narrative reconstruction.

Practical Exercise: The Dependency Map

✓ List recurring behaviors in past and current relationships (e.g., fear of leaving, compulsive caretaking, avoidance of conflict).

✓ Identify triggers for these behaviors (childhood trauma, social pressure, economic reliance).

✓ *Note outcomes when these behaviors were enacted (conflict, emotional exhaustion, feeling trapped).*

✓ Reflect on alternative responses that align with autonomy and self-respect.

Narrative Insight: Aisha, New York City

Aisha grew up witnessing domestic abuse and financial instability. She noticed she repeatedly chose partners who were emotionally unavailable but financially stable. By mapping her dependency, she realized the pattern was survival-driven, not love-driven. This awareness became the first step toward breaking free.

3. Step Two: Healing Trauma Bonds

Trauma bonds, formed through cycles of abuse and reconciliation, make it psychologically difficult to leave unhealthy relationships. Addressing these bonds requires both emotional and cognitive strategies.

Practical Exercise: Emotional Disconnection Practice

Identify one specific emotional trigger related to your partner or past trauma.

Sit in a quiet space and observe the physical and emotional sensations without judgment.

Visualize separating your emotional energy from the trigger, understanding that the intensity does not define your choice.

Reinforce self-soothing behaviors: deep breathing, journaling, or mindfulness meditation.

Narrative Insight: Nomvula, Khayelitsha

Nomvula repeatedly returned to her abusive partner, believing she couldn't survive alone.

Through guided exercises, she learned to recognize the trauma bond and emotionally separate herself from the attachment, ultimately enabling her to leave safely and rebuild her life.

4. Step Three: Reclaiming Economic and Emotional Independence

Financial dependence is a major factor keeping individuals in toxic marriages. Economic empowerment, coupled with emotional independence, lays the foundation for freedom.

Practical Exercise: Independence Plan

✓ Audit personal financial resources and skills.

✓ Set clear short-term goals (e.g., saving a specific amount, completing a course).

✓ Develop medium- and long-term plans for career growth or business initiatives.

✓ Pair financial goals with emotional goals: building self-esteem, cultivating hobbies, strengthening social networks.

Narrative Insight: Michael, New York City

Michael realized he remained in a partner's shadow due to fear of losing material comfort. By creating an independence plan, he secured a financial buffer and pursued passions that reinforced self-worth, making it easier to assert himself in relationships.

5. Step Four: Building Healthy Relational Skills

Moving from survival to thriving also involves learning to cultivate relationships that are conscious, supportive, and mutually beneficial.

Practical Exercise: Relational Reflection

List past relationships and identify behaviors you tolerated out of fear or dependency.

Reflect on qualities you value in a partner and boundaries you wish to maintain.

Role-play scenarios where you assert needs and practice saying no without guilt.

Narrative Insight: Thandi, Johannesburg

Thandi married young, repeatedly sacrificing her desires to maintain her husband's approval. Through reflection exercises, she learned to communicate needs without fear of conflict and started attracting relationships aligned with mutual respect.

6. Step Five: Practicing the Freedom of Love (Eric Fromm)

Fromm emphasizes that love is an act of freedom, not need. Thriving relationships are not about filling gaps, but about sharing wholeness. Applying this principle requires:

Loving intentionally rather than compulsively

Embracing vulnerability without dependence

Maintaining individuality while nurturing connection

Narrative Insight: Lindiwe, Khayelitsha

Lindiwe spent years entering relationships out of societal expectation and fear. By embracing Fromm's philosophy, she learned to love from freedom, rejecting relationships driven by survival or social approval. She cultivated a partnership rooted in shared joy rather than necessity.

7. Step Six: Sustaining Transformation

Ending dependency syndrome is not a one-time event; it is a lifelong practice of awareness, boundary maintenance, and self-affirmation.

Sustaining Practices:

Regular self-reflection and journaling
Participation in supportive communities or therapy groups
Revisiting independence goals
Periodic reassessment of relationships against personal values

Narrative Integration: Across the Globe

New York City: Professionals escaping high-pressure social expectations can apply financial and emotional independence exercises to avoid survival-driven marriages.

Johannesburg: Young adults in townships with limited opportunities learn skills to reclaim autonomy and self-respect.

Khayelitsha: Rural women and men, often constrained by cultural norms, utilize guided reflection and community workshops to break cycles of dependency.

8. From Survival to Thriving

Dependency syndrome in marriage is deeply rooted in childhood trauma, economic constraints, and cultural pressures. However, practical strategies—mapping dependency, healing trauma bonds, reclaiming independence, building relational skills, and practicing freedom in love—enable both women and men to move from survival-driven existence to thriving lives.

The path from survival to thriving is challenging but transformative. By reclaiming autonomy, integrating self-awareness, and cultivating conscious relationships, individuals can experience marriages and partnerships as spaces of growth, freedom, and authentic love.

Chapter 19: Practical Tools and Exercises Workbook – Breaking Marriage Dependency Syndrome

This workbook is designed to guide readers through hands-on exercises that promote self-awareness, emotional freedom, and healthy relationship practices. Each section combines theory, reflection, and action steps rooted in psychology, Freudian identity theory, Carl Jung's concepts of individuation, and Eric Fromm's principles of love and freedom.

Section 1: Mapping Your Dependency Patterns

Objective: Recognize recurring patterns that keep you in survival-driven relationships.

Exercise: The Dependency Map

✓ Take a notebook or journal.

✓ Draw a table with three columns:

✓ Behavior: Examples include fear of leaving, over-accommodating, or avoiding conflict.

✓ Trigger: Note events, thoughts, or feelings that prompt the behavior.

✓ Outcome: Identify consequences, both positive and negative.

✓ Reflect: Which patterns are repeated across relationships? What childhood experiences might be influencing them?

Narrative Reflection

Aisha in NYC realized she repeatedly chose partners who were emotionally unavailable. By mapping her behaviors, she could identify patterns rooted in childhood exposure to instability.

Tip: Repeat this exercise weekly to track progress.

Section 2: Healing Trauma Bonds

Objective: Emotionally disconnect from unhealthy attachments while fostering self-compassion.

Exercise: Emotional Separation

- Identify a specific trigger or toxic attachment.
- Sit quietly and visualize separating your emotional energy from it.
- Observe the feelings without judgment—acknowledge pain, anger, or fear.
- Replace attachment energy with self-soothing behaviors: deep breathing, mindfulness, or journaling.

Narrative Reflection

Nomvula in Khayelitsha learned to leave an abusive relationship after practicing emotional separation, enabling her to regain clarity and courage.

Tip: Pair this exercise with daily affirmations such as: *"I am worthy of love and freedom."*

Section 3: Reclaiming Economic Independence

Objective: Build financial autonomy as a foundation for emotional freedom.

Exercise: Independence Plan

List your financial resources: savings, skills, and assets.

Set short-term goals: e.g., saving R5000 in three months or completing a course.

Develop long-term goals: career advancement, entrepreneurship, or investment plans.

Link emotional goals: self-esteem, hobbies, social connections.

Narrative Reflection:

Michael in NYC remained in a partner's shadow due to fear of losing comfort. Through structured financial planning, he built confidence and autonomy, freeing himself from dependence.

Tip: Track progress monthly and celebrate milestones, no matter how small.

Section 4: Building Healthy Relational Skills

Objective: Develop conscious relationship behaviors that promote mutual respect and personal integrity.

Exercise: Relational Reflection

List past relationships and note behaviors you tolerated out of fear or dependency.

Identify qualities you value in a partner.

Role-play scenarios asserting needs or saying no without guilt.

Narrative Reflection

Thandi in Johannesburg learned to communicate her needs assertively, replacing fear-driven compliance with confidence and self-respect.

Tip: Practice in front of a mirror or with a trusted friend for reinforcement.

Section 5: Practicing Freedom of Love (Eric Fromm)

Objective: Love consciously and independently, avoiding relationships driven by survival or social pressure.

Exercise: The Freedom Journal

Reflect on your current relationship motivations. Are you acting from fear, need, or genuine love?

Write a letter to yourself describing the qualities of a free, mutually respectful relationship.

Commit to actions that reflect love from freedom, e.g., setting boundaries, choosing partners consciously.

Narrative Reflection

Lindiwe in Khayelitsha applied Fromm's principles, learning to leave survival-driven relationships and cultivate love rooted in joy, autonomy, and respect.

Tip: Revisit the journal monthly to track evolution in thinking and behavior.

Section 6: Sustaining Transformation

Objective: Make progress sustainable through consistent practices.

Exercise: Daily and Weekly Check-ins

Daily: Journal emotions, affirmations, and reflections on interactions.

Weekly: Evaluate relationship choices, financial progress, and personal boundaries.

Monthly: Reflect on long-term goals, identity development, and emotional freedom.

Narrative Reflection

Across NYC, Johannesburg, and Khayelitsha, individuals who practiced consistent self-reflection reported increased confidence, reduced dependency, and healthier relationships.

Tip: Pair these exercises with support networks or therapy groups to maintain accountability.

Section 7: Optional Guided Practices

Mindfulness and Meditation: 10–20 minutes daily to reduce stress, improve clarity, and reconnect with the self.

Art Therapy: Use creative expression to process trauma and explore personal identity.

Community Workshops: Attend sessions on relationship skills, independence, and personal development.

Conclusion of the Workbook

This practical workbook transforms the theories in this book into tangible actions. By mapping dependency, healing trauma, reclaiming independence, cultivating relational skills, and embracing freedom of love, readers can break cycles of marriage dependency syndrome.

The journey from survival-driven relationships to thriving, emotionally fulfilling partnerships is challenging—but entirely possible with commitment, reflection, and consistent action.

30-Day Action Plan Workbook:

Breaking Marriage Dependency Syndrome

Purpose

This 30-day program combines reflection, practical exercises, and guided journaling to help readers recognize dependency patterns, process trauma, and reclaim emotional and financial autonomy. Each day takes 15–30 minutes, with a mix of journaling, reflection, and actionable tasks.

Week 1: Awareness and Mapping Dependency Patterns

Day 1: *Identify Your Dependency Patterns*

- Journal: List three ways you rely on others for emotional, financial, or social validation.
- Reflection: Are these patterns rooted in childhood, culture, or past relationships?

Day 2: *Mapping Your Triggers*

- Exercise: Write down events, thoughts, or people that trigger dependency behaviors.
- Action: Notice moments you feel anxious or fearful about being alone.

Day 3: *Consequences of Dependency*

- Journal: Write three outcomes—positive and negative—of staying in dependency-driven relationships.
- Reflection: Which consequences are most harmful to your well-being?

Day 4: *Storytelling Reflection*

- Narrative exercise: Write a short story about a relationship where you felt trapped or pressured.
- Identify lessons and patterns repeated from the past.

Day 5: *Cultural and Social Influences*

- Journal: How have your family, religion, or community shaped your understanding of marriage and dependency?
- Reflection: Are these influences empowering or limiting?

Day 6: *Projection Patterns*

- Reflect on Freud's id, ego, and superego: How might unresolved childhood conflicts affect your partner choices?
- Exercise: Write one way you project old fears or unmet needs onto current relationships.

Day 7: *Weekly Reflection*

- Journal: Summarize insights from the week.
- Task: Identify one small change you can implement next week to reduce dependency behaviors.

Week 2: Healing Trauma Bonds

Day 8: *Recognizing Trauma Bonds*

- Journal: Identify one relationship where you feel emotionally stuck despite harm.
- Reflection: What past trauma might be keeping you attached?

Day 9: *Emotional Separation Practice*

- Guided exercise: Visualize detaching your emotional energy from the toxic relationship.
- Reflection: Write down emotions that arise without judgment.

Day 10: *Mindfulness & Self-Observation*

- Task: 10 minutes of mindful breathing. Observe your thoughts about attachment and control.
- Journal: Note insights and sensations.

Day 11: *Affirmations for Freedom*

- Create 3 affirmations focused on autonomy and self-worth (e.g., "I am enough," "I deserve love without fear").
- Repeat aloud 3 times daily.

Day 12: *Jungian Individuation Exercise*

- Identify qualities in yourself you've suppressed to maintain relationships.
- Journal: How can embracing these traits improve your independence?

Day 13: *Freedom of Love Reflection (Fromm)*

- Write about what love means when it is not tied to survival or societal expectation.
- Task: Identify one act of self-love you will do today.

Day 14: *Weekly Reflection*

- Summarize insights from trauma-bond exercises.
- Task: Choose one attachment behavior to consciously change next week.

Week 3: Reclaiming Identity and Economic Independence
Day 15: *Self-Worth Inventory*

- List strengths, skills, and accomplishments unrelated to relationships.
- Reflection: How can you nurture these qualities independently?

Day 16: *Financial Independence Assessment*

- List your resources, skills, or income sources.
- Task: Identify one financial goal to achieve in the next 3 months.

Day 17: *Practical Action: Independence Step*

- Take one step toward financial autonomy: open a savings account, enroll in a course, or start a small project.

Day 18: *Healthy Boundaries Exercise*

- Journal: Identify two boundaries you need to set with your partner or family.
- Task: Plan how to communicate these respectfully.

Day 19: *Visioning a Healthy Relationship*

- Write down qualities of a partner who complements your life rather than completes it.
- Reflection: How does this vision differ from past relationships?

Day 20: *Role-Playing Assertiveness*

- Practice saying "no" or expressing needs in front of a mirror or with a trusted friend.
- Journal: Note emotional reactions and improvements.

Day 21: *Weekly Reflection*

- Summarize insights from independence and boundary exercises.
- Task: Commit to one action for maintaining autonomy in the coming week.

Week 4: Sustaining Emotional Freedom and Healthy Love

Day 22: *Daily Check-in Routine*

- Begin a 5-minute morning and evening check-in: emotions, desires, and behaviors.

Day 23: *Relational Reflection*

- Evaluate current relationships: Are they supportive, neutral, or harmful?
- Journal: Decide what adjustments or boundaries are necessary.

Day 24: *Celebrating Progress*

- List 5 positive changes you've made since Day 1.
- Reflection: How has your perception of love and marriage evolved?

Day 25: *Commitment to Self-Love*

- Write a personal letter of affirmation.
- Task: Read aloud daily for one week.

Day 26: *Mindfulness & Visualization*

- Visualize your life free from dependency-driven relationships.
- Journal: What feelings, opportunities, and changes do you see?

Day 27: *Creating a Support Network*

- Identify friends, mentors, or groups to support ongoing

growth.

- Task: Reach out to at least one person for accountability.

Day 28: *Practicing Freedom of Choice*

- Journal: Reflect on decisions you can now make from love, not fear.

Day 29: *Rewriting Your Relationship Story*

- Write a short narrative imagining your future relationships rooted in autonomy, respect, and mutual support.

Day 30: *Closing Reflection and Celebration*

- Summarize insights, growth, and next steps.
- Task: Plan a self-reward or ritual to honor your journey toward emotional freedom.

- **Daily Journaling**

Encourage reflection on emotions, triggers, and progress.

- **Mindfulness & Meditation**

Practice at least 10 minutes daily to reinforce self-awareness.

- **Optional Exercises**

Art therapy, creative writing, or community workshops.

This 30-day workbook transforms the theoretical concepts of your book into practical, achievable steps that empower readers to break free from marriage dependency syndrome, heal trauma, reclaim identity, and cultivate conscious love.

30-Day Workbook: Breaking Marriage Dependency Syndrome

- *Breaking Free: A 30-Day Action Plan to Overcome Dependency in Love and Marriage*

- *Guided Exercises for Emotional Freedom, Self-Healing, and Conscious Love*

"This workbook belongs to: ________________________________"

"Freedom is not given—it is reclaimed from within." — Inspired by Eric Fromm

Layout Overview

Each day follows the same consistent structure for clarity and ease:

1. **Daily Focus / Topic**
2. **Reflection Prompt**
3. **Exercise / Action Step**
4. **Journaling Space** (5–10 lines minimum)
5. **Notes / Insights**

Day 1 – Identify Your Dependency Patterns
Focus: Awareness of your dependency in relationships.
Reflection Prompt:

- List three ways you rely on others for emotional, financial, or social validation.
- How do these patterns affect your relationships?

Exercise / Action Step:

- Write one situation this week where you notice a dependency-driven reaction.
- Reflect on alternative choices you could make.

Journaling Space:

Notes / Insights:

Day 2 – Mapping Your Triggers

Focus: Recognize what situations, people, or events trigger dependency behaviors.

Reflection Prompt:

- Write down your top three triggers.
- How do these triggers affect your emotional responses?

Exercise / Action Step:

- For each trigger, write one small action to respond differently next time.

Journaling Space:

Notes / Insights:

- **Weekly Overview**

At the start of each week, summarize the focus and provide a short motivational message.

- **Progress Tracker**

Include a table for each week where readers can tick off completed exercises.

- **Visual Prompts**

Use boxes, circles, or arrows to highlight reflection questions.

- **Mindfulness Corners**

Include small side prompts like *"Take 5 deep breaths"* or *"Visualize your best self today."*

Week 1: Awareness & Dependency Mapping

- Daily pages with exercises for recognizing triggers, dependency patterns, and cultural pressures.

Week 2: Healing Trauma Bonds

- Exercises on trauma identification, emotional separation, and self-love.

Week 3: Reclaiming Identity & Independence

- Focus on financial independence, boundary-setting, and personal goals.

Week 4: Sustaining Freedom & Healthy Love

- Reflection, visualization, relationship evaluation, and long-term action planning.

End of Workbook:

- **Summary Reflection Pages** – 2–3 pages to write insights, growth, and commitments.
- **Resource Section** – Links or references for therapy, support groups, and further reading.
- **Inspirational Quotes** – Sprinkled throughout the workbook for motivation.

Chapter 20: The Fear of Happiness – Zinhle's Journey

Chapter summary - Cultural and Global Considerations

This chapter expands the discussion beyond individual experiences, exploring how culture shapes emotional expression and identity formation. It compares rural African expectations of marriage, gender roles, and community approval with Western urban pressures rooted in independence, success, and personal branding.

Drawing on experiences from South Africa, Mozambique, Nigeria, and global cities like New York, it shows how the struggle for identity is universal, even when expressed differently.

It argues that healing requires balancing cultural expectations with personal autonomy and emotional health.

Zinhle stared at her reflection in the cracked bathroom mirror, her eyes tired, her shoulders slumped. At twenty-nine, she had lived a life that most people only whispered about. Born in a rural village outside Johannesburg, she had left home at fourteen after years of neglect, witnessing violence, and sleeping in rooms that were never truly hers.

With no education and no family support, she had learned quickly that survival often came at the cost of her dignity. For years, survival had meant trading her body for money, safety, and fleeting moments of care.

Now, she lived with Sibusiso, a man she barely knew but who had promised security. On paper, their life looked stable—food on the table, a small rented apartment, a neighbor who nodded politely. But inside, Zinhle felt suffocated. Sibusiso's moods swung violently; some nights he was affectionate, and others he shouted over imagined slights. Zinhle had learned to anticipate his anger, to shrink herself into corners, to silence her needs. She was trapped—not just physically, but emotionally and psychologically.

Her fear of happiness was invisible to most, yet constant. Whenever a quiet moment settled over their apartment—when the dishes were done, the sun streamed through the curtains, and nothing urgent demanded her attention—panic began to rise in her chest.

Happiness felt dangerous. Being content, even briefly, triggered memories of vulnerability, exposure, and loss. She feared that joy might demand change, or worse, make her visible and unsafe.

Understanding the Trap

Zinhle's life illustrated the pattern Branny Mthelebofu calls *Emotional Indigestion*: the body and mind carry unresolved trauma that manifests as chronic stress, anxiety, and even physical illness. Every fear she swallowed—the shame, the anger, the longing—stayed lodged in her chest, tightening around her heart like an invisible vice.

Her story was not uncommon. Many uneducated women, and even some men, become trapped in survival-based relationships. Dependency becomes normalized: safety, food, and shelter outweigh emotional health or personal freedom. The trauma of early life—neglect, abuse, exposure to violence—creates a psychological habit of seeking security in others, even at the cost of autonomy.

Psychologists like Sigmund Freud would say Zinhle's ego had adapted to survive, building defense mechanisms to manage anxiety.

Carl Jung might suggest that her shadow—the parts of herself she feared or repressed—was influencing every decision she made, keeping her in a loop of repetitive harm.

Eric Fromm would argue that true freedom of love requires conscious choice, not fear-driven survival.

The First Step Toward Freedom

Change began the day Zinhle met Lerato, a volunteer at a local women's center. Lerato didn't scold her. She didn't demand that Zinhle leave Sibusiso immediately. Instead, she spoke about agency, safety, and self-compassion. "You may not be able to leave yet,"

Lerato said gently, "but you can start to reclaim your heart and your mind."

Lerato taught Zinhle a simple daily ritual:

Sit quietly, hand on your chest.

Breathe slowly in for four counts, hold for four, exhale for four. Repeat five times.

Name one small thing you did today for yourself—ate a full meal, washed your hair, spoke your mind.

Close your eyes and imagine a bubble of protection around your heart, impenetrable by anger or judgment.

At first, Zinhle felt foolish. But over weeks, the panic that had always accompanied moments of calm began to lessen. She could breathe without expecting an emotional storm to follow. Slowly, she began to experience fleeting moments of joy—sunlight on her skin, laughter at a neighbor's joke, the satisfaction of completing a task. Each moment, no matter how small, became a seed of resilience.

Redefining Safety and Control

Zinhle also learned mental separation techniques. When Sibusiso yelled, she visualized his anger as separate from her own heart. She refused to internalize blame. She gave herself permission to feel, to think, to plan for her future—even while living in the same apartment with a man who could harm her emotionally.

She started journaling, writing letters to herself as her own protector. "You are not what happened to you," she wrote repeatedly. "You are more than survival. You deserve choice, safety, and peace."

Practical Strategies for Those Who Cannot Leave Yet

Protect your emotional space – Use visualization and breathing to maintain inner calm.

Micro-choices matter – Eating properly, walking outside, reading a book—small acts of autonomy reinforce self-worth.

Document trauma – Journaling or storytelling helps process what happened without becoming overwhelmed.

Build a support network – Community centers, friends, volunteers, or counselors can provide guidance even if immediate escape isn't possible.

Reframe dependency – Recognize it as survival, not moral failure.

The Turn Toward Hope

Months passed, and Zinhle began to feel a subtle but profound shift. The fear of happiness no longer ruled her mind. Her heart ached less at the thought of joy. She could laugh without guilt, rest without terror, and imagine a life where her choices were hers alone. She still lived with Sibusiso, but she had learned that freedom of the mind comes before freedom of circumstance.

By reclaiming small measures of autonomy and healing her *emotional indigestion*, Zinhle had not only preserved her mental and physical health, but also laid the groundwork for eventual escape or reconciliation on her own terms. She had begun to understand Fromm's idea of love as freedom—a love that does not bind through fear, but builds through choice.

Reflection Exercise for Readers: Emotional Freedom Within Constraints

Breathing and Visualization – Place a hand on your heart, breathe deeply, and imagine your fear separating from your body.

Micro-acts of Agency – Identify one thing today you can do for yourself without approval or permission.

Write a Protective Letter – Speak to yourself as a guardian, validating your courage and choices.

Plan a Step Toward Independence – Even if small, think of one actionable step to increase safety or autonomy.

This story chapter highlights how emotional freedom is possible even when escape is not immediately feasible, focusing on internal empowerment, resilience, and health.

Zinhle's narrative becomes a guide for women and men trapped in survival-based relationships, showing that the first steps toward liberation often begin inside the mind and heart.

Psychoeducation for Young People

- Psychoeducation is central to prevention. It involves teaching adolescents and young adults about:
- Healthy emotional development
- The difference between love and survival mechanisms
- Boundaries, consent, and self-respect
- Recognizing co-dependent and controlling behaviors
- The psychological impact of unresolved childhood trauma
- Programs in schools, community centers, and digital platforms can raise awareness and normalize discussions about mental health and healthy relationships.

Early Therapeutic Interventions

Therapy is not just for adults. Introducing developmentally appropriate interventions in adolescence can prevent the entrenchment of dependency patterns:

Individual therapy: Helps youth process trauma, develop self-esteem, and strengthen identity.

Group therapy and support circles: Provides peer validation, teaches conflict resolution, and models healthy relationships.

Family therapy: Educates parents about emotional neglect, communication styles, and boundary-setting.

Studies show that young people who receive trauma-informed support are less likely to use relationships as escape routes in adulthood.

Mentorship and Role Modeling

Mentors play a vital role in preventing dependency:

Community mentors

Successful individuals who model emotional and financial independence.

Relational mentors

Adults who demonstrate healthy partnerships without dependency.

Peer mentors

Slightly older youth who have successfully navigated challenges of adolescence.

Mentorship provides young people with examples of how autonomy, love, and identity coexist harmoniously.

Financial Literacy and Economic Empowerment

Economic dependence is a key driver of marital dependency. Preventive strategies must therefore integrate:

Financial education

Budgeting, saving, and entrepreneurship skills.

Scholarships and vocational training:

Reducing pressure to seek marriage as a financial lifeline.

Career guidance

Encouraging goal-setting and long-term planning independent of relational obligations.

By achieving financial independence, young people can make relationship choices based on compatibility and emotional readiness rather than survival.

Cultural and Social Reframing

Communities play a critical role in shaping relational norms.

Preventive strategies must challenge unhealthy cultural scripts:

Promote the idea that marriage is a choice, not a requirement for survival or identity.

Encourage open dialogue about emotional health, sexuality, and boundaries.

Create safe spaces for adolescents to explore identity without judgment.

Globally, programs in Brazil, New York, and Mozambique show that cultural reframing can reduce early marriage rates and dependency-driven relationships.

Leveraging Technology and Media

Digital platforms offer innovative ways to prevent dependency:

Educational apps on emotional intelligence and healthy relationships

Social media campaigns challenging co-dependency norms

Online counseling and peer support networks

Technology can reach youth in both urban and rural contexts, bridging gaps in access to mentorship and therapy.

Integrating Psychoanalytic Theory in Prevention

Freud's theories on identity formation, projection, and defense mechanisms inform preventive strategies:

Projection awareness

Teaching youth to recognize when they transfer unresolved childhood needs onto partners.

Strengthening the ego

Encouraging self-reflection and decision-making independent of external validation.

Superego balance

Helping young people internalize ethical and relational standards without shame or fear of rejection.

Understanding these mechanisms allows young people to build conscious, intentional relationships rather than reactive, dependency-driven ones.

Preventing dependency syndrome in marriage requires a holistic, proactive approach. Education, therapy, mentorship, economic empowerment, cultural reframing, and technology all contribute to equipping young people with the tools to form healthy, autonomous relationships. By addressing the roots of dependency early, society can reduce the cycle of trauma, escape-driven marriage, and identity confusion, creating generations capable of loving freely and building partnerships based on choice rather than survival.

Key Takeaway

Healing and prevention are interconnected. When young people learn self-worth, emotional intelligence, and independence before entering adult relationships, dependency syndrome loses its power, and marriage becomes a space of mutual growth and love rather than a psychological refuge.

Chapter: Therapeutic Models and Interventions – Breaking the Cycle of Dependency Syndrome in Marriage

Introduction

Dependency syndrome in marriage is not an inevitable or irreversible phenomenon. While its roots lie in childhood trauma, poverty, and cultural pressures, therapeutic intervention can interrupt this cycle, fostering emotional independence, self-awareness, and healthier relational patterns. This chapter explores evidence-based therapeutic models, psychoanalytic approaches, and practical interventions that help individuals and couples address dependency, reclaim autonomy, and rebuild identity.

1. Understanding the Therapeutic Need

The first step in intervention is acknowledging the depth of the problem:

Emotional entrapment

Many individuals remain in marriages to escape economic or social hardship.

Trauma transference

Unresolved childhood experiences are projected onto partners, leading to conflict and co-dependency.

Identity confusion

Individuals may struggle to distinguish their own needs from relational expectations.

Sigmund Freud's psychoanalytic theory is particularly useful here. Freud posited that unresolved conflicts in childhood (between the id, ego, and superego) influence adult relationships. Dependency syndrome often arises when the ego is underdeveloped and unable to mediate between unconscious desires and reality, resulting in reliance on a partner for emotional and social validation.

2. Individual Therapy: Rebuilding the Self

Individual therapy addresses the internalized causes of dependency:

Trauma-focused therapy

Techniques like EMDR (Eye Movement Desensitization and Reprocessing) or trauma-informed cognitive behavioral therapy help process childhood wounds.

Psychoanalysis

Uncovering unconscious motivations and relational projections allows clients to understand why they seek security in dependency.

Self-esteem building

Exercises in self-reflection, journaling, and affirmations empower clients to recognize intrinsic worth beyond relational approval.

Boundary training

Clients learn to assert needs, manage expectations, and differentiate themselves from their partners.

Individual therapy restores autonomy, helping clients recognize patterns of dependence and gradually reduce reliance on a partner for emotional survival.

1. Couples Therapy: Transforming Relationship Dynamics

Marriage counseling is essential when both partners are invested in change:

Communication restructuring

Teaching couples to express needs without blame or manipulation.

Conflict resolution skills

Reducing destructive patterns rooted in dependency, such as excessive control, jealousy, or emotional withdrawal.

Mutual autonomy reinforcement

Encouraging partners to maintain individual identities while nurturing the relationship.

Projection identification

Helping partners recognize when they are attributing past trauma or unmet needs to the other.

Research shows that couples therapy reduces co-dependency, enhances relational satisfaction, and prevents the transgenerational transmission of trauma.

4. Group Therapy and Peer Support

Group interventions provide validation and community:

Support groups for women and men

Offer shared experiences and strategies for managing dependency.

Workshops on relational skills

Focused on emotional intelligence, boundary-setting, and self-awareness.

Mentorship circles

Encourage role modeling and social learning from individuals who have overcome dependency patterns.

Group therapy reduces isolation, normalizes discussion of dependency, and provides practical tools for relational independence.

5. Culturally Sensitive Approaches

Effective therapy must consider cultural context:

In South Africa, therapy addresses the historical and socio-economic pressures linking marriage to survival.

In Nigeria, counseling must navigate strong extended-family involvement and expectations of early marriage.

In Mozambique, interventions consider rural poverty, gender norms, and community hierarchy.

Culturally sensitive therapy validates the client's lived experience while guiding them toward healthier relational choices.

6. Psychoeducation as a Therapeutic Tool

Psychoeducation helps clients understand the mechanisms of dependency:

Dependency syndrome explained

Clients learn the psychological, emotional, and cultural roots of their patterns.

Projection awareness

Highlighting unconscious transference helps clients recognize why they expect partners to fulfill unmet childhood needs.

Identity reconstruction

✓ Exercises and discussions help clients separate self-concept from relational survival.

✓ By translating psychoanalytic insights into accessible language, psychoeducation fosters conscious, deliberate change.

7. Integrating Freud's Identity Theory in Therapy

Freud's theory remains highly relevant:

Id impulses: Unmet childhood desires for safety and affection manifest as dependence on a partner.

Ego development: Therapy strengthens decision-making and emotional regulation, allowing individuals to balance personal desires with reality.

Superego influences: Clients learn to internalize ethical and relational standards without guilt or shame.

Therapists help clients map past experiences onto current behaviors, enabling conscious choices rather than automatic dependency-driven responses.

8. Preventing Relapse: Long-Term Strategies

Breaking dependency is an ongoing process:

Continued self-reflection: Journaling, mindfulness, and personal goal-setting reinforce autonomy.

Community involvement: Engagement in supportive networks mitigates isolation.

Therapeutic maintenance: Periodic counseling or check-ins prevent regression under stress.

Intergenerational education: Teaching children about healthy attachment prevents transgenerational dependency.

Recovery is iterative. Each successful intervention strengthens emotional resilience, allowing individuals to enter relationships based on love, not survival.

Therapy offers a scientifically grounded pathway out of the psychological prison of dependency syndrome in marriage. Individual, couples, and group interventions—supported by psychoanalytic theory, trauma-informed approaches, and cultural sensitivity—can restore identity, build autonomy, and foster relational health.

Dependency syndrome is not a moral failing but a psychological, social, and cultural response to complex adversity. Healing is possible when individuals confront their past, understand relational projections, and embrace personal growth. With structured, compassionate interventions, marriages can transform from survival mechanisms into genuine partnerships rooted in love, respect, and mutual emotional support.

Key Takeaway

Effective therapy does not simply reduce dependency; it empowers individuals to reclaim their identity, exercise choice, and experience love as freedom rather than necessity.

Chapter 21: Case Studies and Real-Life Narratives – Dependency Syndrome Across Africa and Globally

Introduction

While theory and psychoanalysis provide the framework to understand dependency syndrome in marriage, real-life examples illuminate its pervasive impact. Across Africa and globally, the syndrome manifests differently depending on socio-economic, cultural, and historical contexts. This chapter presents case studies from Nigeria, Mozambique, and New York, highlighting how childhood trauma, poverty, cultural expectations, and identity confusion converge to shape dependency patterns in marriage.

1. Case Study: Nigeria – The Weight of Cultural Expectation

In rural Nigeria, many young women experience extreme pressure to marry early:

Background

In communities such as the Niger Delta and northern Nigeria, cultural norms emphasize marriage as the central life goal for girls. Education, career aspirations, and personal identity are often secondary.

Living conditions

Overcrowded homes, poverty, and limited parental guidance force girls to view marriage as both escape and survival.

Impact

Many young women enter marriages without emotional readiness, relying entirely on husbands for financial support, social identity, and decision-making authority.

Psychological outcome

Unprocessed childhood trauma leads to emotional dependence, anxiety, and depression. Men, likewise, may remain in marriages to escape economic instability or social pressure.

Observation

Freud's identity theory explains this phenomenon. Girls internalize societal and familial expectations (superego) while their ego struggles to mediate between personal desires and external pressures. The result is a marriage driven more by obligation than authentic relational choice.

1. Case Study: Mozambique – Poverty and Early Marriage

Mozambique presents a slightly different dynamic:

Background: In rural districts like Zambezia and Nampula, extreme poverty and limited schooling increase early marriage rates. Families often view daughters' marriages as economic transactions to secure survival.

Living conditions

Children grow up in single-room houses or mud-brick dwellings, witnessing domestic conflict and sexualized behavior, mirroring patterns observed in South African townships.

Impact

Dependency manifests as both financial and emotional reliance on partners. Women rarely negotiate roles in the marriage, fearing social stigma or familial reprisal if they challenge patriarchal norms.

Psychological outcome

The marriage often perpetuates cycles of trauma, especially when children inherit parental dysfunction and poverty.

Observation

Identity confusion emerges early; girls project their longing for safety and love onto older partners, interpreting marriage as emotional salvation rather than partnership. Therapy or psychoeducation is rarely accessible, leaving dependency unchallenged.

3. Case Study: New York – Urban Poverty and Relational Survival

In a contrasting Western urban setting, dependency syndrome manifests differently but shares psychological roots:

Background

In New York City, young women from low-income neighborhoods—often raised in foster care, overcrowded apartments, or single-parent homes—experience emotional neglect and instability.

Living conditions

Exposure to substance abuse, domestic violence, and neighborhood crime produces trauma. Privacy is limited; emotional needs are unmet.

Impact

Marriage or long-term partnerships are sought primarily for financial security and emotional stability. Women may prioritize a partner's resources over compatibility or love, echoing patterns seen in African contexts.

Psychological outcome

Emotional dependence, co-dependency, and repeated cycles of relational failure are common. Men may also enter relationships out of need for emotional rescue or housing stability.

Observation

Freud's theory of projection is evident: partners unconsciously fulfill unmet childhood needs. Early trauma shapes relational choices, perpetuating cycles of dependency even in urban Western contexts.

4. Cross-Cultural Patterns

Despite differences in geography, culture, and economic conditions, several patterns are consistent:

Early trauma and instability drive the need for relational rescue.

Marriage as survival strategy transcends socio-economic status; it often compensates for poverty, emotional neglect, or lack of opportunity.

Identity confusion is a common thread; individuals project unresolved desires onto partners.

Therapeutic absence worsens outcomes; where counseling is accessible, dependency patterns can be mitigated.

Conclusion

Dependency syndrome in marriage is both culturally shaped and globally prevalent. Across continents, it functions as a psychological adaptation to adversity, rather than a moral failing.

5. Implications for Therapy and Intervention

The case studies highlight the need for multi-layered interventions:

Individual therapy to address trauma, restore ego strength, and clarify identity.

Couples therapy to correct relational projections and improve communication.

Community psychoeducation to destigmatize mental health support and promote healthy relational expectations.

Policy initiatives to reduce poverty, improve housing, and expand educational opportunities, especially for girls.

By integrating individual, relational, and societal interventions, dependency cycles can be broken and healthier marriages fostered.

Dependency syndrome is a complex, multidimensional phenomenon affecting women and men across the globe.

Real-life narratives from Nigeria, Mozambique, and New York demonstrate how childhood trauma, socio-economic hardship, and cultural norms converge to create marriages rooted in survival rather than choice. Understanding these lived experiences is essential for developing effective therapeutic interventions and societal reforms.

Ultimately, this chapter underscores a universal truth: marriage should be a partnership born of love and choice, not a refuge from adversity. Psychoanalytic insight, therapeutic support, and culturally informed interventions provide a pathway to break dependency and reclaim personal identity.

Chapter 22: Strategies for Breaking Dependency Syndrome – Prevention, Education, and Policy Recommendations

Introduction

Dependency syndrome in marriage is not an inherent flaw in individuals but a response to systemic trauma, cultural norms, and socio-economic constraints. While the preceding chapters outlined its origins, manifestations, and consequences, this chapter focuses on actionable strategies to interrupt these cycles. By integrating therapeutic, educational, and policy-level interventions, societies can foster healthier relationships, stronger identities, and emotional autonomy for both women and men.

1. Individual-Level Interventions

1.1 Psychoeducation and Self-Awareness

The foundation of breaking dependency begins with self-knowledge.

Individuals must

Understand how early-life trauma, neglect, and environmental pressures shape relational expectations.

Identify unconscious motivations for entering or staying in marriages.

Recognize projection patterns where unmet childhood needs are placed onto partners.

Application

Psychoeducation workshops and online resources can help individuals explore identity formation, emotional regulation, and attachment styles. Freud's theory of the ego, superego, and id provides a framework to understand the internal conflicts driving dependency behaviors.

1.2 Individual Therapy and Trauma Processing

Therapeutic intervention is essential for:

Addressing unresolved trauma from childhood exposure to abuse, neglect, or poverty.

Developing emotional independence and healthy coping mechanisms.

Reducing anxiety, depression, and co-dependency in adult relationships.

Recommended approaches include:

Cognitive Behavioral Therapy (CBT) for reframing relational beliefs.

Psychoanalytic therapy to explore unconscious motivations and identity projections.

Narrative therapy to reconstruct personal histories and redefine self-worth.

2. Relational Interventions

2.1 Couples Therapy

Many marriages influenced by dependency syndrome involve two individuals carrying unprocessed trauma. Couples therapy:

Facilitates mutual understanding of each partner's history and emotional needs.

Encourages communication strategies that prevent projection and co-dependency.

Helps establish healthy boundaries, shared responsibilities, and emotional reciprocity.

Observation

Addressing dependency at the relational level reduces the perpetuation of trauma into subsequent generations, particularly when children are involved.

2.2 Mentorship and Support Networks

Peer mentorship and support groups create safe spaces for:

Discussing marital challenges without judgment.

Sharing coping strategies and successful examples of independence.

Normalizing therapeutic engagement and reducing stigma around mental health.

3. Community and Cultural-Level Strategies

3.1 Psychoeducation Campaigns

Conduct culturally sensitive workshops in rural and urban communities.

Educate families about the psychological effects of forcing marriage as a survival strategy.

Provide practical tools for parents to nurture autonomy, emotional literacy, and resilience in children.

3.2 Redefining Social Norms

Engage traditional and religious leaders to shift narratives: marriage as partnership, not escape.

Highlight stories of women and men who achieved independence before marriage.

Promote alternative pathways to financial stability and social recognition beyond marriage.

4. Policy and Societal Interventions

4.1 Education and Economic Empowerment

Ensure access to quality education for girls and boys, reducing reliance on marriage as an escape.

Promote vocational training and entrepreneurship programs that provide financial autonomy.

4.2 Legal Protections

Enforce laws preventing child marriage and gender-based violence.

Provide social safety nets for women leaving abusive relationships, reducing economic dependency.

4.3 Mental Health Infrastructure

Increase accessibility to affordable therapy and counseling services.

Train mental health professionals to address culturally specific dependency patterns.

Develop school-based mental health programs to identify trauma early and prevent relational maladaptations.

5. Global Examples of Success

Brazil: Community-based psychoeducation in favelas decreased early, survival-driven marriages.

South Africa: NGO-led workshops on emotional literacy and financial independence empowered township women.

USA: Foster care programs incorporating therapy reduced dependency patterns in adulthood.

Observation

Multi-layered interventions—individual, relational, community, and policy-level—show the highest effectiveness in breaking cycles of dependency.

6. Integrating Psychoanalytic Insight

Freud's theories of identity formation, projection, and the dynamics between the id, ego, and superego illuminate why interventions must address both internal psychological structures and external social conditions:

Projection awareness

Individuals learn to recognize unmet childhood needs projected onto partners.

Ego strengthening

Therapy helps build self-regulation and autonomy.

Superego recalibration

Social norms are reinterpreted to value individual identity alongside relational roles.

This integrated approach ensures that interventions do not only mitigate symptoms but transform underlying psychological mechanisms.

Breaking dependency syndrome in marriage requires a comprehensive, multi-layered approach:

Individual: Psychoeducation, trauma processing, and self-awareness.

Relational: Couples therapy, mentorship, and communication training.

Community: Social norm transformation, workshops, and role-model advocacy.

Policy: Education access, economic empowerment, legal protections, and mental health infrastructure.

Ultimately, the goal is to enable individuals to enter marriage or partnerships from a place of choice, emotional readiness, and self-awareness, rather than necessity or survival. By combining psychoanalytic insights with practical interventions, societies can foster healthier marriages, stronger identities, and generational healing.

Chapter 223: Reclaiming Love and Identity – A Roadmap to Healthy Marriages Beyond Dependency Syndrome

Introduction

Dependency syndrome in marriage is both a symptom and a consequence of deep-seated trauma, socio-economic challenges, and cultural expectations. As explored throughout this book, many individuals—especially women in African communities but increasingly globally—enter marriages as a survival strategy rather than a conscious choice. This chapter consolidates insights from earlier chapters and presents a roadmap to reclaim love, autonomy, and identity. It emphasizes that healthy relationships arise not from necessity, but from emotional readiness, self-awareness, and shared commitment.

1. Understanding the Foundations of Change

To break the cycle of dependency, individuals must first understand its roots:

✓ **Childhood trauma:** Exposure to neglect, abuse, and unstable home environments shapes relational patterns.

✓ **Cultural and societal pressure:** Marriage is often framed as the ultimate solution to poverty, insecurity, or lack of social acceptance.

Psychological mechanisms

Freud's psychoanalytic theory shows how unresolved conflicts between the id, ego, and superego influence partner selection, emotional dependency, and identity projection.

Recognizing these factors allows individuals to identify why they entered a relationship, and to distinguish between needs driven by survival and those grounded in authentic desire.

2. Emotional Healing and Self-Reclamation

2.1 Individual Therapy

✓ **Trauma processing:** Address unresolved childhood experiences to prevent repetition in adult relationships.

✓ **Identity work:** Explore personal values, desires, and life goals independent of social expectations.

✓ **Self-esteem building:** Develop confidence to make choices based on preference, not fear.

2.2 Self-Education and Reflection

Journaling, mindfulness, and guided reflection can help individuals map the trajectory from past experiences to current relational patterns.

Understanding projection—placing unmet emotional needs onto partners—helps mitigate dependency behaviors.

Key Insight: True freedom in relationships begins with self-understanding and self-compassion.

3. Building Healthy Relationships

3.1 Communication and Boundaries

Establishing clear boundaries prevents co-dependency and emotional exhaustion.

Open communication encourages honesty, empathy, and shared responsibility.

3.2 Mutual Growth and Respect

Relationships should be partnerships, not rescues.

Both partners must cultivate self-sufficiency, while offering emotional support.

Couples therapy can assist in identifying relational patterns that perpetuate dependency.

3.3 Shared Vision

Develop shared goals for emotional, financial, and family life.

Align values and expectations before making commitments to reduce conflict and reliance on marriage as a survival strategy.

4. Community and Societal Roles in Reclaiming Identity

Education campaigns

Normalize therapy and self-exploration in communities.

Economic empowerment

Provide opportunities for women and men to achieve independence before marriage.

Role modelling

Highlight examples of individuals who pursue relationships by choice, not necessity.

These societal interventions reduce the external pressures that push individuals toward dependency-driven marriages.

5. Policy and Legal Frameworks

Enforce laws against child marriage and gender-based abuse.

Provide social support systems for those leaving dependent or abusive relationships.

Expand access to mental health services in schools, communities, and workplaces.

Impact

When structural support is combined with personal growth, dependency syndrome diminishes over generations.

6. Psychoanalytic Insights Applied

Freud's ideas of identity formation, projection, and ego development remain crucial:

Projection awareness

Individuals learn to distinguish their unmet needs from the needs of their partner.

Ego development

Stronger self-regulation allows conscious choice in relationships.

Superego recalibration

Cultural and moral expectations are reframed to respect autonomy while valuing partnership.

This approach integrates the psychological with the social, emphasizing both internal and external pathways to relational health.

7. Global Lessons and Case Studies

New York

Foster care interventions reduced survival-based partnerships by teaching self-efficacy.

Nigeria

Community workshops addressing child marriage and trauma created generational shifts in marriage expectations.

Mozambique

Programs integrating therapy with economic support helped women delay marriage, pursue education, and enter relationships from choice rather than necessity.

These examples illustrate that dependency syndrome is not inescapable—even in the most challenging social conditions, structural and personal interventions can foster change.

8. The Roadmap to Healthy Marriages

Self-awareness

Understand past trauma and unconscious motivations.

Therapy

Engage in individual and, where applicable, couples therapy to heal and rebuild identity.

Education

Acquire emotional literacy, communication skills, and relational knowledge.

Independence

Pursue financial, social, and emotional autonomy before marriage.

Community support

Utilize mentorship, support groups, and role models.

Policy engagement

Advocate for laws and programs that prevent dependency-driven marriages.

Conscious partnership

Enter relationships from a place of choice, compatibility, and mutual respect.

Reclaiming love and identity is both an individual and societal endeavour.

Dependency syndrome in marriage is a complex interplay of childhood trauma, cultural expectations, and socio-economic pressures. Breaking free from this cycle requires honesty, courage, and structured support.

Therapy, self-reflection, education, and societal change are the pillars that allow individuals to enter marriages—or remain single—with autonomy, dignity, and genuine desire.

Final Insight

Marriage, in its healthiest form, is a partnership of equals. When entered consciously, it becomes a space for love, growth, and mutual support—not a lifeline from trauma or survival. By applying the lessons in this book, individuals can transform not only their relationships but the cycles that have shaped generations.

Dependency Syndrome as a Survival Mechanism

When girls enter adolescence, many begin searching for older male partners who can offer financial stability, accommodation, or a sense of protection.

This pattern is not a product of immorality but a survival response to overwhelming environmental pressures.

Women without education or employment opportunities view marriage as their only pathway to dignity. Ironically, even highly educated and financially successful women often internalise the belief that emotional fulfillment and identity must be completed through marriage.

In this way, dependency syndrome becomes a cultural norm.

Women are taught that not being chosen for marriage reflects failure, and those who do not secure a stable partner may experience deep shame, depression, or substance abuse.

Survival Mechanism in the Modern Century

As society advances technologically and economically, the emotional landscapes of young women are paradoxically becoming more precarious.

Dependency syndrome in marriage, once primarily rooted in poverty and traditional gender expectations, has evolved in the twenty-first century to intersect with new cultural pressures, social media influences, and shifting definitions of success.

Today, the survival mechanism of dependency manifests not only in early marriages or cohabitation but also in the subtle psychological entrapment of social validation, emotional insecurity, and maladaptive coping strategies.

1. Early Vulnerability and Societal Pressures

When girls enter adolescence, many begin seeking older male partners who promise financial stability, accommodation, or emotional protection.

In some communities, pregnancies by the age of 14 or 15 have become alarmingly common, a stark indicator of vulnerability and survival-based decision-making. These relationships are often misinterpreted by outsiders as immorality, yet they are frequently the only perceived lifelines out of unstable, overcrowded, or neglectful homes.

Modern environments compound this problem.

Exposure to social media portrays idealized lifestyles where female success is increasingly measured by relational status: having a partner, living with a man, or being perceived in a romantic relationship.

Consequently, even highly educated and financially independent women may internalize the belief that their emotional fulfillment and social identity are incomplete without a man.

Success is no longer merely professional achievement; it is validated publicly through relational associations.

2. Cultural Reinforcement and Emotional Conditioning

Dependency syndrome has become a cultural norm in which societal approval is closely tied to relational visibility.

Women are taught that not being chosen for marriage, or not living with a partner, reflects personal failure.

This cultural messaging fuels a profound internalized pressure to seek a man at all costs.

The consequences are multifaceted:

Shame and self-devaluation

Women perceive singlehood as inadequacy, reinforcing internalized negative self-perception.

Depression and anxiety

The constant comparison to societal ideals creates chronic stress, fear of judgment, and emotional fatigue.

Substance abuse

Alcohol, in particular, has emerged as a cornerstone escape mechanism. Unlike therapy, which requires confronting uncomfortable truths and deep emotional work, alcohol and other substances offer immediate, temporary relief from stress, shame, and existential anxiety.

For many, it becomes a surrogate partner—filling emotional voids without the demands of vulnerability or self-reflection.

3. Therapy as a Double-Edged Sword

While therapy is widely promoted as a solution for dependency syndrome, in the modern context, it is sometimes perceived as a threat to internal freedom and instantaneous emotional satisfaction.

Confronting the roots of trauma requires patience, introspection, and sustained effort—qualities often at odds with contemporary demands for instant gratification.

For young women seeking quick relief from social pressure, therapy may feel like a cage rather than a pathway, pushing them toward faster, more tangible escapes such as alcohol, relationships, or cohabitation.

The paradox is clear: the very institutions designed to heal and empower can feel constraining, while socially acceptable vices provide ephemeral comfort. This tension underscores the urgency of reconciling cultural expectations with psychological resilience.

4. Modern Dependency and Identity Projection

Dependency syndrome today is as much about identity projection as survival. Women project desires for safety, respect, and recognition onto male partners, while men may similarly project their need for control, approval, or emotional rescue.

The relational dynamic often becomes a continuous negotiation of internal inadequacies, shaped by societal narratives and reinforced by economic realities.

Social media exacerbates this cycle, broadcasting curated lives in which romantic validation equals worth.

A successful woman without a partner is often subtly positioned as incomplete, while relationships—regardless of quality—are glorified as markers of achievement. Emotional dependence is thus normalized, perpetuating a cycle of relational survival rather than conscious choice.

5. Implications for Mental Health and Society

The modern expression of dependency syndrome has profound implications:

Rising teenage pregnancies and early cohabitation indicate the urgency of intervention at community and educational levels.

Substance use as an emotional coping mechanism highlights gaps in accessible, culturally sensitive, and engaging mental health resources.

Shifting definitions of success embed dependency within the aspirational psyche, making singlehood or self-sufficiency psychologically challenging.

Without structural interventions—ranging from policy reform and economic empowerment to social campaigns redefining success—the cycle of dependency will continue to reproduce itself, even among the most educated and economically independent women.

Dependency syndrome in the modern era is not simply about marriage or economic survival; it is a complex entanglement of social pressure, identity insecurity, and maladaptive coping strategies.

Alcohol, relationships, and social validation have become surrogate mechanisms for emotional escape, offering immediate relief but perpetuating long-term dependency.

Breaking this cycle requires a profound cultural shift: recognizing the value of emotional autonomy, decoupling identity from relational status, and creating spaces where healing and self-understanding are not perceived as constraints, but as true pathways to freedom.

Trauma, Silence, and Emotional Burdens

When women enter marriage with high levels of unprocessed trauma, they unknowingly carry unresolved psychological pain into the relationship. The marriage that was supposed to save them becomes another space of suffering.

Many marriages begin under pressure—women insisting on commitment because their home environment feels unbearable, or men agreeing because they also seek escape. These marriages, formed through desperation rather than genuine compatibility, frequently deteriorate into conflict, resentment, or emotional distance.

Once children are born, divorce becomes nearly impossible.

Women may stay in painful marriages because returning home means returning to poverty, overcrowding, unemployment, and possibly the same traumatic environment they escaped.

Men, too, may remain in unhappy marriages—afraid of judgment, financial loss, or the insecurity of starting over.

Trauma, Silence, and Emotional Burdens in Modern

Marriage Dependency

Marriage is often idealized as a sanctuary—a space of emotional support, stability, and personal fulfillment. Yet, for many individuals, it becomes a continuation of trauma rather than a resolution.

Dependency syndrome in marriage thrives not only in impoverished or underprivileged contexts but also among educated women and men, whose decisions are deeply influenced by social expectations, identity confusion, and cultural conditioning.

1. The Educated Woman and the Pressure to Marry

Even among highly educated women, marriage is frequently perceived as a societal milestone, a confirmation of personal success, and a validation of worth.

Academic achievement and financial independence, while empowering, do not insulate women from cultural messaging that equates relational status with social acceptance.

In modern contexts:

Marriage as Social Currency

Women are often judged not solely by their professional achievements but by their ability to secure a life partner. Societal norms suggest that a woman, no matter her accomplishments, is incomplete without a man.

Fear of Social Stigma

Single women, even in urban and professional spaces, may encounter subtle or overt judgment, reinforcing anxiety and feelings of inadequacy.

Early Commitment Despite Readiness

Educated women may enter marriages prematurely—not because of emotional readiness but to conform to expectations, satisfy family pressures, or align with perceived social success.

This pursuit often masks internal struggles: unresolved childhood trauma, low self-esteem, and the unconscious search for validation through relational attachment.

Marriage becomes less about authentic partnership and more about social acceptance and internalized cultural definitions of success.

2. Educated Men and the Conformity of Identity

Men, too, are affected by dependency syndrome, though often in ways shaped by societal ideals of masculinity and identity. Highly educated men may possess economic independence and social capital, yet still marry for reasons that have little to do with personal fulfillment:

Marriage as Social Expectation

In many cultures, men are evaluated by their ability to provide, settle, or maintain family structures. Remaining single beyond a socially accepted age may trigger judgment, ridicule, or a perception of failure.

Identity Uncertainty

Men grappling with unresolved personal trauma, emotional immaturity, or unclear life goals may view marriage as a stabilizing force or a socially sanctioned escape from self-reflection.

Marriage as Performance

Some men enter relationships to satisfy external expectations, demonstrating their conformity to societal ideals rather than their internal desire for connection. This dynamic mirrors the pressures faced by women: the partnership is performed to meet society's gaze rather than to cultivate emotional intimacy.

1. **The Intersection of Trauma and Relational**

Performance

When both partners carry unprocessed trauma—whether from childhood neglect, domestic instability, or identity confusion—the marriage often becomes a crucible of unresolved emotional patterns.

Key features include:

Silent Suffering

Individuals conceal their pain to maintain appearances, avoid judgment, or meet societal expectations. Silence becomes a coping mechanism, creating emotional distance.

Compounded Pressure

The societal imperative to sustain the marriage intensifies internalized anxiety. Couples remain together not out of compatibility but due to fear of financial instability, loss of social respect, or perceived failure.

Parenthood as Constraint

The birth of children often solidifies marital entrapment. Divorce or separation carries not only logistical and financial burdens but also emotional and societal consequences, perpetuating dependency cycles across generations.

1. Psychological Mechanisms Underlying These

Patterns

Sigmund Freud's theories on identity and the interplay of the id, ego, and superego provide insight into these patterns:

Id-driven impulses

Early trauma and unmet emotional needs push individuals toward relationships that promise immediate emotional or social satisfaction.

Ego negotiation

The ego attempts to reconcile personal desires with external pressures—balancing the need for autonomy with the demand to conform.

Superego influence

Cultural, familial, and societal expectations act as the internalized moral authority, compelling individuals to marry, perform, or remain in relationships even when emotionally detrimental.

In educated men and women, this triad manifests in complex ways: they may consciously pursue personal and professional goals while unconsciously engaging in relationships to resolve childhood conflicts, gain validation, or avoid social censure.

5. Consequences of Survival-Based Marriages

Marriages formed under pressure, cultural expectation, or identity uncertainty carry significant emotional and psychological burdens:

Emotional Distance and Resentment

Couples struggle to connect authentically, leading to chronic dissatisfaction.

Reinforcement of Trauma

Unprocessed pain resurfaces through conflict, co-dependency, or projection of unresolved feelings onto partners.

Mental Health Implications

Anxiety, depression, substance misuse, and psychosomatic symptoms are frequent outcomes of survival-driven marital choices.

6. Breaking the Cycle

Understanding the intersection of trauma, identity, and societal expectation is crucial for addressing dependency syndrome in marriage. Interventions must:

Encourage self-reflection and identity work independent of relational validation.

Challenge cultural narratives that equate marital status with success.

Promote emotional literacy and trauma processing as prerequisites to relational health.

Provide alternatives to marriage as a sole source of validation, including economic independence, social support networks, and personal fulfillment strategies.

Marriage, when entered without full emotional readiness or self-understanding, transforms from a sanctuary into a pressure chamber of trauma, expectation, and relational performance. Educated women may marry for social approval rather than authentic desire, while educated men may conform to external expectations despite personal uncertainty.

Recognizing these patterns is the first step toward breaking cycles of dependency, fostering autonomy, and cultivating relationships grounded in mutual respect, emotional maturity, and authentic love.

Therapy, Identity Reconstruction, and Modern Dependency

In the contemporary landscape, traditional therapy is increasingly viewed with skepticism, sometimes perceived as an obstacle rather than a pathway to emotional freedom.

Many individuals, especially those entangled in dependency syndrome, experience therapy as confronting, destabilizing, or even threatening to their constructed sense of identity. In this context, alternative coping mechanisms—such as alcohol, casual relationships, or social media validation—emerge as substitutes for structured healing, often exacerbating dependency patterns.

1. Therapy as the Perceived "Enemy" of Freedom

Therapy requires introspection, honesty, and the dismantling of internalized narratives that have sustained dependency. For individuals whose identities have been built around relational survival, this process can feel like a loss of freedom:

Fear of Self-Exposure

Confronting childhood trauma and emotional wounds threatens the identity many have constructed to survive societal and familial pressures.

Dependency on Relationships

When marriage or partnership has been the primary source of validation, therapy can feel like an affront to the very structure that defines one's social existence.

Cultural Resistance

In many communities, admitting to emotional or psychological struggles carries stigma. Therapy is sometimes framed as weakness or indulgence, discouraging engagement.

Consequently, individuals often resist formal therapeutic intervention, turning instead to coping mechanisms that provide immediate relief but do not address root causes.

2. Alcohol and Substance Use as a Coping Mechanism

One of the most visible alternative strategies is alcohol consumption. Alcohol provides a temporary escape from anxiety, unresolved trauma, and relational stress. In contemporary society:

Normalization of Alcohol Use

Drinking has become socially acceptable in many urban and rural contexts, often integrated into celebrations, social gatherings, and even coping routines.

Temporary Emotional Relief

Alcohol numbs emotional discomfort and creates an illusion of independence, masking the underlying dependency.

1. **Reinforcement of Dependency Cycles**

While alcohol may reduce immediate stress, it frequently exacerbates relational conflict, impulsive behaviour, and health complications, deepening the dependency trap.

This pattern is evident across diverse contexts—from New York's urban neighborhoods to township settlements in South Africa—where young adults and even highly educated professionals may resort to alcohol to cope with internal and relational pressures.

4. Social Media, Validation, and the Illusion of Independence

Modern dependency extends beyond physical partnerships. Social media platforms have created new arenas where relational validation is pursued externally:

Comparison and Insecurity

Constant exposure to curated images of success, marriage, and lifestyle generates anxiety and reinforces the need for relational validation.

Projection of Identity

Individuals project idealized versions of themselves online, creating a facade that conceals unresolved trauma and dependence.

Temporary Gratification

"Likes," comments, and online recognition provide fleeting emotional relief, echoing the survival-based validation historically sought through marriage.

Ironically, these digital coping mechanisms mimic the emotional patterns of dependency syndrome: reliance on external approval and avoidance of self-confrontation.

1. **Educated Individuals, Therapy Resistance, and Societal Expectations**

Highly educated women and men, while possessing cognitive tools to analyze their experiences, are not immune to these patterns. They may resist therapy for several reasons:

Fear of Identity Disruption

Therapy challenges deeply ingrained beliefs about success, marriage, and self-worth.

Cultural and Professional Pressure

Maintaining an image of composure and stability in professional or social circles can make vulnerability feel unsafe.

Substitution with Temporary Escapes

Alcohol, workaholism, or short-term relationships often serve as substitutes for structured healing, offering immediate relief without confronting the dependency cycle.

This resistance perpetuates marriages and relationships built on survival, societal performance, or cultural expectation rather than authentic connection.

1. **Toward Identity Reconstruction and Sustainable Independence**

Breaking the cycle of dependency requires an integrated approach:

Reframing Therapy

Therapy should be reframed as a tool for empowerment, not a threat to freedom. Psychoeducation, culturally sensitive counseling, and community-based interventions can reduce stigma.

Building Self-Validation Mechanisms

Individuals must cultivate self-worth independent of relational or societal approval. Education, hobbies, community engagement, and mentorship programs can provide alternative sources of identity.

Integrating Mind-Body Practices

Meditation, journaling, and somatic therapies allow individuals to process trauma without relying on immediate relational validation.

Creating Supportive Communities

Peer groups, mentorship networks, and discussion forums provide relational practice in a safe, non-judgmental environment, reducing the urgency to marry for survival.

7. The Psychoanalytic Perspective

Freud's theory of identity formation illuminates why therapy feels threatening to individuals entrenched in dependency syndrome:

Id Dominance

The instinctual drives for security, love, and acceptance dominate decision-making when trauma is unresolved.

Ego Vulnerability

The ego struggles to reconcile personal desires with societal expectations, creating tension and avoidance behaviors.

Superego Pressure

Internalized norms about marriage, gender roles, and success act as moral constraints, making self-exploration anxiety-provoking.

Therapy, therefore, is perceived as a challenge to the superego's authority—a confrontation with long-held beliefs about identity, worth, and relational success.

In the modern era, dependency syndrome in marriage is compounded by the rejection of therapy, the normalization of alcohol use, and the pursuit of social validation through external mechanisms.

Both educated and less-educated individuals may enter marriages not for love or compatibility, but as a survival strategy or social performance.

Breaking this cycle requires redefining freedom—not as avoidance of responsibility or pain, but as mastery over one's own identity, emotional independence, and relational authenticity. Only by confronting trauma, resisting societal coercion, and cultivating internal validation can individuals transform marriage from a survival mechanism into a partnership founded on genuine love and self-awareness.

Global Case Studies: Dependency Syndrome in New York, Nigeria, and Mozambique

Dependency syndrome in marriage is not confined to African communities; it manifests globally wherever socio-economic instability, trauma, and rigid cultural expectations intersect. By examining case studies from New York, Nigeria, and Mozambique, we can understand how structural pressures, psychological dynamics, and societal norms converge to create dependency patterns in both men and women.

Freud's psychoanalytic theories provide a lens to analyze how early experiences, identity confusion, and unconscious drives influence adult relational choices.

1. New York: Urban Poverty and Survival Marriages

In the urban landscape of New York, dependency syndrome manifests among populations exposed to poverty, familial instability, and systemic neglect. Young women and men often grow up in overcrowded housing projects, foster care, or single-parent households, where emotional neglect and exposure to violence are frequent.

Early Trauma

Children witness substance abuse, domestic conflict, and unsafe sexual behavior, resulting in unresolved psychological pain. This often leads to the premature search for secure adult attachments.

Marriage as Survival

Young adults, particularly women from under-resourced neighborhoods, may enter cohabitation or early marriage to access stability, protection, or housing. Marriage or partnership becomes a functional tool rather than a relational choice.

Societal Pressure

Even in Western societies, social validation is strongly tied to relational status. Highly educated women may feel compelled to marry or cohabit to align with peer expectations, while men may enter relationships to assert social maturity despite internal identity confusion.

Freudian Analysis

Freud's model of the id, ego, and superego explains this behavior: the id drives the pursuit of security and attachment, the superego imposes societal and moral expectations, and the ego struggles to balance these forces, often resulting in survival-driven relational choices rather than authentic connection.

2. Nigeria: Cultural Expectations and Gendered Dependency

In Nigeria, traditional gender roles and cultural narratives about marriage amplify dependency syndrome. The societal expectation that women marry young to secure financial security, social recognition, and familial honor places immense psychological pressure on adolescent girls and young women.

Cultural Pressures

Proverbs, religious teachings, and family expectations often frame marriage as the ultimate measure of success for women. Girls are socialized to view marriage as essential for social acceptance, while men are subtly pressured to assert their roles as providers.

Economic Constraints

High youth unemployment and limited educational opportunities exacerbate dependency. Women may pursue marriage with older men who offer financial stability, and men may enter partnerships to maintain societal status rather than personal fulfillment.

Trauma and Identity

Early exposure to domestic conflict, polygamy, or societal inequality contributes to identity confusion. Women may internalize the belief that their self-worth is inseparable from relational status, while men may struggle with emotional suppression and fear of vulnerability.

Freudian Perspective

The unresolved conflicts between id-driven desires for security and superego-enforced cultural norms create unconscious motives that shape marriage choices. Therapy is often stigmatized, and emotional expression is constrained, reinforcing dependency behaviors.

3. Mozambique: Poverty, Migration, and Survival Strategies

Mozambique's social and economic landscape creates unique pressures on young adults. Widespread poverty, rural-to-urban migration, and post-conflict trauma have left many families struggling to provide basic stability for children.

Overcrowding and Early Exposure

Rural households and informal settlements often lack privacy, with children exposed to adult sexual behavior, domestic conflict, and emotional neglect. Early sexual curiosity and premature pregnancies are common.

Marriage as an Escape

For girls and young women, marriage or cohabitation with older men is often perceived as a route to safety, financial support, and social mobility. Men, too, may marry to assert independence from extended family or escape economic precarity.

Intergenerational Trauma

Families affected by past conflicts and economic instability pass down unresolved trauma. Children internalize fear, longing, and identity confusion, shaping their relational choices as adults.

Psychoanalytic Interpretation

Freud's theories illuminate the psychological mechanism behind these choices: unmet childhood needs drive adult dependency patterns, while societal norms and moral expectations (superego) reinforce survival-based relational decisions.

4. Comparative Observations

Across New York, Nigeria, and Mozambique, several patterns emerge:

Trauma as a Root Cause

Early exposure to neglect, violence, or unsafe living conditions generates identity confusion, low self-esteem, and heightened dependency needs.

Marriage as Survival

In contexts of economic or social instability, marriage becomes a strategic choice, providing temporary

security rather than authentic relational fulfillment.

Societal and Cultural Enforcement

Norms and expectations shape dependency behaviors for both genders, pressuring educated individuals to conform even when personal identity is unformed or conflicted.

Resistance to Therapy

Across contexts, therapy is underutilized due to stigma, fear of self-exposure, or cultural resistance, leaving maladaptive coping strategies like substance use, social validation, or survival marriages intact.

Freudian Insight

Unconscious drives, unresolved trauma, and superego pressures converge to perpetuate dependency. Both women and men often enter marriages not for love, but to satisfy survival needs, societal expectations, or identity anxieties.

Dependency syndrome in marriage is a global phenomenon, shaped by cultural expectations, poverty, trauma, and internalized identity conflicts.

While the manifestations differ—cohabitation in New York, traditional marriage in Nigeria, early unions in Mozambique—the underlying psychological patterns remain similar: unresolved trauma drives dependency, social and cultural norms enforce relational survival strategies, and therapy or self-reflection is often resisted.

Breaking the cycle requires an integrated approach: destigmatizing therapy, fostering emotional literacy, and promoting self-knowledge so that marriage can become a partnership of choice rather than a survival mechanism.

Recognizing the global footprint of dependency syndrome also highlights the universality of human vulnerability and the urgent need for culturally sensitive interventions that address both structural and psychological determinants.

Educated Individuals and the Paradox of Societal Compliance: Why Success Does Not Prevent Dependency Syndrome

In modern society, education and financial success are often assumed to provide individuals with the autonomy, self-confidence, and critical thinking necessary to make independent life choices. Paradoxically, even highly educated men and women frequently fall prey to dependency syndrome in marriage.

Despite access to resources, information, and social mobility, these individuals may still marry or enter long-term partnerships not out of genuine emotional alignment, but to satisfy societal expectations, maintain appearances, or achieve a symbolic status of success.

1. The Societal Pressure of "Visible Success"

Education and professional achievement, while empowering in some areas, do not inoculate individuals from cultural and social pressures. In many communities—urban or rural, African or Western—society measures a woman's success not by her degrees, career achievements, or entrepreneurial endeavors, but by her relational status: being married, cohabiting, or visibly partnered with a man.

Women and Marriage

Highly educated women face implicit and explicit pressures to "settle down." Peer comparisons, family expectations, and media narratives reinforce the idea that personal worth is incomplete without a male partner.

Men and Marriage

Similarly, educated men may experience societal scrutiny if they remain single past a certain age. Marriage or cohabitation becomes a marker of maturity, respectability, and stability, even when personal identity is unresolved.

This pressure often leads individuals to make relational choices that prioritize appearance over authenticity, resulting in marriages that reinforce dependency rather than genuine emotional interdependence.

2. The Psychological Dynamics of "Conditional Choice"

Freud's theories of the psyche offer insight into why educated individuals, despite awareness, succumb to dependency syndrome:

Id-driven Needs

Even accomplished individuals harbor unconscious needs for security, validation, and love. The id pushes them toward relationships that promise these satisfactions, especially when early trauma or emotional neglect remains unresolved.

Superego Enforcement

Cultural and societal expectations function as the superego, imposing moral and social norms. The educated individual may internalize messages such as "success is meaningless without marriage" or "you must maintain appearances," which override authentic desires.

Ego Mediation

The ego struggles to reconcile the unconscious desires of the id with the normative pressures of the superego. In many cases, the compromise is marriage or partnership that satisfies social approval, even if it perpetuates emotional dependency or identity suppression.

1. Identity Confusion Among Educated Women and Men

Education and career success do not automatically resolve underlying identity conflicts. In fact, they can sometimes exacerbate tension:

Women

Highly educated women may feel a dissonance between independence and relational expectation. While capable of self-sufficiency, they may pursue marriage to adhere to cultural or familial norms, suppressing personal desires in favor of relational validation.

Men

Educated men may enter marriages to project success, stability, or social conformity. Insecure about emotional competence or fearful of solitude, they may seek relational approval rather than personal fulfillment.

Consequence

Both genders risk perpetuating cycles of dependency: emotionally, financially, and socially. They may prioritize marital appearance over relational satisfaction, unintentionally modeling co-dependent dynamics to their children.

4. The Role of Therapy and the Fear of Emotional Freedom

In modern society, therapy is widely recognized as a tool for emotional awareness, healing, and personal growth. Yet paradoxically, for some educated individuals, therapy is perceived as a threat to internal freedom:

Exposure Anxiety

Therapy requires confronting unresolved trauma, suppressed emotions, and unconscious patterns—processes that challenge one's self-image and relational narratives.

Freedom vs. Conformity

Many prefer the "comfort" of marriage or cohabitation as a socially sanctioned structure rather than risking the uncertainties of emotional autonomy. Dependency becomes safer than self-exploration.

Substance and Coping Mechanisms

In the absence of therapeutic engagement, some individuals resort to alcohol, social validation, or overachievement to mask unresolved pain and sustain dependent relational patterns.

5. Marriage as Symbolic Validation

Marriage among educated individuals often functions less as an intimate partnership and more as a socially sanctioned validation of personal worth:

Women

Marriage symbolizes that they are desirable, capable of sustaining a family, and socially accomplished.

Men

Marriage signals maturity, competence, and social reliability, even if emotional readiness is absent.

Identity Projection

Both genders project onto marriage a solution to unresolved childhood issues, unprocessed trauma, or identity confusion. Freud's concept of projection explains this: unconscious desires and fears are redirected onto the partner and marital institution.

6. Implications and Risks

The paradox of educated dependency is particularly insidious:

Marriages built on societal compliance rather than authentic alignment risk emotional stagnation, conflict, and dissatisfaction.

Children in these households may inherit modeled dependency behaviors, normalizing co-dependency and reinforcing identity confusion across generations.

Individuals may remain trapped in relational cycles where personal growth is subordinated to social approval, perpetuating trauma and limiting emotional autonomy.

Dependency syndrome transcends economic and educational achievement. Highly educated men and women are not immune to its influence; in fact, social pressures and identity uncertainty can intensify its effects. Marriage, instead of being a space of mutual growth and authentic partnership, often becomes a vehicle for validation, escape, or conformity.

Breaking the cycle requires courage: engaging in self-reflection, confronting unresolved trauma, and redefining personal measures of success beyond relational status. Only through conscious emotional work can marriage evolve from a mechanism of dependency to a genuine partnership grounded in mutual respect, autonomy, and love.

Therapy, Emotional Education, and Breaking the Cycle: Redefining Marriage Beyond Dependency

Introduction

Dependency syndrome in marriage, as explored in previous chapters, is deeply rooted in childhood trauma, socio-economic pressures, cultural expectations, and identity confusion. While education, financial independence, and societal success can reduce some vulnerabilities, they do not automatically resolve the psychological patterns that perpetuate dependency.

Therapy and emotional education emerge as critical tools to break this cycle—yet in modern contexts, they are often misunderstood or resisted.

Many individuals perceive introspective work as a threat to freedom, preferring the temporary escape offered by relationships, societal validation, or substances such as alcohol.

This chapter examines the role of therapy and emotional education in fostering autonomy, healthy relational patterns, and authentic selfhood, while critically analyzing why some modern individuals resist these tools, perpetuating dependency despite apparent success.

1. Therapy as a Path to Freedom

Therapy provides a structured environment to explore unresolved trauma, emotional patterns, and unconscious projections that influence relational choices:

Uncovering Childhood Trauma

Through guided exploration, individuals confront experiences of neglect, abuse, or emotional abandonment that shaped their expectations of love and marriage.

Understanding Projection in Relationships

Freud's theory of projection is central here. Many individuals project unresolved desires, fears, or unmet needs onto their partners. Therapy helps identify these projections, allowing individuals to separate their authentic self from the unconscious narratives influencing their choices.

Developing Emotional Autonomy

Therapy empowers individuals to cultivate self-awareness, self-esteem, and personal boundaries. Emotional autonomy reduces the need to rely on a partner for validation, safety, or identity completion.

However, in the modern century, therapy is sometimes framed as an encroachment on personal freedom.

Individuals fear confronting uncomfortable truths, preferring the illusory security of co-dependent marriages or escapist behaviors like alcohol consumption.

2. Emotional Education: The Underrated Tool

Beyond formal therapy, emotional education is essential for breaking dependency cycles. It involves teaching individuals how to:

Recognize and regulate emotions

Identify relational patterns and unhealthy dynamics

Communicate needs and boundaries effectively

Make conscious, informed choices in relationships

Emotional education is particularly relevant in communities where cultural norms equate marriage with social achievement. By providing knowledge and tools for self-reflection, individuals can resist societal pressures and redefine success as personal fulfillment rather than relational conformity.

3. Societal Pressures and the Resistance to Therapy

Modern dependency syndrome is perpetuated by societal norms that valorize marriage as a measure of success:

Women

Despite higher education and career achievements, women may feel compelled to marry early or maintain relationships for social validation, fearing judgment, loneliness, or perceived failure.

Men

Similarly, men may marry or remain in marriages for appearances, financial gain, or social approval, even if emotional readiness or identity clarity is absent.

Substance Use as Coping

Alcohol and other substances often serve as coping mechanisms for unprocessed trauma or relational dissatisfaction. Rather than engaging in introspection, individuals may seek temporary relief through numbing or avoidance.

The resistance to therapy reflects a paradox: individuals desire freedom and happiness, yet perceive the exploration of self and past trauma as threatening to their emotional comfort. Without confronting these fears, dependency persists.

4. Redefining Marriage Beyond Survival

Therapy and emotional education facilitate a redefinition of marriage from a survival mechanism to a conscious partnership:

Mutual Autonomy

Partners maintain individual identity while fostering interdependence based on choice rather than need.

Authentic Compatibility

Decisions to marry or cohabit are grounded in emotional, intellectual, and relational alignment, not escape or societal expectation.

Healthy Emotional Expression

Couples learn to express needs, negotiate conflict, and cultivate intimacy without recreating childhood trauma dynamics.

Breaking Intergenerational Cycles

Children raised in these partnerships witness healthy relational patterns, reducing the likelihood of perpetuating dependency in the next generation.

5. Global Perspectives on Therapy and Dependency

Cross-cultural studies reveal that dependency syndrome is not confined to Africa. In New York, Brazil, and Mozambique, individuals with access to therapy or emotional education demonstrate:

Greater ability to resist societal pressures

More intentional partner selection

Reduced reliance on marriage as an identity-defining milestone

Lower rates of co-dependent behaviors and substance misuse

However, even where therapy is accessible, cultural stigma, cost, or lack of awareness can prevent engagement. Recognizing and addressing these barriers is essential for meaningful change.

6. The Path Forward: Practical Interventions

To dismantle dependency syndrome at individual and societal levels, the following interventions are crucial:

Accessible Therapy

Subsidized counseling services in schools, communities, and workplaces.

Emotional Literacy Programs

Workshops and curricula focused on self-awareness, relationships, and trauma recovery.

Community Engagement

Normalizing conversations about mental health and relational autonomy.

Parenting Education

Guiding caregivers to provide emotional security, boundaries, and healthy role modeling.

Policy Support

Government and NGOs can promote mental health, social equity, and educational opportunities to reduce systemic pressures that drive dependency.

Dependency syndrome in marriage is a multifaceted phenomenon rooted in trauma, cultural expectations, socio-economic pressures, and identity confusion. While therapy and emotional education provide

pathways to autonomy and healthy relational patterns, modern individuals often resist these tools, perceiving them as threats to comfort or freedom.

Breaking the cycle requires courage: confronting personal trauma, challenging societal norms, and redefining the purpose of marriage. When therapy, education, and self-reflection are embraced, marriage transforms from a survival strategy into a conscious partnership grounded in authenticity, emotional maturity, and mutual respect.

Chapter 24: Identity Reconstruction – From Childhood Trauma to Healthy Adult Relationships

Chapter Summary - When the Mind Remembers What Life Forgets

Here the focus shifts to memory, emotion, and the unconscious. Drawing from psychoanalytic theory and lived experience in African rural settings, the chapter explains how the mind stores distressing experiences not through logic but through sensations and triggers. It examines repressed memories, emotional fragmentation, and the subtle ways trauma resurfaces—through dreams, bodily tension, relationship patterns, and sudden emotional shifts. The chapter emphasizes that memory is not linear but layered, often revealing itself only when the person is ready.

Introduction

The journey toward emotional independence and healthy relationships begins with identity reconstruction.

Dependency syndrome in marriage, as explored in previous chapters, often originates from unresolved childhood trauma, social pressures, and distorted cultural expectations.

When individuals enter adulthood without a secure sense of self, they are vulnerable to co-dependent behaviors, emotional compromise, and relational dysfunction.

This chapter explores how identity is formed, disrupted, and can be reconstructed using insights from psychoanalytic theory, modern psychological approaches, and cross-cultural perspectives. It examines how men and women, across socio-economic and geographic contexts—including townships in South Africa, urban centers in New York, and communities in Mozambique and Nigeria—struggle with identity confusion in the context of love and marriage.

1. Childhood Trauma and Its Impact on Identity Formation

Freud's psychoanalytic framework provides a foundational understanding of identity formation:

The Id, Ego, and Superego:

Trauma in early childhood disrupts the balance between instinctual drives (id), conscious decision-making (ego), and internalized moral standards (superego). A child exposed to neglect, abuse, or domestic chaos often develops a fragile ego, making the adult self vulnerable to external validation and dependency.

Attachment Patterns

Insecure attachment to caregivers produces a persistent fear of abandonment, driving a search for stability through marriage or partnerships.

Identity Projection

Individuals may project unresolved needs onto partners, expecting them to compensate for emotional deficits, often unconsciously recreating familial dynamics in their adult relationships.

2. Educational and Socio-Cultural Influences on Adult Identity

Even highly educated individuals are not immune to dependency patterns:

Women

Educated women often internalize societal messages that success is measured by relational status. Despite career achievements, the absence of a partner is equated with failure, prompting marriages motivated by external validation rather than emotional readiness.

Men

Educated men may marry to conform to societal norms, family expectations, or economic appearances, even when uncertain of their identity or emotional capacity. Their marriages may reflect social performance rather than authentic desire or partnership.

Societal Reinforcement

Across cultures, status, reputation, and gender norms create invisible pressures to conform to relational milestones, making independent identity formation challenging.

3. Identity Reconstruction: Breaking the Cycle

Reconstructing identity requires deliberate self-awareness, therapeutic intervention, and cultural critique:

Self-Awareness and Reflection

Individuals must examine their childhood experiences, beliefs about love, and relational patterns. Journaling, guided introspection, and mentorship can help identify unconscious motivations.

Therapy and Trauma Processing

Psychological interventions—including individual therapy, cognitive-behavioral techniques, and trauma-focused modalities—help reframe negative beliefs, regulate emotions, and establish boundaries.

Redefining Success and Fulfillment

Identity reconstruction includes separating personal worth from relational status. Self-esteem must be cultivated independently of social approval or marital achievement.

Developing Emotional Literacy

Recognizing and managing emotions enables individuals to communicate needs effectively, prevent co-dependency, and engage in mutually respectful relationships.

4. Global Perspectives: Identity Challenges Across Contexts

New York

In urban environments, young adults raised in foster care or overcrowded housing may rush into partnerships to secure housing, emotional security, or societal validation. Therapy access is available but often underutilized due to stigma or fear.

Nigeria

Cultural emphasis on early marriage, parental authority, and gendered roles produces pressure on young adults, particularly women, to marry before achieving full autonomy. Identity is often shaped around expected relational performance.

Mozambique

Economic instability and high poverty rates intensify dependency behaviors. Limited access to education or mental health services exacerbates identity confusion, prompting early or transactional marriages as survival strategies.

5. The Role of Relationship Projections

Freud's concept of projection is central to understanding adult relational choices:

Unrealistic Expectations

Individuals unconsciously project childhood needs onto partners, expecting them to resolve unhealed trauma.

Cycle of Repetition

Without intervention, unresolved childhood patterns repeat across generations, manifesting as dependency, control struggles, or emotional neglect within marriages.

Therapy as Correction

Professional guidance helps identify these projections, distinguish past from present, and cultivate authentic relational choices.

6. Practical Steps for Identity Reconstruction

Mapping Personal History

Understand how upbringing, culture, and societal expectations influenced identity.

Therapeutic Intervention

Engage in professional support to process trauma, identify co-dependency, and rebuild self-concept.

Boundary Setting

Learn to define personal limits and communicate them clearly in relationships.

Independent Goal Setting

Pursue education, career, hobbies, and social networks that reinforce autonomy.

Cultivating Mindful Relationships

Enter partnerships consciously, seeking compatibility and emotional reciprocity rather than escape or survival.

Identity reconstruction is both a personal and societal imperative. Dependency syndrome in marriage cannot be fully addressed without empowering individuals to reclaim selfhood and autonomy. By confronting trauma, cultivating emotional literacy, and resisting societal pressures, individuals can reconstruct their identities, form healthy relationships, and redefine marriage as a partnership rooted in choice, respect, and authentic love.

Ultimately, breaking the cycle of dependency begins with the self. When adults achieve clarity, emotional independence, and resilience, they not only transform their marriages but also influence the next generation, fostering a culture where love is a source of fulfillment, not survival.

Chapter 25: Breaking Free – The Intersection of Cultural Expectations, Gender Roles, and Emotional Liberation in Marriage

Introduction

Dependency syndrome in marriage is not only a product of individual trauma or identity confusion; it is deeply reinforced by cultural expectations and gender norms. Societies shape what it means to be a "successful" woman or man, often linking personal worth to relational achievement. Breaking free from these constraints requires examining the intersection of cultural pressures, gender roles, and emotional liberation, and understanding how these forces perpetuate cycles of dependency in both men and women.

This chapter explores the ways societal expectations influence marital dependency, the role of gender in shaping relational behavior, and strategies for fostering emotional autonomy and liberation in modern marriage contexts.

1. Cultural Expectations and Marriage Dependency

Marriage as a Social Mandate

In many communities—from African villages in Limpopo, Nigeria, and Mozambique to urban centers like New York and São Paulo—marriage is portrayed as the pinnacle of social achievement. Women are often raised to believe that marital status validates personal worth, while men are expected to demonstrate financial and emotional stability through partnership.

Family Pressure

Parents and extended families exert strong influence, encouraging early marriage for daughters as a form of protection and social security. For men, societal perception of competence and adulthood is often measured by marital status.

Religious and Traditional Norms

Biblical or cultural directives emphasizing that "a woman shall leave her home to join her husband" have been interpreted as moral imperatives. While intended to maintain family continuity and social cohesion, they inadvertently reinforce dependency by prioritizing marital conformity over personal autonomy.

2. Gender Roles and Their Influence on Dependency

Women and Emotional Labour

Women often internalize the role of caretaker, emotional mediator, and nurturer within marriage. This role reinforces dependency when women feel obligated to maintain the household and secure male approval, even at the cost of their own mental health.

Men and Provider Pressure

Men, even when educated and capable, may marry primarily to meet societal expectations of provision, control, or status. Emotional readiness and genuine relational desire may be secondary to societal validation.

Mutual Survival Marriages

These marriages, based on external pressures rather than internal alignment, frequently result in co-dependency, emotional dissatisfaction, and suppressed identity for both partners.

3. Emotional Liberation: Overcoming Societal Constraints

Self-Awareness and Conscious Choice

Liberation begins with recognizing how cultural and gender expectations shape relational decisions. Individuals must critically examine why they pursue marriage and what unmet emotional needs are being projected onto partners.

Deconstructing Gender Norms

Challenging traditional roles allows partners to renegotiate responsibilities and expectations. For example, men can share emotional labor and caregiving responsibilities, while women can assert autonomy in financial and personal decisions.

Therapeutic Support

While therapy may be perceived as intrusive or countercultural in some settings, it provides critical tools for emotional processing, boundary-setting, and identity reinforcement. Alternatives, such as support groups, mentorship, and culturally sensitive counseling, can also facilitate liberation.

4. Case Studies Across Contexts

New York

Urban youth raised in foster systems or overcrowded homes often enter partnerships for housing, financial security, or emotional stability. Breaking free involves accessing therapy, mentoring programs, and supportive social networks that validate self-worth outside relational status.

Nigeria

Early marriage pressures and patriarchal structures reinforce dependency. Women often marry young, prioritizing family approval over personal choice. Emotional liberation requires education, financial independence, and community programs challenging restrictive gender norms.

Mozambique

Economic hardship and cultural expectations intertwine, creating cycles where both men and women remain in unsatisfying marriages. Liberation strategies include vocational training, access to mental health resources, and community advocacy for gender equity.

5. The Psychology of Breaking Free

Freud's Influence on Identity and Projection

Individuals often project unresolved childhood trauma onto partners. Emotional liberation involves recognizing these projections, separating past experiences from present relationships, and building self-defined identity.

The Role of Resilience

Resilient individuals actively challenge societal pressures, redefine personal goals, and pursue relationships that reflect mutual growth rather than survival.

Mindfulness and Emotional Regulation

Conscious awareness of emotional triggers, communication patterns, and dependency tendencies enables adults to engage in healthy relational dynamics.

1. Strategies for Fostering Independence Within

Marriage

Mutual Boundary-Setting

Partners must identify and respect personal boundaries, creating space for individual growth.

Shared Decision-Making

Egalitarian relationships reduce dependency by promoting agency and accountability for both partners.

Financial and Emotional Autonomy

Cultivating independence in income, social networks, and personal interests diminishes the pressure to remain in a relationship for survival.

Cultural Reframing

Communities must reimagine success, valuing individual fulfillment alongside marital status. Educational campaigns and advocacy can shift social norms toward empowerment.

Breaking free from dependency syndrome requires more than individual insight; it demands confronting entrenched cultural expectations, redefining gender roles, and fostering emotional independence. Marriage should evolve from a survival strategy into a conscious choice based on compatibility, mutual respect, and authentic love.

By challenging societal pressures, cultivating self-awareness, and embracing emotional liberation, individuals can reconstruct relationships that honor identity, autonomy, and mutual fulfillment. In doing so, dependency is replaced with partnership, trauma is addressed rather than perpetuated, and marriage becomes a space for growth rather than a mechanism for escape.

Chapter 26: Therapy, Culture, and Liberation – Redefining Mental Health in the Modern Marriage

Introduction

In contemporary society, therapy and mental health practices are increasingly recognized as essential for emotional well-being. Yet, in the context of marriage dependency syndrome, therapy is often misunderstood, resisted, or even feared. Some perceive it as an external imposition, a challenge to personal freedom, or a critique of cultural norms. This chapter examines the complex relationship between therapy, culture, and emotional liberation, exploring why traditional approaches to mental health sometimes clash with societal expectations, and how new, contextually sensitive frameworks can foster independence within marital relationships.

1. Therapy and the Modern Perception of Freedom

Therapy as Threat vs. Tool

Many individuals, particularly in African and other collectivist societies, view therapy as a potential threat to personal and familial autonomy. The fear is that introspection may reveal uncomfortable truths, challenge accepted cultural practices, or destabilize the carefully maintained social image.

The Conflict Between Internal Happiness and External Expectations

While therapy encourages self-awareness and emotional processing, societal pressures often prioritize conformity over authenticity. In marriages shaped by dependency, confronting unresolved trauma may seem threatening, as it could disrupt the perceived stability of the relationship.

Alcohol and Escapism

In the absence of accessible or culturally acceptable therapeutic resources, individuals increasingly rely on substances such as alcohol to self-medicate. Alcohol becomes a coping mechanism for stress, trauma, and emotional dissatisfaction, providing temporary relief but perpetuating dependency and relational dysfunction.

2. Cultural Barriers to Mental Health

Stigma and Shame

Mental health issues are often stigmatized, interpreted as weakness, or associated with moral failure. Women who express emotional vulnerability may be labeled as unstable, while men may be pressured to suppress feelings entirely, reinforcing cycles of emotional dependency.

Collectivist vs. Individualist Values

In many African and Latin American communities, family and community needs supersede personal growth. Therapy's focus on individual autonomy may conflict with these collective expectations, creating tension for those seeking emotional liberation.

Generational Transmission of Trauma

Unresolved trauma is often passed from one generation to the next. Families that prioritize survival and marriage over emotional processing inadvertently teach younger generations to use marriage as a coping mechanism rather than a conscious choice.

3. Therapy as a Path to Liberation

Understanding the Self

Therapy allows individuals to explore the roots of dependency syndrome, including childhood trauma, identity confusion, and societal pressures. By understanding these patterns, people can consciously choose partners rather than unconsciously reproducing cycles of co-dependency.

Reframing Marriage

Therapy challenges the notion that marriage is a solution to poverty, emotional neglect, or identity struggles. Couples learn to engage in partnerships based on mutual respect, emotional compatibility, and shared goals, rather than survival or social validation.

Tools for Emotional Independence

Cognitive-behavioral strategies, mindfulness practices, and trauma-informed counseling provide practical methods for regulating emotions, building self-esteem, and asserting boundaries. These tools help individuals maintain identity and agency within the marital context.

4. Global Comparisons of Therapeutic Resistance

New York

Urban populations often have access to formal therapy but face societal skepticism. Young adults may avoid therapy due to financial constraints or fear of judgment, turning instead to informal coping mechanisms like alcohol, partying, or early sexual relationships.

Nigeria

Traditional healers and religious institutions are commonly preferred over psychotherapy. While these practices provide community-based support, they may reinforce dependency norms by emphasizing conformity and moral obedience over self-exploration.

Mozambique

Rural communities often lack trained mental health professionals. Women and men in dependency-driven marriages rely heavily on family networks or community elders, who may unintentionally perpetuate cycles of dependency by prioritizing survival over emotional insight.

1. **Psychoanalytic Perspectives on Therapy and Dependency**

Freud's Identity Theory

According to Freud, unresolved childhood conflicts create internalized anxieties that influence adult relationships. Dependency syndrome can be understood as a projection of these conflicts, where individuals seek partners to compensate for unmet needs or unresolved trauma.

Projection in Marriage

Individuals may unconsciously project ideals, fears, or desires onto their spouse, expecting the partner to provide validation, security, or identity. Therapy helps identify these projections, enabling individuals to separate past trauma from present relational dynamics.

The Role of the Superego, Ego, and Id

The superego enforces cultural and societal expectations, the id pursues immediate satisfaction, and the ego negotiates between the two. Therapy strengthens the ego, allowing individuals to navigate social pressures while maintaining personal autonomy.

6. Alternative Approaches to Emotional Liberation

Community-Based Programs

Culturally sensitive workshops on parenting, relationships, and emotional literacy can provide education without threatening traditional values.

Peer Support Networks

Groups for women and men navigating dependency and marital challenges offer safe spaces to share experiences, build resilience, and learn coping strategies.

Digital and Telehealth Platforms

Access to online counseling, guided therapy programs, and self-help resources can circumvent stigma and provide support in otherwise underserved areas.

7. Recommendations for Reclaiming Emotional Freedom

Normalize Emotional Exploration

Societies must reframe therapy from a mark of weakness to a tool for personal growth and relational health.

Integrate Cultural Context

Mental health services should respect local customs while promoting self-awareness and autonomy.

Educate on Dependency Syndrome

Awareness campaigns can help couples recognize unhealthy relational patterns and seek intervention before trauma escalates.

Promote Gender Equity

Empowering women and men to share responsibilities and validate each other's individuality reduces relational dependency.

Address Substance Abuse

Programs addressing alcohol and other coping mechanisms are critical to breaking cycles of avoidance and emotional suppression.

Therapy, when culturally contextualized and accessible, becomes a powerful tool for reclaiming personal freedom and emotional autonomy within marriage.

While dependency syndrome thrives on silence, unresolved trauma, and societal pressure, intentional emotional exploration allows individuals to transform survival-based relationships into partnerships grounded in love, respect, and self-knowledge.

By integrating psychoanalytic insights, culturally sensitive approaches, and practical interventions, individuals can break cycles of dependency, resist the lure of escapist behaviors such as alcohol use, and cultivate marriages that enhance, rather than compromise, personal growth and happiness.

Chapter 27: Identity Reconstruction and Love Beyond Dependency

Chapter summary - Illusion, Identity, and Romantic Attachments

This chapter analyses how people build identities around love, relationships, and external validation. It explores the fantasy of being "saved" by a partner, the illusion of perfection in romance, and the emotional collapse that follows heartbreak. The chapter uses psychological theory to explain projection, idealization, trauma bonding, and the self-blame that often follows relational disappointment. It demonstrates how identity becomes entangled with another person's presence—leaving individuals feeling empty when that connection ends.

Introduction

Dependency syndrome in marriage does not merely distort relationships—it reshapes individual identity. When marriage is approached as a survival mechanism, personal growth, self-concept, and emotional autonomy are often subordinated to the perceived needs of the partnership or societal expectations.

This chapter examines how adults can reconstruct identity post-dependency, drawing on psychoanalytic frameworks, sociocultural understanding, and modern therapeutic approaches, with a focus on building authentic love and self-directed fulfillment.

1. Identity and the Psychoanalytic Lens

Freud's Identity Theory Revisited

Freud posited that identity emerges from the dynamic interplay between the id, ego, and superego.

In dependency-driven marriages, unresolved childhood trauma—emotional neglect, abuse, and instability—often leads to an overdeveloped superego, internalizing societal pressures and expectations, while the id remains suppressed or misdirected.

The ego, tasked with mediating between internal desires and external demands, becomes overwhelmed, producing confusion in personal desires, relationship choices, and self-concept.

Projection in Dependent Marriages

Individuals unconsciously project unresolved needs onto their partners, expecting the spouse to provide validation, stability, and a sense of identity.

These projections create relationships that are less about mutuality and more about compensating for childhood deficits. Without intervention, such projections perpetuate cycles of emotional dependency, dissatisfaction, and conflict.

2. The Modern Context: How Educated Individuals Experience Dependency

Educated Women

Many women with higher education and financial independence still marry for reasons rooted in societal expectations rather than personal fulfillment.

Marriage is seen as the ultimate marker of success, social validation, or completion of identity. Even accomplished women often feel pressure to conform, fearing judgment or marginalization if they remain single.

Emotional dependency persists because cultural conditioning equates marital status with worth.

Educated Men

Similarly, men who are not fully secure in their own identity may enter marriages to satisfy societal norms or to avoid being perceived as failures.

These men may have achieved professional or academic success, yet struggle internally with self-definition, intimacy, or emotional expression.

Marriage becomes a public performance rather than a reflection of genuine relational desire.

3. Trauma, Silence, and Identity Erosion

Carrying Forward Childhood Trauma

Unprocessed childhood trauma—ranging from witnessing violence to neglect or emotional absence—creates internalized patterns of fear, shame, and self-doubt.

When entering marriage under pressure, these unresolved wounds amplify dependency.

Partners become surrogate parents or emotional caretakers, reinforcing unhealthy relational dynamics.

The Silent Suffering

Both men and women often remain silent about dissatisfaction, fear of rejection, or emotional needs.

Children born into these marriages may inadvertently inherit these patterns, perpetuating cycles of dependency and identity confusion across generations.

4. Reconstructing Identity Post-Dependency

Self-Reflection and Awareness

Rebuilding identity begins with self-awareness. Individuals must examine the motivations behind their marital choices, including fear, societal pressure, or financial necessity. Journaling, guided introspection, or counselling can help illuminate unconscious patterns.

Separating Self from Relationship

Identity reconstruction requires differentiating personal values, desires, and emotional needs from those of the partner.

This process challenges internalized messages that marriage defines worth and encourages authentic self-expression.

Therapy as a Tool, Not a Constraint

While some view therapy as a threat to freedom, psychoanalytic and trauma-informed approaches can provide structured spaces for safe exploration of identity.

Therapy helps individuals dismantle projections, identify triggers, and establish boundaries, supporting autonomy within and beyond marriage.

5. Building Love Beyond Dependency

Mutual Respect and Emotional Reciprocity

Healthy love is rooted in choice, not survival. Partners consciously recognize each other's individuality, strengths, and vulnerabilities.

Shared Responsibility

Dependency syndrome often arises when one partner assumes disproportionate responsibility for emotional or financial security.

Reconstructing identity involves redistributing these responsibilities to promote equality and interdependence.

Authentic Intimacy

Intimacy becomes a shared exploration rather than a transactional exchange.

Couples learn to communicate desires, fears, and boundaries openly, reducing emotional projection and dependency.

6. Global Insights: Cultural Variations in Identity and Dependency

New York

Highly urbanized environments provide access to mental health resources, but social pressures to succeed and "appear normal" lead many to adopt performative marriages.

Therapy, while accessible, is often delayed due to stigma or fear of vulnerability.

Nigeria

Patriarchal expectations and religious norms strongly influence marital decisions.

Educated individuals may suppress personal desires to maintain social approval, perpetuating identity compromises.

Mozambique

Limited access to mental health services and economic instability mean that marriage often remains the default pathway to security. Individuals internalize dependency norms, delaying the development of independent identity and authentic emotional expression.

7. Steps Toward Emotional Autonomy and Relational Freedom

Acknowledgement

Recognize and validate patterns of dependency and unresolved trauma.

Education

Learn about psychological concepts, including projections, identity formation, and attachment theory.

Self-Care Practices

Implement routines that promote self-esteem, emotional regulation, and self-expression.

Therapeutic Engagement

Use culturally sensitive therapy or support networks to process past trauma and restructure identity.

Conscious Relationship Decisions

Enter partnerships based on alignment of values, mutual respect, and shared goals, not fear or societal pressure.

Dependency syndrome in marriage is not simply a relational issue—it is a profound challenge to personal identity, emotional autonomy, and the capacity for authentic love. By reconstructing identity through self-awareness, cultural insight, and therapeutic intervention, individuals can move beyond survival-based relationships toward partnerships grounded in respect, choice, and mutual growth.

True liberation begins within the self.

Only when identity is reconstructed can marriage transform from a vehicle of escape into a space for authentic love, fulfillment, and freedom.

Chapter: Redefining Marriage in the 21st Century – Independence, Equality, and Emotional Literacy

Introduction

The institution of marriage, historically rooted in economic survival, social cohesion, and cultural continuity, is undergoing a profound transformation in the 21st century.

Traditional norms that tied a woman's worth to marital status or a man's success to being a provider are being challenged by increased education, global connectivity, and psychological awareness. However, dependency syndrome continues to shape relational patterns, often hidden beneath modern appearances of choice and freedom.

This chapter explores how marriage can be redefined through independence, emotional literacy, and equality, emphasizing that the health of a relationship depends less on social performance and more on individual psychological development and mutual respect.

1. Independence as a Core Value

Economic and Emotional Autonomy

True independence in marriage involves more than financial stability—it encompasses the ability to make decisions, set boundaries, and maintain personal identity.

Educated women, historically pressured to marry for security, now have the opportunity to define self-worth outside of partnerships.

Similarly, men must cultivate emotional self-sufficiency to avoid using marriage as a compensatory mechanism for unresolved identity issues.

Challenges in Modern Contexts

Despite progress, social pressures persist.

Women are often still judged by marital status, while men face societal expectations to be providers and protectors. These pressures can perpetuate dependency behaviours if not consciously addressed.

2. Emotional Literacy as a Relational Tool

Defining Emotional Literacy

Emotional literacy is the capacity to recognize, understand, and manage one's own emotions, while empathically engaging with the emotions of others.

In marriages shaped by dependency syndrome, partners frequently lack these skills, leading to miscommunication, projection, and co-dependence.

Benefits for Couples

Couples who cultivate emotional literacy can:

- Reduce conflict through mindful communication
- Recognize unhealthy dependency patterns
- Develop authentic intimacy and trust
- Foster resilience in the face of external stressors

3. Equality in Modern Marriages

Balancing Roles and Responsibilities

Marriage in the modern century requires flexibility.

Traditional gender roles—where men solely provide and women solely nurture—are increasingly inadequate for contemporary socio-economic realities.

Equality entails:

- Shared decision-making
- Fair distribution of household and emotional labor
- Mutual respect for career aspirations and personal goals

Social and Cultural Barriers

In many African and Western societies, equality in marriage remains aspirational.

Cultural norms, familial expectations, and internalized beliefs about gender roles continue to reinforce dependency, despite educational attainment or financial independence.

1. Healing Past Trauma to Prevent Dependency Patterns

Psychological Legacies of Childhood

Unresolved trauma from early life—such as neglect, abuse, or exposure to instability—can manifest in adult relationships as over-reliance, fear of abandonment, or co-dependent behavior.

Therapeutic Interventions

Therapy can help individuals:

- Identify the origins of dependency patterns
- Process unresolved trauma
- Rebuild self-esteem and self-concept
- Develop healthier relational strategies

Skepticism About Therapy

In modern contexts, some view therapy as an intrusion or as inhibiting internal happiness.

While therapy is not a universal solution, it is an essential tool for building self-awareness and emotional autonomy.

5. Modern Case Studies: Applying Independence and Equality

New York

Urban professionals increasingly enter marriages with high education and financial stability.

Dependency manifests subtly—through emotional avoidance, performance-based relationships, and prioritization of social image over personal fulfillment. Couples benefit from workshops on communication, emotional intelligence, and boundary-setting.

Nigeria

Patriarchal expectations influence marital decisions, even among educated couples. Women may compromise identity to meet family or religious expectations.

Programs promoting gender equality, leadership, and financial independence help reduce dependency patterns.

Mozambique

Limited mental health infrastructure and economic instability amplify traditional dependency norms.

Community-based interventions, peer support, and education on self-concept are crucial for promoting independent relational choices.

6. Strategies for Building Modern Marriages

Self-Assessment Before Partnership

Individuals should evaluate motives for marriage—security, love, social acceptance, or escape—and identify patterns of dependency.

Open Dialogue About Expectations

Partners must communicate openly about emotional needs, financial responsibilities, and long-term goals.

Mutual Growth and Learning

Couples should cultivate shared experiences that promote intellectual, emotional, and social growth, rather than relying solely on one partner for fulfillment.

Cultural Navigation

Recognize societal pressures and intentionally negotiate which norms to follow and which to redefine.

Creating Safety Nets

Financial planning, personal development, and emotional support outside the marriage reduce the pressure to remain in unhealthy relationships.

7. Reimagining Love and Fulfillment

Modern marriages are not defined by escape or dependency but by choice, authenticity, and shared growth.

Love becomes a collaborative journey where partners honor individuality while cultivating connection.

Dependence shifts to interdependence—a balanced dynamic where autonomy and mutual support coexist.

Autonomy Within Togetherness

Both partners retain distinct identities and pursue personal goals while building relational intimacy.

Sustainable Fulfillment

Emotional satisfaction derives not from societal validation but from self-understanding, healthy communication, and shared purpose.

Redefining marriage in the 21st century requires a paradigm shift: from survival-driven unions to partnerships founded on independence, equality, and emotional literacy.

By integrating self-awareness, cultural insight, and psychological understanding, couples can break cycles of dependency, reconstruct identity, and cultivate relationships rooted in authentic love.

Marriage becomes not a societal checkpoint but a space of growth, freedom, and mutual fulfillment—transforming dependency into choice, and obligation into joy

Chapter 28: Breaking the Cycle of Dependency – Practical Steps for Emotional Freedom and Healthy Relationships

Introduction

Dependency syndrome in marriage, while deeply rooted in culture, trauma, and social pressures, is not immutable. Breaking the cycle requires intentional effort, self-awareness, and strategies that foster autonomy, emotional intelligence, and authentic connection. This chapter provides practical guidance for women and men seeking to reclaim their emotional freedom, build healthy relationships, and reconstruct identity beyond survival-based dependency.

1. Understanding Your Dependency Patterns

Self-Reflection

Examine why you enter or remain in relationships.

✓ Are you motivated by fear, social expectation, financial need, or emotional insecurity?

✓ Journaling, mindfulness, and reflective exercises can reveal hidden patterns.

Early Life Influences

- Identify experiences that shaped dependency tendencies, such as:
- Childhood neglect or abuse
- Exposure to unhealthy relationships
- Poverty or unstable living conditions
- Cultural messaging equating marriage with survival

Signs of Dependency

Look for behaviors like over-pleasing, fear of being alone, over-reliance on a partner for validation, or avoidance of conflict to maintain connection. Recognizing these patterns is the first step toward change.

2. Building Emotional Autonomy

Emotional Regulation

Learn to manage your emotions without relying on a partner as a stabilizer. Techniques include meditation, breathing exercises, and cognitive reframing.

Self-Validation

Cultivate internal sources of approval rather than seeking constant reassurance from others.

Celebrate accomplishments, talents, and personal growth.

Healthy Boundaries

Clearly define what is acceptable in relationships, from communication to personal space, finances, and decision-making. Boundaries protect identity and reduce co-dependency.

3. Strengthening Identity and Self-Esteem

Reclaiming Individuality

Engage in activities that nurture your identity outside the relationship—hobbies, career goals, education, and community involvement.

Addressing Trauma

Unprocessed trauma can perpetuate dependency. Seek professional support through therapy, counseling, or trauma-informed workshops.

If therapy feels restrictive, structured self-help programs, support groups, and culturally-sensitive mentorship can serve as alternatives.

Freud's Insight on Identity

Sigmund Freud's theory of the id, ego, and superego explains how unresolved childhood conflicts influence adult relational patterns. By becoming aware of these unconscious drivers, individuals can prevent projection of old wounds onto current partners.

4. Financial and Social Independence

Economic Empowerment

Financial security reduces pressure to remain in unhealthy relationships.

Prioritize career development, savings, and skill-building.

Social Networks

Build supportive communities outside your partner, including friends, family, or professional networks.

These connections provide validation, advice, and emotional support without reinforcing dependency.

5. Redefining Love and Partnership

From Dependency to Interdependence

Shift from relying on your partner for survival to mutual support based on equality and respect.

Healthy Communication

Practice expressing needs clearly, listening actively, and negotiating disagreements constructively.

Choosing Compatibility over Obligation

Select partners based on shared values, emotional maturity, and long-term compatibility, not social expectation or fear of loneliness.

6. Strategies for Couples

Joint Growth

Engage in activities that promote mutual learning, such as workshops, shared hobbies, or volunteer projects.

Therapeutic Collaboration

Even reluctant partners benefit from structured relationship coaching or counseling to resolve recurring conflicts and reinforce healthy interdependence.

Conflict as Opportunity

Treat disagreements as a chance to improve communication, understanding, and compromise rather than as threats to the relationship.

7. Overcoming Societal Pressures

Question Cultural Norms

Analyze traditions or social expectations that reinforce dependency. Decide consciously which norms to embrace, adapt, or reject.

Resisting Judgment

✓ Avoid measuring success by marital status or external validation. Focus on personal growth and emotional well-being as markers of fulfillment.

Role Models

✓ Look to individuals and couples who exemplify independent, emotionally intelligent, and egalitarian partnerships.

8. Tools and Practices for Sustaining Freedom

Journaling

✓ Track emotional triggers, relationship patterns, and progress toward autonomy.

✓ Mindfulness and Meditation

Develop present-moment awareness to reduce anxiety and reliance on partners for emotional regulation.

Workshops and Seminars

Attend programs on self-development, gender equality, and relational skills.

Mentorship

Engage with mentors who model emotional independence and balanced partnerships.

Creative Expression

Art, music, and writing provide outlets for emotions, helping prevent unhealthy projection onto partners.

Breaking the cycle of dependency is both a personal and societal endeavor.

Individuals reclaim freedom by understanding their psychological patterns, building emotional and financial autonomy, and redefining love as a partnership of equals rather than a survival mechanism.

Couples who integrate these strategies cultivate marriages rooted in mutual respect, choice, and growth.

True freedom begins within—the marriage becomes a reflection of self-awareness, not a remedy for unmet needs.

By embracing independence, identity, and emotional literacy, modern relationships can transform dependency into authentic interdependence, where love is liberating rather than confining.

Chapter 29: Rebuilding Identity After Marriage Dependency – Therapy, Self-Discovery, and Emotional Resilience

Introduction

This chapter explores strategies for self-discovery, emotional resilience, and rebuilding a sense of self after years of dependency, drawing on psychoanalytic insights, contemporary psychology, and culturally informed approaches.

Dependency in marriage often leaves individuals with blurred boundaries, fractured self-esteem, and unresolved trauma.

When a relationship ends—through divorce, separation, or even emotional detachment—the challenge becomes reclaiming identity and reconstructing a life independent of survival-driven choices.

1. Understanding the Identity Loss in Dependency

Internalized Beliefs

Many individuals internalize the idea that self-worth is tied to being chosen, loved, or married.

Ending a dependent marriage can trigger existential crises, anxiety, and depression.

Projection Patterns

Following Freud's theory, unresolved conflicts from childhood—id, ego, and superego dynamics—often shape adult relationships.

Individuals may have projected unmet needs onto partners, creating illusions of love or compatibility.

Recognizing these projections is essential to reclaim authenticity.

Societal Pressure

Social norms often reinforce dependency patterns.

Women, in particular, may feel failure after divorce, while men may struggle with perceived loss of control or status.

Understanding the external pressures helps contextualize emotional responses and reduces self-blame.

Chapter 30: Freedom, Love, and Healing – Escaping the 21st Century Marriage Syndrome

Chapter summary: Self-Compassion as a Path to Recovery

This chapter teaches that healing cannot begin without self-compassion. It reframes dependency, mistakes, and emotional struggles not as weaknesses but as responses to difficult circumstances. The chapter guides the reader through forgiving past choices, recognizing survival mechanisms, and celebrating personal progress. It offers tools for internal validation, emotional regulation, and building a sense of self that is grounded, resilient, and independent of external approval.

In the small village of Makholeng, life moves at the rhythm of tradition.

Women rise early, prepare food, tend to children, and maintain the household, while men leave for work in nearby towns or cities.

Yet beneath the surface of this seemingly simple life, emotional currents run deep.

Many marriages here—like in townships or corporate offices across Johannesburg or New York—carry hidden burdens: dependency, fear, and unresolved trauma.

Lindiwe, a 34-year-old corporate manager in Johannesburg, is an example of this modern paradox. Highly educated, financially independent, and professionally successful, she appears to have achieved what society says defines fulfillment: career success, social status, and a stable partner. Yet her marriage has become a pressure cooker. Every conversation with her husband feels like a negotiation. Every argument triggers the echoes of her childhood—years of emotional neglect, exposure to parental conflict, and the internalized belief that love is conditional.

Internalized Beliefs and the Trap of Self-Worth

From a young age, Lindiwe absorbed the message that her value was tied to being chosen. "Who will marry you?" relatives asked. "Without a husband, what will people think?" These questions shaped her self-perception. Ending a dependent marriage, therefore, is not just a logistical or financial decision—it triggers existential anxiety.

According to Eric Fromm, true love requires freedom, self-awareness, and the ability to give without need.

When people are conditioned to believe their worth hinges on marriage, they confuse survival with love.

Lindiwe struggles with this daily.

Even though her husband no longer respects her boundaries, she hesitates to leave.

The fear of social judgment, of returning to loneliness, of failing to meet the invisible checklist of success, keeps her trapped. This is the essence of what Branny Mthelebofu calls *Emotional Indigestion*: unresolved internal conflicts, unexpressed anger, and suppressed desire for autonomy, which manifest not only as psychological strain but also as physical symptoms—high blood pressure, insomnia, and chronic stress, all risk factors for diabetes and obesity.

Projection Patterns and Freud's Influence

Sigmund Freud's theories provide insight into why Lindiwe remains entangled in her marriage. The interplay of the id, ego, and superego creates a psychological landscape where unmet childhood needs are projected onto adult partners. Lindiwe's ego attempts to mediate between her deep desire for unconditional acceptance (id) and the moralized, socially enforced idea that a woman's worth is tied to marriage (superego).

Her husband, meanwhile, unconsciously carries his own projections—fear of inadequacy, pressure to be the provider, and unresolved trauma from his own family.

Both are trapped in a feedback loop: each partner unconsciously reenacts childhood conflicts through the marriage.

Freud suggests that without conscious recognition of these patterns, individuals will continue to repeat them, mistaking familiarity for love.

In Lindiwe's case, she often finds herself defending behaviors she dislikes or tolerating disrespect, projecting her longing for parental approval onto her spouse. She perceives his attention or avoidance as validation, feeding her dependency, while her physical and mental health quietly deteriorates.

Societal Pressure and Cultural Context

Beyond the personal, societal pressures weigh heavily. In Makholeng, as in Johannesburg's high-rise apartments or New York's corporate towers, failure to maintain a marriage is stigmatized. Women face whispers, judgment, or pity. Men experience diminished social status or perceived loss of control.

These external pressures reinforce internal dependency, making separation feel not only impossible but morally wrong.

Cultural and religious institutions often reinforce these patterns.

Churches, community gatherings, and even corporate cultures reward endurance over self-care. Lindiwe recalls advice from a well-meaning pastor: *"Marriage is a sacred bond; don't abandon it for personal comfort."* While intended as guidance, it amplified her fear of happiness, cementing the belief that self-fulfillment is secondary to duty.

Rural Therapy Methods in the 21st Century

Branny Mthelebofu's rural therapy method, *Emotional Indigestions*, offers a framework for addressing these challenges even when formal therapy is rejected. The method emphasizes:

Narrative Sharing

Participants recount their life stories within a safe circle, externalizing internalized beliefs and recognizing patterns.

Lindiwe, for example, shared her childhood experiences of neglect and societal pressure, discovering parallels with other women.

Somatic Awareness

Recognizing physical symptoms of suppressed emotion—tight chest, stomach tension, sleep disturbances—and linking them to specific relational stressors.

Freedom of Self Exercises (Fromm-Inspired)

Practicing daily decisions that honor personal choice without fear of judgment. This could be as simple as taking time alone, pursuing hobbies, or asserting boundaries at work and home.

Projection Identification

Using group dialogue and reflective journaling to identify where childhood needs are projected onto partners. Participants explore alternative ways to meet those needs independently.

Community Integration

In rural villages, the method encourages social support, mentorship, and safe spaces that validate autonomy rather than enforce conformity.

For women in urban centers, this translates into peer support groups, mindful therapy practices, and structured mentorship programs.

The goal is the same: reclaim autonomy, reduce dependency, and foster authentic love.

Practical Application for Health and Well-Being

The physical health aspect cannot be ignored. Chronic stress from unresolved *Emotional Indigestion* contributes to high blood pressure, obesity, diabetes, and cardiovascular disease. Lindiwe's daily practices now include:

Mindful Movement: Yoga, walking, or dance to release emotional tension.

Nutritional Awareness: Mindful eating to counter stress-related metabolic disorders.

Reflective Journaling: Daily acknowledgment of feelings and autonomous decisions.

Boundary Reinforcement: Small, daily assertions to reclaim control over her emotional space.

By integrating psychological insight with physical care, the method recognizes that dependency syndrome is both a mental and bodily phenomenon. Healing requires attention to both.

In modern contexts, healing from dependency syndrome demands more than intellectual insight—it requires the body and mind to work in harmony.

Consider the young woman navigating life in a bustling township, or the corporate executive juggling deadlines and societal expectations; both carry emotional tension that is often unacknowledged but palpably affects their physical well-being.

One way to address this tension is through mindful movement.

Practices such as yoga, walking through quiet streets, or expressive dance allow the body to release stress accumulated over years of internalized pressure.

These activities are not mere physical exercises; they become a language through which the body communicates unresolved emotional burdens.

As readers, one might ask themselves: in my daily life, how often do I allow my body to release what my mind cannot yet name? How does my posture, gait, or even restlessness signal unresolved dependency or suppressed fear?

Equally important is nutritional awareness, which is often overlooked in discussions about emotional dependency.

Food becomes both sustenance and a mirror of the self. Stress-related metabolic issues, including obesity and diabetes, are frequently physical manifestations of unprocessed psychological trauma.

By practicing mindful eating, individuals begin to observe their patterns: Are we eating out of hunger, or out of a desire to soothe anxiety, loneliness, or fear of abandonment? Do our food choices reflect self-care or self-neglect? These questions prompt a deeper recognition that dependency syndrome is as much a physiological phenomenon as it is psychological.

Reflective journaling offers another avenue for reclaiming agency. Writing daily—acknowledging emotions, decisions made autonomously, or moments when one succumbs to societal pressure—creates a mirror for the mind. This practice encourages individuals to confront their projections, revisit childhood lessons internalized without awareness, and examine the subtle ways dependency manifests in relationships.

The act of recording one's thoughts can be transformative, prompting readers to question: Which choices are truly mine, and which are echoes of fear or cultural expectation?

Finally, reinforcing boundaries through small, daily assertions allows for the gradual reclamation of emotional space. Saying "no" when necessary, expressing discomfort, or choosing personal time may seem trivial in isolation, yet they constitute a radical act of self-sovereignty for someone conditioned to subordinate their needs.

These small acts accumulate, strengthening the capacity to maintain emotional autonomy even in challenging relational dynamics.

By integrating these approaches, the method recognizes that dependency syndrome cannot be addressed solely through introspection or therapy; it requires a holistic engagement with both mind and body. Healing is iterative, reflective, and embodied. It invites the reader not only to observe patterns of thought and behavior but also to feel and act differently within their own lives. In doing so, one begins to cultivate a sense of freedom—freedom of thought, movement, and emotional expression—that is the cornerstone of authentic love, self-respect, and psychological resilience.

Toward Authentic Freedom and Capacity to Love

The 21st-century woman, whether in a rural village, corporate office, or cosmopolitan city, faces pressures unique to her context. Dependency syndrome is amplified by societal expectations, internalized beliefs, and projections from unresolved trauma. Freud illuminates the mechanisms; Fromm inspires the possibility of freedom; Branny Mthelebofu's rural therapy approach provides practical tools for those unwilling or unable to attend conventional therapy.

Lindiwe's story demonstrates that the capacity to love authentically begins with self-freedom.

True love, as Fromm explains, is an active, conscious choice—a union of two whole, autonomous individuals, not a survival strategy. By understanding projections, releasing internalized pressures, and addressing both emotional and physical health, individuals can break the cycle of dependency, reclaim autonomy, and embrace genuine happiness—even in the most restrictive social or cultural environments.

Chapter 31: Men, Dependency, and Emotional Indigestion – Breaking the Invisible Chains

In the dusty township of Alexandra, 38-year-old Themba wakes before dawn. His small flat is cluttered, a reflection of his inner turmoil. Despite a stable job in a corporate office downtown, a car he barely uses, and a partner who appears loving on the surface, Themba feels trapped. The pressures of masculinity, success, and societal expectations weigh on him heavily.

The Silent Burden of Dependency

Unlike the stereotypical image of men as emotionally unshakable, many men live in silent struggle.

Themba's dependency is subtle, often unnoticed by peers:

Financial Dependence on Status

He feels compelled to maintain an image of wealth and control, partly to validate himself and partly to satisfy his partner and social circles.

Fear of Vulnerability

Opening up emotionally risks judgment, ridicule, or perceived weakness. He has learned that expressing needs or insecurities is socially forbidden.

Projection of Childhood Trauma

Freud's framework explains that Themba projects unresolved needs from an absent, critical father and an emotionally distant mother onto his partner. Every argument echoes those childhood wounds, reinforcing patterns of anxiety and fear.

Like many men, Themba remains in a marriage that erodes his sense of self. Fromm's philosophy of freedom and love offers a lifeline: the capacity to love is intrinsically linked to the ability to be free within oneself. When autonomy is sacrificed for social approval or to escape fear, love becomes a transaction rather than a union.

Cultural and Societal Pressures

Themba's experience is not unique. Across South African townships, rural villages in Limpopo, or urban neighborhoods in New York, societal pressures shape men's emotional lives:

Masculinity Expectations

Men are expected to be providers, stoic, and dominant. Failure in these roles is perceived as weakness.

Marriage as Social Proof

Remaining in a marriage—regardless of unhappiness—signals stability, responsibility, and conformity. Divorce or separation is stigmatized.

Corporate and Professional Pressures

In high-pressure jobs, emotional needs are sidelined. Men like Themba may cope with alcohol, overeating, or overworking, masking emotional distress that contributes to *Emotional Indigestion*.

These pressures create a feedback loop: societal expectations reinforce dependency, which in turn erodes mental and physical health. Themba experiences insomnia, high blood pressure, and weight gain—physical manifestations of unprocessed emotional conflict.

Rural and Urban Therapy Approaches

Branny Mthelebofu's *Emotional Indigestion* can be adapted for men, both rural and urban.

Practical steps include:

Group Reflectionz

Men share personal histories in confidential spaces, revealing projections, internalized beliefs, and patterns of dependency.

Somatic Therapy

Recognizing bodily symptoms of emotional strain—tight chest, neck stiffness, digestive issues—and linking them to specific stressors in relationships.

Freedom of Self Exercises (Fromm-Inspired)

Daily practices that encourage autonomy: setting personal boundaries, making independent choices, and acknowledging one's own needs.

Projection Recognition

Journaling and mentorship help men identify where childhood trauma is projected onto partners, colleagues, and themselves.

Community Integration

Peer support networks reduce isolation, normalize vulnerability, and encourage authentic self-expression.

In Themba's journey, weekly circles provided safe spaces to explore his father's absence, societal pressures, and the fears that kept him trapped. Over time, he learned that self-worth is not dependent on fulfilling societal roles but on acknowledging and embracing his authentic self.

Practical Health Interventions

Dependency syndrome has a profound impact on men's physical health.

Chronic stress, untreated anxiety, and repressed emotions contribute to:

Hypertension and cardiovascular disease

Diabetes and metabolic disorders

Obesity and digestive issues

Insomnia and chronic fatigue

Themba incorporated simple practices into his routine:

Mindful Movement: Daily walks, yoga, or boxing to release tension.

Nutritional Awareness: Addressing emotional eating linked to stress.

Reflective Journaling: Writing daily reflections on autonomy, emotional projections, and relationship dynamics.

Boundary Setting: Practicing assertive communication and personal decision-making in both home and workplace.

These steps allowed him to reduce *Emotional Indigestion*, reclaim freedom, and create space for authentic love—not dependent on fear, social validation, or survival needs.

The Art of Freedom and Love for Men

Just as Lindiwe's story highlights the female experience, Themba's narrative illuminates the male side of dependency syndrome. Freud's theories explain the psychological mechanics, Fromm provides a vision of freedom and authentic love, and Branny Mthelebofu's practical rural therapy model offers tangible steps for emotional healing.

Dependency in marriage is not merely a personal problem—it is a social, cultural, and psychological phenomenon that affects health, well-being, and relationships. Men and women alike must recognize projections, confront societal pressures, and cultivate freedom within themselves to love authentically.

The journey is neither easy nor linear, but through awareness, practical exercises, and community support, men and women can break the cycles of dependency, reclaim autonomy, and heal emotionally, physically, and spiritually.

2. Therapy as a Tool, Not a Trap

While therapy has sometimes been criticized as a "constraint" on natural self-exploration, it can serve as a structured tool to process trauma and guide identity reconstruction:

Trauma Processing

Therapy provides a safe space to explore past abuse, neglect, or emotional manipulation. Techniques like EMDR (Eye Movement Desensitization and Reprocessing) and CBT (Cognitive Behavioral Therapy) can reduce residual trauma impacts.

Self-Exploration

Guided sessions help uncover

authentic desires, values, and life goals that were overshadowed by dependency patterns.

Boundary Reconstruction

Individuals learn to establish and maintain healthy personal and relational boundaries.

Alternative Approaches

For those wary of traditional therapy, culturally-sensitive mentors, support groups, spiritual counseling, and structured self-help programs can provide similar guidance while respecting autonomy.

3. Practical Steps to Rebuild Identity

Self-Reflection and Journaling

Identify habits, beliefs, and patterns formed by dependency. Track emotional triggers and instances of autonomy.

Reclaim Personal Interests

Re-engage with hobbies, passions, and activities that nurture individuality and confidence.

Set Clear Goals

Financial independence, career development, and social engagement rebuild self-esteem and provide structure.

Social Reintegration

Reconnect with family, friends, or supportive communities who validate identity without reinforcing dependency.

Mindfulness and Meditation

Cultivate emotional regulation, present-moment awareness, and self-compassion.

1. Emotional Resilience and Coping

Handling Loneliness

Being alone after a dependent marriage is a necessary stage. Embrace solitude as a learning space for self-discovery rather than a void to be filled.

Managing Anxiety and Shame

Many individuals experience shame or societal judgment. Cognitive restructuring and affirmations help reshape negative beliefs.

Developing Coping Skills

Exercise, creative expression, volunteer work, and skill-building provide outlets for stress and reinforce self-efficacy.

Chapter 32 Exercise: Building Emotional Resilience After Dependency

Recovering from dependency, especially after a marriage built on survival rather than choice, is rarely a linear process.

Emotional wounds linger, identity feels fragmented, and societal pressure amplifies shame or anxiety.

This exercise provides practical tools to cultivate emotional resilience, restore autonomy, and develop coping strategies—tools that readers can integrate into daily life.

1. Handling Loneliness: Learning to Be Alone

The Story:

Nandi, a 32-year-old woman from Khayelitsha, spent a decade in a marriage where her choices were shaped by fear of abandonment. After leaving, she felt an overwhelming emptiness. Initially, she viewed solitude as punishment, a reminder of failure. But over time, she began to see her alone time as a classroom, a space to rediscover who she truly was beyond relational expectations.

Exercise:

Daily Reflection Window

Spend 15–30 minutes each day in solitude. Observe thoughts without judgment. Ask yourself: *"Who am I when no one is watching? What brings me joy independent of others?"*

Embrace Rituals

Create small daily rituals—morning tea, walking in a garden, listening to music—that celebrate your presence without external validation.

Journaling Prompt

Write three new things you learn about yourself each week. Identify patterns of strength, curiosity, or creativity that emerge in solitude.

2. Managing Anxiety and Shame: Cognitive Restructuring

The Story:

Tariq, a corporate manager in Johannesburg, ended a co-dependent marriage after eight years. Despite his professional success, he felt constant judgment from colleagues and family. Shame compounded his anxiety, triggering sleep disturbances and loss of appetite. By challenging his inner dialogue and consciously reframing beliefs, he began reclaiming mental freedom.

Exercise:

Thought Awareness

Identify recurring self-critical or shame-inducing thoughts (e.g., *"I am incomplete without a partner"*).

Reframe and Affirm

Replace each thought with evidence-based affirmations (e.g., *"I am whole, and my worth is not dependent on another person"*). Repeat aloud, morning and night.

Visualization Technique

Imagine stepping outside a judgmental crowd and entering a space where your decisions are honored. Notice the physical sensations of relief and freedom.

3. Developing Coping Skills: Engaging Body, Mind, and Community

The Story:

Amara, from New York City, struggled to navigate life after leaving a toxic relationship. Loneliness and residual trauma fueled emotional eating and sedentary habits. Integrating movement, creativity, and service into her routine gradually reshaped her mental and physical well-being. She discovered that resilience was cultivated through small, consistent acts of self-care.

Exercise:

Mindful Movement

Commit to daily movement, whether yoga, walking, or dancing. Focus on how your body feels rather than on appearance or performance. Reflect afterward: *"What tension did I release? How does my body feel connected to my emotions?"*

Creative Expression

Engage in painting, writing, music, or crafting for 30–60 minutes daily. Allow expression of unresolved feelings without self-criticism.

Volunteer or Skill-Build

Identify a community project, workshop, or skill-building course. Active contribution fosters autonomy and reinforces your sense of competence and purpose.

4. Integration and Self-Assessment

At the end of each week, pause to assess your emotional state:

- What patterns of dependency or fear surfaced?
- Which coping strategies brought relief or clarity?
- How did solitude, affirmation, and active engagement shift your internal dialogue?

By consciously combining reflection, physical care, creative expression, and community engagement, individuals can gradually break cycles of dependency and build resilience.

As Fromm emphasizes in *The Art of Loving*, freedom of self is a prerequisite for authentic love—not only for others but for oneself.

Jung's notion of individuation aligns here: confronting shadow aspects and projecting conscious awareness fosters integration of mind, body, and spirit.

5. Redefining Relationships

Choosing Partners Consciously

Rebuilding identity allows individuals to select partners based on compatibility, shared values, and mutual respect—not survival or societal expectation.

Healthy Interdependence

Relationships should complement identity, not define it. Mutual growth, support, and autonomy become core pillars.

Setting Realistic Expectations

Understanding one's emotional needs and boundaries prevents re-entering dependency patterns.

6. Cultural and Global Considerations

Context Matters

Dependency and identity challenges vary across cultures. In African contexts, societal expectations for marriage are strong, while in Western urban settings, pressures may stem from professional success and social image.

Learning from Global Patterns

Comparing approaches in New York, Nigeria, Mozambique, and other regions shows that rebuilding identity requires balancing cultural expectations with personal growth. Empowerment, mentorship, and social support remain universal solutions.

Cultural and Global Considerations

Understanding dependency syndrome and the challenges of identity requires acknowledging the profound influence of culture and context. In many African communities, the expectation to marry is deeply ingrained.

From rural villages in Limpopo to township settlements like Khayelitsha and Alexandra, young women and men grow up absorbing a clear social script: securing a partner is not only a personal milestone but also a pathway to social respect, safety, and even survival.

These expectations shape behaviors long before adulthood, creating patterns of dependency that are reinforced by extended families, religious teachings, and community norms.

In contrast, urban Western settings such as New York or London present a different set of pressures. Here, the emphasis may not be survival or family expectation, but professional achievement, social image, and the perceived "success" of relationships.

Even highly educated women and men, thriving in corporate or academic spheres, may find themselves caught in dependency patterns, driven by the fear of loneliness or societal judgment.

In both contexts, whether in an African village or a Manhattan high-rise, the underlying struggle is similar: individuals seek validation outside themselves, often sacrificing authenticity and emotional health to meet external expectations.

Looking beyond borders provides a unique perspective. Observing patterns in Nigeria, Mozambique, Brazil, or urban

Western cities shows that rebuilding identity requires balancing cultural norms with personal growth.

While the pressures differ—poverty, family honor, or professional image—the universal strategies remain strikingly similar. Empowerment programs, mentorship opportunities, and consistent social support networks are crucial.

Whether a woman in Lagos learning financial independence or a man in New York confronting emotional vulnerability, the path to freedom begins with understanding the interplay between societal pressures and internalized beliefs.

7. The Role of Self-Compassion

Forgiving Past Choices

Recognize that dependency was often a survival response, not a personal failing.

Embracing Growth

Celebrate progress, however incremental, and view setbacks as learning opportunities.

Internal Validation

Cultivate self-worth that is independent of external approval or romantic validation.

The Role of Self-Compassion

Recovery from dependency and the reconstruction of self-identity begins with cultivating self-compassion. It requires a shift in perspective: recognizing that past choices, including staying in dependent or toxic relationships, were often survival responses rather than personal failings. Nandi, a young woman from Khayelitsha, once blamed herself for every failed relationship, believing she was weak or undeserving of love. Over time, she began to understand that her decisions were shaped by circumstances—poverty, trauma, and social expectations—and that forgiving herself was the first step toward freedom.

Self-compassion also involves embracing growth in all its forms.

Progress is rarely linear; setbacks are inevitable, but they are not failures—they are opportunities to learn and refine one's understanding of self.

Each step toward emotional autonomy, no matter how small, is a victory. Reflecting on her journey, Nandi learned to celebrate even the simplest achievements: setting a boundary, asserting a preference, or choosing solitude over compromise.

Finally, internal validation becomes the cornerstone of lasting change. Cultivating a sense of self-worth independent of external approval or romantic validation is essential. By affirming their intrinsic value, individuals can begin to engage in relationships not out of fear or obligation but from authentic desire.

When Tariq in Johannesburg learned to honor his own needs and feelings, he discovered that love no longer demanded surrendering his identity. Self-compassion, therefore, is not merely a therapeutic exercise—it is the foundation for freedom, resilience, and the ability to love both oneself and others authentically.

Rebuilding identity after marriage dependency is a multifaceted process requiring awareness, self-compassion, and deliberate action. By processing trauma, reclaiming autonomy, and reconstructing emotional resilience, individuals can emerge with a stronger sense of self, prepared to engage in healthy, mutually supportive relationships. True freedom and fulfillment come from understanding that love and partnership are extensions of identity—not substitutes for it.

Chapter 33: The Fear of Happiness – Zinhle's Journey

Zinhle stared at her reflection in the cracked bathroom mirror, her eyes tired, her shoulders slumped. At twenty-nine, she had lived a life that most people only whispered about. Born in a rural village outside Johannesburg, she had left home at fourteen after years of neglect, witnessing violence, and sleeping in rooms that were never truly hers. With no education and no family support, she had learned quickly that survival often came at the cost of her dignity. For years, survival had meant trading her body for money, safety, and fleeting moments of care.

Now, she lived with Sibusiso, a man she barely knew but who had promised security. On paper, their life looked stable—food on the table, a small rented apartment, a neighbor who nodded politely. But inside, Zinhle felt suffocated. Sibusiso's moods swung violently; some nights he was affectionate, and others he shouted over imagined slights.

Zinhle had learned to anticipate his anger, to shrink herself into corners, to silence her needs. She was trapped—not just physically, but emotionally and psychologically.

Her fear of happiness was invisible to most, yet constant. Whenever a quiet moment settled over their apartment—when the dishes were done, the sun streamed through the curtains, and nothing urgent demanded her attention—panic began to rise in her chest. Happiness felt dangerous. Being content, even briefly, triggered memories of vulnerability, exposure, and loss. She feared that joy might demand change, or worse, make her visible and unsafe.

Understanding the Trap

Zinhle's life illustrated the pattern Branny Mthelebofu calls *Emotional Indigestion*: the body and mind carry unresolved trauma that manifests as chronic stress, anxiety, and even physical illness. Every fear she swallowed—the shame, the anger, the longing—stayed lodged in her chest, tightening around her heart like an invisible vice.

Her story was not uncommon. Many uneducated women, and even some men, become trapped in survival-based relationships.

Dependency becomes normalized: safety, food, and shelter outweigh emotional health or personal freedom. The trauma of early life—neglect, abuse, exposure to violence—creates a psychological habit of seeking security in others, even at the cost of autonomy.

Psychologists like Sigmund Freud would say Zinhle's ego had adapted to survive, building defense mechanisms to manage anxiety. Carl Jung might suggest that her shadow—the parts of herself she feared or repressed—was influencing every decision she made, keeping her in a loop of repetitive harm.

Eric Fromm would argue that true freedom of love requires conscious choice, not fear-driven survival.

The First Step Toward Freedom

Change began the day Zinhle met Lerato, a volunteer at a local women's center. Lerato didn't scold her. She didn't demand that Zinhle leave Sibusiso immediately. Instead, she spoke about agency, safety, and self-compassion. "You may not be able to leave yet," Lerato said gently, "but you can start to reclaim your heart and your mind."

Lerato taught Zinhle a simple daily ritual:

Sit quietly, hand on your chest.

Breathe slowly in for four counts, hold for four, exhale for four. Repeat five times.

Name one small thing you did today for yourself—ate a full meal, washed your hair, spoke your mind.

Close your eyes and imagine a bubble of protection around your heart, impenetrable by anger or judgment.

At first, Zinhle felt foolish. But over weeks, the panic that had always accompanied moments of calm began to lessen. She could breathe without expecting an emotional storm to follow. Slowly, she began to experience fleeting moments of joy—sunlight on her skin, laughter at a neighbor's joke, the satisfaction of completing a task. Each moment, no matter how small, became a seed of resilicnce.

Redefining Safety and Control

Zinhle also learned mental separation techniques.

When Sibusiso yelled, she visualized his anger as separate from her own heart. She refused to internalize blame. She gave herself permission to feel, to think, to plan for her future—even while living in the same apartment with a man who could harm her emotionally.

She started journaling, writing letters to herself as her own protector. "You are not what happened to you," she wrote repeatedly. "You are more than survival. You deserve choice, safety, and peace."

Practical Strategies for Those Who Cannot Leave Yet

Protect your emotional space – Use visualization and breathing to maintain inner calm.

✓ Micro-choices matter – Eating properly, walking outside, reading a book—small acts of autonomy reinforce self-worth.

✓ Document trauma – Journaling or storytelling helps process what happened without becoming overwhelmed.

✓ Build a support network – Community centres, friends, volunteers, or counselors can provide guidance even if immediate escape isn't possible.

✓ Reframe dependency – Recognize it as survival, not moral failure.

The Turn Toward Hope

Months passed, and Zinhle began to feel a subtle but profound shift. The fear of happiness no longer ruled her mind. Her heart ached less at the thought of joy. She could laugh without guilt, rest without terror, and imagine a life where her choices were hers alone. She still lived with Sibusiso, but she had learned that freedom of the mind comes before freedom of circumstance.

By reclaiming small measures of autonomy and healing her *emotional indigestion*, Zinhle had not only preserved her mental and physical health, but also laid the groundwork for eventual escape or reconciliation on her own terms. She had begun to understand

Fromm's idea of love as freedom—a love that does not bind through fear, but builds through choice.

Reflection Exercise for Readers: Emotional Freedom Within Constraints

Breathing and Visualization – Place a hand on your heart, breathe deeply, and imagine your fear separating from your body.

✓ Micro-acts of Agency – Identify one thing today you can do for yourself without approval or permission.

✓ Write a Protective Letter – Speak to yourself as a guardian, validating your courage and choices.

✓ Plan a Step Toward Independence – Even if small, think of one actionable step to increase safety or autonomy.

Chapter 34: Shackled by Expectations – Sipho's Silent Struggle

Sipho adjusted the tie he didn't like but knew his colleagues admired. From the outside, his life seemed enviable: a decent job in Johannesburg's bustling financial district, a spacious apartment, and a partner, Lerato, who was admired by their friends for her beauty and charm. Yet beneath the surface, Sipho felt hollow.

Raised in a crowded township, Sipho had learned early that a man's worth was measured by provision. His father was often absent, leaving him to navigate a violent neighborhood and unstable home alone. He learned to suppress emotions, hide fear, and perform the role society demanded: the strong, unemotional man.

Love, tenderness, and vulnerability were luxuries he could not afford.

The Trap of Dependency in Men

Sipho's relationship with Lerato had begun with excitement, laughter, and shared dreams. But soon, the pressure of societal expectation weighed heavily.

Friends, family, and even coworkers reminded him—subtly or openly—that he should *settle down*, buy property, and maintain the image of success. The marriage became less about connection and more about performance, a shield against judgment.

Even with a stable job, Sipho felt dependent—dependent on Lerato to validate his worth, dependent on appearances to mask his fear of inadequacy. He could not show weakness, cry, or voice dissatisfaction.

Each argument left him more anxious, yet leaving felt impossible. He feared losing status, control, and the illusion of a normal life.

Psychological Roots of Male Dependency

Freud's theory of the ego, id, and superego helps explain Sipho's inner conflict. His superego—the internalized voice of society—demanded success, stoicism, and control. His id craved connection, intimacy, and freedom to express vulnerability. The ego struggled to mediate these opposing forces, often failing, leaving Sipho trapped in emotional paralysis.

Carl Jung would note that Sipho's shadow—the suppressed emotions and unacknowledged trauma—was manifesting through anxiety, irritability, and a compulsion to maintain outward appearances. He lived in conflict with his own needs, unknowingly projecting inner fears onto his partner.

Eric Fromm's idea of the **Freedom of Love** offers a pathway out: true love requires choice, self-awareness, and emotional autonomy. Sipho's struggle illustrated the opposite: love as a performance, constrained by fear, obligation, and social pressure.

Living With Emotional Indigestion

Sipho's physical health mirrored his inner turmoil. Chronic stress manifested in insomnia, elevated blood pressure, and heart palpitations. Branny Mthelebofu's concept of *Emotional Indigestion* described this exact phenomenon: unresolved trauma and unexpressed feelings create psychosomatic distress, eroding mental and physical well-being.

He had stayed silent for years, believing that enduring was strength. Yet every day, the weight of repression grew heavier. Arguments with Lerato left him numb.

Moments of joy felt foreign, even dangerous, triggering guilt or fear. He feared happiness, because it demanded authenticity he felt unprepared to claim.

Practical Steps Toward Emotional Freedom

One evening, Sipho met Thabo, an older mentor who had faced similar struggles. Thabo didn't offer solutions, only guidance:

Internal Dialogue – Begin each day by

acknowledging one suppressed emotion: fear, sadness, longing, or anger. Speak it silently, without judgment.

Micro-acts of Autonomy – Make small decisions independently of Lerato, such as planning meals, managing finances, or taking a personal day. These build confidence and self-trust.

Physical Expression – Exercise, walk, or move the body to release stress and prevent the mind from becoming a prison.

Boundary Setting – Clearly define emotional limits with Lerato. For example, agree to step away during arguments to prevent escalation.

Therapeutic Reflection – Journaling, meditation, or conversations with trusted mentors to process the past and present.

A Turning Point

Sipho's breakthrough came gradually. One Sunday, sitting on the balcony overlooking the city, he realized that happiness did not require approval. It did not demand perfection, social validation, or constant performance. He could feel joy quietly, safely, within himself.

He began practicing Fromm's **Freedom of Love**: embracing connection with Lerato without needing her to complete him, loving her as a choice rather than a dependency. Slowly, emotional indigestion eased. He felt more energetic, focused, and alive. He had not changed his circumstances entirely—he still worked, still lived in the same apartment, still maintained social appearances—but his internal freedom allowed him to thrive.

Reflection Exercise for Male Readers

Name Your Suppressed Emotions *– Identify one feeling you've ignored today.*

Assert One Small Boundary *– Practice saying no, or taking a step for yourself without guilt.*

Engage the Body *– Walk, run, or stretch for 15–20 minutes to release tension.*

Practice Freedom of Love *– Reflect on a relationship where you feel dependent. Consider how love could exist as a choice, not obligation.*

Journal a Daily Victory *– Record one action that honored your autonomy or well-being.*

Closing Note

Sipho's journey shows that men, too, experience dependency syndrome. It is not always about financial reliance; often, it is about emotional captivity, social expectation, and fear of vulnerability. By cultivating awareness, setting boundaries, and reclaiming inner freedom, men can heal, thrive, and experience authentic love—even within the constraints of modern life.

Chapter 35: Breaking the Intergenerational Cycle – How Families and Societies Can Prevent Dependency Syndrome

Chapter summary - Reclaiming the Self

The final chapter brings the themes together, guiding the reader toward reclaiming identity, agency, and emotional autonomy. It focuses on practical and psychological steps for rebuilding life after emotional fragmentation: creating boundaries, developing a sense of self separate from others, reconnecting with the body, seeking therapy or traditional healing when needed, and cultivating meaningful social support. The chapter ends with a message of empowerment: healing is not a return to the person one used to be but the creation of someone wiser, stronger, and deeply aware of their emotional landscape.

Introduction

This chapter examines how societies can intervene, using scientific insights from psychology, sociology, and cultural studies, to prevent dependency from becoming the default survival strategy.

Dependency syndrome in marriage is not just an individual problem; it is often a reflection of intergenerational trauma, social norms, and structural inequality.

The patterns that create dependency—poverty, emotional neglect, early exposure to adult behaviours, and societal pressure to marry—are frequently passed down from one generation to the next. Breaking this cycle requires a multifaceted approach, involving families, communities, educational systems, and government policies.

1. Understanding the Transmission of Dependency

Family Dynamics

Children raised in homes with unresolved trauma, poor communication, and overemphasis on marriage as a survival tool internalize dependency patterns. Girls see marriage as the ultimate solution to poverty and instability, while boys may adopt controlling behaviors or fear vulnerability in relationships.

Cultural Reinforcement

Societal norms glorify marriage as a measure of success. Families, religious institutions, and media often reinforce the idea that life is incomplete without a partner, creating pressure to marry regardless of readiness.

Psychological Projection

According to Freud's psychoanalytic theory, unresolved conflicts from childhood—manifesting in the id, ego, and superego—shape relational expectations. Children project unmet needs onto future partners, replicating the dependency they observed in parental figures.

2. Early Intervention: Education and Awareness

Life Skills and Emotional Education

Schools can incorporate programs that teach emotional intelligence, healthy boundaries, self-esteem, and financial literacy. These programs empower children to view marriage as a choice rather than a necessity for survival.

Sexual Education

Comprehensive sexual education helps adolescents understand consent, sexual health, and identity formation, reducing early pregnancies and coerced relationships.

Mentorship Programs

Positive role models—both male and female—can demonstrate alternative pathways to stability and self-fulfillment, breaking the cycle of marrying solely for survival.

3. Family-Based Strategies

Parental Guidance

Parents who model healthy relationships, emotional expression, and autonomy provide children with frameworks for independence.

Open Communication

Encouraging dialogue about emotions, relationships, and personal ambitions prevents children from internalizing fear and secrecy as norms.

Supportive Structures

Families that emphasize education, skill-building, and personal growth create environments where marriage is a choice, not an escape.

4. Community and Societal Interventions

Economic Empowerment

Access to microfinance, vocational training, and entrepreneurship reduces the economic pressure to marry early. Women and men with financial independence are less likely to enter survival-driven marriages.

Social Campaigns

Media and community programs can redefine success and self-worth, portraying marriage as one of many fulfilling life paths rather than the ultimate goal.

Safe Spaces for Youth

Youth centers, recreational programs, and counseling hubs provide alternatives to early dependency by fostering social and emotional development.

5. Policy-Level Solutions

Child Protection and Housing

Reducing overcrowded living conditions and providing child-safe housing minimizes exposure to trauma and early sexualization.

Education Access

Governments ensuring universal access to quality education help young women and men envision futures independent of marriage dependency.

Healthcare and Mental Health Services

Accessible therapy, counseling, and reproductive health services equip youth and adults to process trauma and make informed decisions about relationships.

6. Redefining Cultural Narratives

Challenging Gender Norms

Promoting equality in domestic responsibilities, financial contributions, and decision-making reduces the societal pressure that drives dependency.

Celebrating Independent Success

Communities should recognize achievements in career, education, personal growth, and social impact, alongside marital milestones.

Intergenerational Dialogue

Facilitating conversations between elders and youth about historical practices, modern challenges, and evolving gender roles encourages critical reflection and change.

1. **The Role of Therapy and Self-Discovery in Prevention**

Preventive Counseling

Therapy should not only be reactive but proactive, equipping adolescents and young adults to navigate relationships without replicating dependency patterns.

Trauma-Informed Practices

Programs designed to address early childhood trauma reduce the risk of dependency forming in adulthood.

Building Emotional Autonomy: Teaching skills like assertiveness, self-reflection, and emotional regulation fosters independent decision-making.

Breaking the intergenerational cycle of dependency syndrome requires a holistic approach that combines individual healing, family support, community engagement, and systemic policy interventions.

By empowering children with education, safe spaces, emotional intelligence, and alternative pathways to self-worth, societies can ensure that marriage becomes a choice, not a survival strategy.

Through conscious effort, communities can foster generations who enter relationships from a place of self-awareness, emotional maturity, and freedom—transforming dependency into autonomy, and survival-driven bonds into partnerships rooted in love and mutual growth.

The Psychological Dimensions of Dependency

Dependency syndrome in marriage is not solely an economic issue. It involves deep emotional wounds formed during childhood:

- ✓ lack of parental love,
- ✓ witnessing violence or substance abuse,
- ✓ observing unhealthy relationships,
- ✓ experiencing neglect or emotional abandonment,
- ✓ unresolved confusion around sex and identity.

Without healing, people unknowingly recreate the same wounds in adulthood. Freud's psychoanalytic theory on the id, ego, and superego helps us understand this cycle: individuals who grow up without stability internalise fear, longing, and confusion.

These feelings shape how they choose partners, how they stay in harmful relationships, and how they define their identity.

Identity Confusion and the Search for Belonging

Identity problems have become increasingly common among young people, especially those raised in environments marked by instability. Children who grow up without consistent love, without a model of healthy relationships, or in homes full of conflict and noise may struggle to understand who they are or what roles they should play in adulthood.

When young people enter adolescence, they begin choosing identities—sometimes in reaction to trauma rather than in alignment with their authentic selves. Without therapeutic intervention, unresolved childhood pain can lead to confusion around gender roles, sexuality, spirituality, or life direction.

The Global Nature of Dependency

Although this book draws heavily from South African contexts, similar patterns are evident in countries such as Brazil, Vietnam, the United States, Russia, and Australia.

Poverty, traumatic home environments, or boarding-home systems can create generations of young adults who search for emotional security through marriage. Marriage becomes a symbol of safety—even when the emotional readiness for it is absent.

The Role of Therapy and Healing

This book argues that therapy—especially individual therapy—is crucial for breaking dependency cycles.

Healing begins with self-honesty: understanding why one entered a relationship, what wounds were carried forward, and how childhood experiences shaped adult choices. Therapy helps individuals rebuild self-esteem, establish boundaries, and develop healthy forms of love that are not rooted in fear or survival.

Healthy marriages require emotional maturity, self-awareness, and the capacity to give and receive love. When couples reach this point, they can renew their vows emotionally, seeing each other not as escape routes but as partners.

Reclaiming Love and Identity

Dependency syndrome in marriage is not a moral failing—it is a psychological, cultural, and economic response to difficult circumstances. To break this cycle, society must encourage healing, emotional education, and safe spaces for self-discovery.

Women and men must learn to redefine marriage from an escape to a partnership. Only then can love become a place of freedom, not dependency.

INDEX LIST

Key Themes in the Book

Marriage Dependency Syndrome
Poverty and Emotional Survival
Cultural Pressure to Marry
Gender Roles in African and Western Societies
Toxic Love Normalization
Mental Health Crisis in Marriage
Economic Vulnerability and Relationships
Sexuality, Trauma, and Identity
Religious Influence on Relationships
Urban vs Rural Relationship Dynamics
Corporate Women and Emotional Burnout
Men's Hidden Emotional Struggles
Emotional Freedom and Self-Healing

Social and Cultural Contexts

African Rural Communities (Limpopo, Bolobedu, Venda)
Christian Churches and Marriage Doctrine
Modern Feminine and Masculine Identities
Mozambique (Traditional Marriage Structures)
New York City (Urban Relationship Stress)
Nigeria (Cultural Marriage Pressure)
Townships (Soweto, Alexandra, Khayelitsha)
Western Marriage Ideals

Health Connections

Depression and Anxiety
Diabetes and Stress
Domestic Violence Trauma Responses
Emotional Fatigue
Obesity and Emotional Eating
Psychosomatic Illness
Stress-Induced Eating Disorders
Substance Abuse (Alcohol as Escape)

Relationship Patterns
Abusive Dynamics and Power Imbalances
Choosing the Same Type of Partner
Co-dependency Cycles
Economic Trap Relationships
Emotional Withdrawal in Men
Fear of Abandonment
Loneliness After Leaving a Marriage
Marrying for Survival vs Love
Shame After Divorce
Staying in Toxic Love

Locations & Case Studies
Johannesburg – Corporate, township, and suburban contrasts
Khayelitsha – Rural-urban poverty patterns
Limpopo Villages – Cultural norms and family pressure
Mozambique – Traditional marriage dynamics
New York City – High-performance relationship pressure
Nigeria – Social expectations and religious norms

Healing Practices
Boundary Building
Building Autonomy
Cognitive Restructuring
Community Support Circles
Journaling and Self-Reflection
Mindful Movement
Narrative Healing
Nutritional Awareness
Self-Compassion Practices
Somatic Healing
Strengthening Internal Validation
Trauma Release Exercises
Village Therapy

New Concepts by Branny Mthelebofu

INDEX LIST WITH DEFINITIONS

A

Abandonment Fear

A deep emotional insecurity rooted in childhood experiences of neglect or inconsistency, leading individuals to cling to unhealthy relationships to avoid feeling alone.

Addictive Love

A compulsive need for emotional connection that mirrors addiction patterns, where the partner becomes a source of relief, validation, and identity.

Attachment Styles

Psychological patterns formed in childhood that shape how individuals relate to partners—secure, anxious, avoidant, or disorganized.

C

Cognitive Restructuring

A therapeutic technique that challenges negative thought patterns and replaces them with healthier beliefs and self-perceptions.

Collective Unconscious (Carl Jung)

The inherited psychological structures shared by all human beings, which influence emotions, relationships, and behavior without conscious awareness.

Co-dependency

A relational pattern where a person becomes overly responsible for another's emotions, often sacrificing their own needs to maintain the relationship.

Cultural Marriage Pressure

Societal expectations that link a woman's or man's value to their marital status, often forcing individuals into unions for acceptance rather than love.

D

Dependency Syndrome

A psychological, emotional, and economic reliance on a partner where identity, survival, and self-worth are tied to the relationship—often resulting in unhealthy attachments.

Dissociation

A coping mechanism where individuals disconnect from their emotions or physical sensations to survive trauma or overwhelming stress.

Divorce Shame

The guilt, stigma, or social judgment experienced after leaving a marriage, often intensified by cultural or religious expectations.

E

Ego (Freud)

The rational part of the mind that balances desires, moral values, and real-world demands; often weakened in individuals raised in chaotic or traumatic homes.

Emotional Burnout

A state of mental and physical exhaustion caused by prolonged emotional stress in relationships, work environments, or family life.

Emotional Indigestion (Branny Mthelebofu)

A condition where unprocessed emotions accumulate—similar to undigested food—resulting in psychological stress, irritability, and psychosomatic illness.

Emotional Resilience

The ability to withstand emotional difficulties and recover from hardships through coping skills, reflection, and self-awareness.

Existential Anxiety

A deep internal fear triggered when individuals confront questions about their purpose, identity, or future—often experienced when leaving a dependent relationship.

F

Fear of Happiness

A subconscious fear of peace or joy due to unprocessed trauma; individuals may sabotage good relationships because stability feels unfamiliar or unsafe.

Freedom of the Mind (Erich Fromm)

A psychological state where individuals detach from societal pressures and relate from genuine self-awareness rather than fear, neediness, or conformity.

I

Identity Confusion

A state where individuals are uncertain about who they are psychologically or socially, often leading them to seek validation from romantic partners.

Id (Freud)

The instinctual part of the psyche driven by desires and impulses such as pleasure, intimacy, and emotional comfort.

Internalized Beliefs

Deep-rooted ideas absorbed from family, culture, or religion that shape an individual's sense of value, relationships, and choices.

J

Jungian Shadow

The hidden part of a person containing traits they deny or suppress, which often drive toxic relationship choices unconsciously.

L

Loneliness Trauma

Emotional discomfort that arises after detaching from a dependent or abusive relationship, where solitude feels threatening rather than healing.

Love as Escape

The belief that romantic relationships can fix financial, emotional, or familial struggles—often leading to dependency.

M

Marriage Syndrome

A societal and psychological condition where individuals feel pressured to marry for status, stability, or identity rather than compatibility or mutual commitment.

Mindful Movement

Physical practices—such as yoga, walking, or dance—used to release emotions stored in the body due to trauma or stress.

P

Projection (Freud)

The unconscious act of placing one's unresolved feelings or wounds onto another person, often creating illusions about partners.

Psychosomatic Illness

Physical health problems caused or worsened by emotional stress, including diabetes, hypertension, obesity, headaches, and heart conditions.

Poverty-Based Attachment

A form of dependency where relationships are chosen for survival—financial security, shelter, food—rather than emotional compatibility.

R

Repetition Compulsion (Freud)

A tendency to repeat destructive relationship patterns in adulthood that mirror childhood wounds, even when the outcome is harmful.

Romantic Idealization

The creation of exaggerated beliefs about a partner, often ignoring red flags or toxic behavior.

S

Self-Compassion

A practice of treating oneself with kindness, patience, and forgiveness, especially after making mistakes or experiencing relationship failures.

Shadow Work

A process of exploring the hidden parts of oneself to break free from unconscious relationship patterns.

Somatic Memory

The body's physical storage of emotional trauma, felt as tension, pain, or illness.

Survival Marriage

A union formed primarily for escape from poverty, abuse, overcrowded homes, or social pressure, rather than emotional compatibility.

T

Trauma Bond

A powerful emotional attachment formed with an abusive or inconsistent partner, reinforced by cycles of pain and intermittent affection.

Toxic Normalization

The cultural acceptance of harmful relationship behaviors, such as emotional neglect, controlling behavior, or financial dependency.

Transgenerational Trauma

The passing down of unprocessed emotional wounds from one generation to another, influencing marriage patterns and identity.

V

Village Therapy (Branny Mthelebofu)

A community-based healing model where cultural storytelling, group reflection, physical movement, and somatic awareness are used as alternatives for individuals who avoid formal therapy.

W

Women's Corporate Burnout

Emotional exhaustion experienced by women working in high-pressure environments who struggle to balance career expectations with societal pressure to marry.

8. Declaration

I declare that there is no conflict of inters in this book.

Did you love *Dependency Syndrome in Marriage*? Then you should read *The Healing We Never Spoke Of: Therapy*[1] by Branny Mthelebofu!

[2]

For professionals, the book acts as a guide for culturally informed therapy, drawing on the works of Freud, Jung, Ferenczi, and integrating film, art, and novel-writing as tools to engage patients creatively. It challenges therapists to listen with cultural humility and emotional curiosity, not clinical distance. What if your sadness isn't just yours—what if it's inherited silence? In the heart of South Africa's villages, and beyond, people carry unspoken burdens—grief that was never named, love that was never returned, questions that were never asked. This is not just a story about therapy—it is a journey into forgotten feelings, buried memories, and the cultural

1. https://books2read.com/u/mZDKx5

2. https://books2read.com/u/mZDKx5

silence that keeps so many from seeking help. It speaks to the widows who never cried, the men who confuse control for love, and the children who inherited pain before they learned to speak. Blending narrative storytelling, psychoanalysis, traditional wisdom, and prayer, this book is a bridge between the modern therapist's couch and the rural fire hearth. Whether you believe in dreams, ancestors, or dialogue—this book invites you to see healing not as betrayal of culture, but as a return to wholeness. Therapy is not introduced as a Western import, but as a tool that can be adapted to fit the language, rhythm, and values of village life.

Read more at https://www.facebook.com/branny.smithsa/.

Also by Branny Mthelebofu

The Healing We Never Spoke Of: Therapy
Emotional Indigestion: Illness Shaping Bodies, Families, and Communities
Emotional Indigestion Illness Shaping Bodies, Families, and Communities
Research and Innovation: Strategies for Managers and Entrepreneurs
Dependency Syndrome in Marriage

Watch for more at https://www.facebook.com/branny.smithsa/.

About the Author

Dr Branny Mthelebofu is a multifaceted South African creative whose work bridges the realms of storytelling, healing, and music. As a public health specialist, filmmaker, nutrition therapist, holistic counsellor, and musician, he channels his diverse talents into narratives that explore the complexities of the human psyche and the pursuit of inner peace.

Under the pen name Branny Smith, Dr Mthelebofu crafts stories that delve into personal challenges, emotional trauma, and the transformative journey toward self-understanding. His literary works, such as The Professor's Descent, Desperation, and Chasing Where There is Love, My Wedding Contract Too, Her Lover is Gone, often feature protagonists grappling with internal conflicts and societal pressures, reflecting his deep interest in mental health and psychoanalysis. Beyond writing, Branny Smith employs his background in holistic therapy to assist clients in achieving emotional well-being through interactive counselling sessions. His approach integrates scriptwriting principles to facilitate character development and personal growth, offering a unique therapeutic experience that resonates with individuals seeking happiness and fulfillment.

As a musician, Branny Smith composes lyrics that address life's challenges, happiness, and the quest for peace of mind, utilizing music as a form of therapy for his audience. His passion for mental health and storytelling converges in his creative endeavors, making his work a compelling exploration of the human condition.

Through his multifaceted career, Dr Branny Mthelebofu continues to inspire and guide others on their journeys toward self-discovery and emotional resilience.

Read more at https://www.facebook.com/branny.smithsa/.

Banny Joma

All about Research

About the Publisher

The publisher produces films, sound tracks, music (different genres) and also publishes books.

www.ingramcontent.com/pod-product-compliance
Lightning Source LLC
LaVergne TN
LVHW090301210926
848480LV00001B/87
* 9 7 9 8 2 3 2 6 9 8 3 8 6 *